dancing bodies, living histories

dancing bodies, living histories

new writings about dance and culture

edited by

Lisa Doolittle
Anne Flynn

The Banff Centre Press

CANADIAN CATALOGUING IN PUBLICATION DATA

Main entry under title:

Dancing bodies, living histories

Includes papers from the conference, Foothills and Footsteps, held
at the University of Calgary, Jan. 1999.
Includes bibliographic references and index.
ISBN: 0-920159-69-9

1. Dance—Research—Congresses. I. Doolittle, Lisa, 1954– II.
Flynn, Anne, 1955– III. Title: Foothills and footsteps.
GV1583.D36 2000 792.8'072 C00-910376-7

COVER AND BOOK DESIGN: Vangool Design & Typography, Calgary
COVER PHOTOGRAPH: Janine Vangool
PRINTED AND BOUND IN CANADA BY HOUGHTON BOSTON PRINTERS, SASKATOON, SK

Le Conseil des Arts du Canada | The Canada Council for the Arts

The Banff Centre Press gratefully acknowledges the support of the Canada Council for the Arts for its support of our publishing program.

Banff Centre Press
The Banff Centre for the Arts
Box 1020-17 Banff, Alberta Canada T0L 0C0
www.banffcentre.ab.ca/Writing/Press

THE BANFF CENTRE
FOR THE ARTS

new
writings
about
dance
and
culture

contents

innovating and perpetuating

retrieving

preface

iro valaskakis tembeck

When I first starting teaching dance history over twenty years ago in Montreal, I was considered an oddball. Dance theory in Canada was then in its infancy and people were not used to reflecting on an art form that, despite the longevity of its presence here and its long-standing universal roots, still lay at the fringes of society. Though marginalized, the oddity of dance studies did somehow manage to flourish within the walls of academe, and several Canadian universities started offering dance majors with a theoretical component. The study of dance integrated knowledge and expertise from the related fields of cultural studies, anthropology, aesthetics, sociology, and politics. It appropriated various contemporary theories and rejected the monopoly of the DWEM (Dead White European Male) canon of cultural traditionalism. Dance sought to remind us that its practice lay at the core rather than at the periphery of the social fabric. These new ways of looking at the art form not only enriched the artistry but also honed our critical thinking and taste.

I remember the uphill struggle of teaching history in those early days. We were at that time too engrossed in the *hic et nunc* mentality. Shunning the need for permanence and immortality, we catered to the here and now while fully experiencing the moment. We wished to be, yet again, ravished by the "shock of the new," little knowing that originality, as George Steiner once said, is in fact also a return to our origins. Fortunately, the sense of history is slowly gaining ground once more and we find ourselves disturbed by the shock of the old, which we are carefully retrieving in fragments. The recovery of traces of past values, inventions, and expressions sheds additional light on present dancemaking. Oral histories, an ethnological approach, and the understanding of cultural differences are all means to determine dance's important role within society and to measure the erosion or mutation of specific mentalities.

In Canada, many believed that because few books were readily available on our choreographic heritage, this was a sign that there was no real legacy to preserve. But as analysis and documentation are brought back into the dance experience, we are discovering countless layers of social, political, and economic information that make age-old borders and simplistic categories vanish. Novel connections have linked indigenous forms with imported ones, and opposing stylistic genres are seen to have common grounds of comparison.

By reflecting on and preserving dance practices, we are, in fact, remembering them and salvaging them from oblivion.

The essays that make up this anthology reveal a wide range of topics researched from various vantage points. They address concerns about gender, ethnicity, and the malleability and adaptation that are essential to understanding our pluralistic reality. Flamenco, classical ballet, Aboriginal, folk, African American, and Queer studies all adopt specific voices to discard cultural colonialism. As we look back in order to go forward, such counter-narratives reveal the complexity and diversity of choreographic expression.

Having just watched the media replay of the year 2000 festivities throughout the world, I was reminded that at the key moments in life we turn to music and dance to express the feelings and realities that overwhelm us.

— *January 2000*

acknowledgements

A collective of individuals graciously contributed knowledge and expertise to create this book. To begin, we thank the writers who contributed such wonderful papers and who brought an enormous spirit of generosity to the project. We are honoured to present their insightful and well-crafted work. Next, we thank Susan Bennett for providing encouragement and practical support at key moments along the way: she opened doors, she held hands, and she taught us a few cool moves by recognizing that our dance fit with the larger choreography of humanities research.

This collection would not have been possible without the mentoring of Susan Foster, and we offer her our deepest thanks. She introduced this particular group of Canadian dance scholars to a group of American dance scholars, who now all know one another and will undoubtedly continue to collaborate in the future. Rather than the isolation that dance scholars can feel, this international exchange has created a fantastic network of colleagues, and we celebrate our good fortune. Susan also read parts of the manuscript and provided very useful suggestions.

We are grateful to the Calgary Institute for the Humanities for sponsoring the "Foothills and Footsteps: New Writings in Dance Studies Research Network and Conference." The research-network model provides an excellent structure for generating new scholarship, and we applaud the Institute for recognizing that dance scholarship matters and should be supported. In particular, we would like to thank Gerry Dyer for her extraordinary skill with details and human relations, and we thank the former director of the Institute, Dr. Jane Kelley. We give special thanks to the Social Sciences and Humanities Research Council for its financial support of both the research network and this book and for the encouraging steps it is taking to include dance scholarship in its portfolio. Both the Alberta Dance Alliance and the Canada Council for the Arts supported aspects of the conference that enriched everyone's experience, and for this support we thank them.

A special thanks goes to Don Stein and Lauri Seidlitz at the Banff Centre Press for envisioning this book and for connecting us with The Banff Centre Artist in Residence Program, which enabled this group of dance writers to meet. The Banff Centre has created some progressive dance programs in recent years, and its institutional commitment to dance artists and scholars is commendable. We would also like to thank Carol Phillips, Keith Turnbull, Tanis Booth, and Carol Holmes, all at The Banff Centre.

Thanks to the students in UNIV 401: Culture in Motion for their liveliness and pointed insights, and to the organizers who team-taught: Susan Bennett from English and Anne Flynn from Dance, Kathleen Foreman from Drama, and Elly Silverman from Women's Studies.

Thanks to Michael Green, curator of the High Performance Rodeo, an annual festival produced by One Yellow Rabbit Performance Theatre. He was enthusiastic about the conference right from the beginning and was willing to make his way through the sometimes clumsy process of connecting universities with the professional arts community.

Thanks to the following individuals for their contributions to the conference and for their support of the growth of dance in universities and other institutions: the University of Calgary B.A. Dance Program, especially Jill Breeck and Eileen Spender; Dr. Ron Zernicke, Dean, Faculty of Kinesiology, University of Calgary; Dr. Maurice Yacowar, Dean, Faculty of Fine Arts, University of Calgary; Dr. Ches Skinner, Dean, Faculty of Fine Arts, University of Lethbridge; Brian Smith, Chair, Drama Department, University of Calgary; Dr. Selma Odom, Dance Department, York University.

The editors would like to express heartfelt appreciation to their spouses and children for their support through all phases of this project.

introduction

lisa doolittle and anne flynn

Dancing histories, living bodies, bodies dancing, bodies living histories. Sometimes the body and its lived dance are captured in written words or spoken words. More often they vanish as one moment surrenders to the next, making space for the present. The collection of essays presented here represents the conscious summoning of particular moments in the lives of the writers and the subjects they have written about. Their bodies, both past and present, which move, think, sense, feel, and create, meet in a dance of words and ideas. *Dancing Bodies, Living Histories* brings to the study of dance a sense of history and culture. To the study of history and culture it brings a sense of embodied life.

This book was born out of a specific gathering that took place in a specific geographic location, which is itself filled with a history. This context is both part of and separate from the stories within these pages, where a past and a present coexist and inform each other. It is with this particular place and circumstance that we begin our entry to the essays. "Foothills and Footsteps: New Writings in Dance Studies Research Network and Conference" took place 2–7 January 1999 at The Banff Centre and the University of Calgary in Alberta, Canada. The conference gathered twelve scholars at varying stages of their careers, seven Canadians and five Americans who write about dance. The drive to organize such an event was inspired by the creation of a new B.A. Dance degree program at the University of Calgary in 1995. The Foothills and Footsteps research network and conference celebrated the arrival of dance as a major area of study on the campus and began a conversation between the University of Calgary and scholars working in the broader world of dance studies.

We will first spend some time on the history of dance at the University of Calgary because it will help establish a context for the creation of the research network and the book. Inside this academic soap opera lurk many of the themes that emerge throughout these collected essays. While this specific history is only one isolated case (and we will summarize rather than detail its many subplots), dance has suffered similar, and often more tragic, fates in other locales. Zooming in on one case helps us see some common beliefs about dance and how we cling to these beliefs, and how belief systems influence institutional structures in an effort to reproduce themselves.

Courses in dance have been offered at the University of Calgary since 1964. The development of a degree program, however, was stalled for almost thirty years because of ideological differences between the dance performers/choreographers in the Faculty of Fine Arts and the dance educators in the Faculty of Kinesiology. The division of dance into these separate spheres of study was institutionalized by the creation of a minor in Dance in the Faculty of Fine Arts and a major in Dance Education for Kinesiology students. Dance in Fine Arts meant dancing for the stage, and dance in Kinesiology meant dancing for schools and communities. No program overlap was allowed.

When these decisions were made in the mid-seventies, breaking up the study of dance into these categories seemed like a workable solution to what was essentially a conflict between the proponents of dance as high art and the proponents of dance as popular activity. In practice, however, this solution had completely negative consequences for both the development of a dance community in Alberta and the growth of dance within the university. The decision to separate dance into two faculties meant there was no university dance major anywhere in Alberta and that students interested in dance were split between these two camps. The ideological and physical division between these faculties was so deep that in the early 1980s the Faculty of Fine Arts proposed a BFA in Dance that completely excluded from the degree requirements all the courses and faculty members in the Dance Education program in Kinesiology. Despite protest that such exclusion was misguided, the university approved the expensive proposal and sent it to the provincial department of advanced education, where it sat unfunded.

Fast forward to the early 1990s, when extreme cuts in government grants to universities forced major budget reductions, and we see the beginning of a move toward combining the resources within these separate programs. There had been enough of a cultural shift to allow for a different kind of discussion about dance to take place. The Canadian dance world found its formerly homogenous identity shifting and expanding. The federal arts-funding body, the Canada Council for the Arts, responded by making fundamental changes to its funding policies and eligibility criteria. Non-European dance forms were presented on the concert stage more frequently. Audiences could now see, for example, African or East Indian dance, and the training of dancers expanded to include a variety of movement practices outside the traditional dance technique class. The growth in sport science and the fitness industry influenced the training of dancers and the choreography being made, providing for more easygoing relations with Kinesiology. Times had changed and dance in Fine Arts and dance in Kinesiology finally had more in common.

Rather than getting bogged down in the discussion of obvious dualisms like performing/teaching and fine arts/sports, the dance faculty could move the discussion along and give consideration to other possibilities. It was evident to the group that dance at this university would simply not survive if it didn't move forward with a collaborative B.A. Dance proposal and, despite continued university-wide budget cuts, in 1995 the collaborative B.A. Dance became one of six dance degree programs in Canada. With such a small number of Canadian universities offering a dance major, demand has been high. In its first four years, the program received almost two hundred applications.

Both the local and the national dance communities in Canada have been affected by the state of affairs at the University of Calgary. Rather than producing dance degree graduates since the mid-1970s, which would have been possible, twenty years were wasted on a divisive and narrow-minded agenda. This is not to say that there was no dance activity going on. Lots of dance happened during these years in both the Fine Arts Dance and Dance Education programs, and the local dance community definitely felt the impact of the students who studied at the University of Calgary. However, Alberta dancers had to leave the province to get a dance degree, and, without the infrastructure of a dance department, Calgary was not able to participate as strongly in the local or national dance community. The development of dance in the public school system has lagged behind those provinces with dance degrees because of the inability to produce dance majors who can pursue teaching certification. Faculty members were limited in their professional endeavours both because of the lack of a departmental infrastructure and because dance was merely servicing students in other majors, which is entirely different from working with majors who study dance in-depth. The acceptance of dance as a legitimate area of study within the academy was also compromised. The ideological conflict between the faculties was well known on campus, and it invited and legitimized the trivialization of dance.

So, what can this particular episode tell us? It tells us that reductive, dualistic thinking about dance in academia is not very useful. Dualist epistemology forces us to think about dance in the simplistic categories of mind/body, thinking/feeling, rational/irrational, male/female, and objective/subjective, where we construct dance as an activity of a subjective, irrational, female, feeling body. The objective, rational, male, thinking mind (which is more valued in our culture) gets omitted from this cultural construct, and we are left with a totally inadequate representation of what it is to dance. Dancers are stereotyped as emotional rather than rational; dance is viewed as a physical activity rather than an intellectual pursuit and therefore can be easily dismissed and relegated to a minor area of study. Despite numerous and thorough critiques of the inadequacy of dualistic thinking, we see evidence of these divisions everywhere. We still talk about "physical education" as though the mind did not participate in movement practices, and students and faculty must spend twice as long in the studio or gym to get the same credit given to lecture courses. As soon as dance embraced a non-dualist, interdisciplinary model, the old barricades began to crumble at the University of Calgary and dance began to flourish.

In just a few short years since the creation of the dance degree program, university administrators have been quick to highlight dance as a model for interfaculty collaboration and exchange. Interestingly, images of dancers have figured prominently in recent University of Calgary promotional materials. The history of faculty conflict is unknown to all the new dance majors, who think they are arriving at a new, young department. In their application letters, many students mention how great it is that they can study dance in both Fine Arts and Kinesiology. The contrast with the previous state of dance activity at the University of Calgary is striking. Into this energized, albeit contested, setting stepped the participants in Foothills and Footsteps.

Institutions like universities reflect divisions in the world outside their walls. But universities are also powerful cultural entities, and the structures we erect within these slow-changing institutions can affect the workings of the profession. They affect the way we perceive and talk about dance and the way we allow ourselves to dance. In choreographing the conference and research network, we wanted to place dance front and centre on the humanities stage and to shift the perception of dance away from limiting dualities like mind/body, thinking/feeling, rational/irrational, male/female, and objective/subjective, dualities that so quickly assert themselves when we dance only inside the frame of physical education or performing arts. And of course this is the way dance inhabits culture itself, not in clean, theoretical categories, but between and among and within the moments of life. Looking at embodied movement, we can see these fleeting moments in new ways, watching how dance might craft a connection between what has been and what might be. The essays in this book explore how dance leaps across disciplinary boundaries — the reinvented gestures of a so-called dying Aboriginal culture guide and support the fancy footwork of land claims lawyers (see Shea Murphy in this collection). Dance weaves together the ordinary and the archetypal — a woman's everyday existence is seen dancing cheek-to-cheek with her life as an onstage icon of femininity (Cordova). Dance unravels the threads that bind form and content — why can't a modern dance also be a Jewish dance (Jackson)? Dancer Katherine Dunham unexpectedly turns us out of an old fieldwork methodology and into a new anthropology (Ramsey), while a walk with a fancy pocketbook turns a consumerized victim of global capitalism into a woman who has something in the bag (Thompson).

Creating a forum for these kinds of intellectual improvisations seemed like a fitting way to celebrate the creation of a new dance degree in Canada. In synchrony with the newness of the degree program and with dance scholarship, particularly in Canada, we chose to highlight the work of new dance scholars from the United States and Canada, and to explore some of the most significant new directions in the emerging field of dance studies. We wanted to explore the idea of dance as a cultural practice influenced by and influencing key values in a given historical moment. We also wanted to enjoy ourselves in a community setting.

One early strategy was to align dance with the Calgary Institute for the Humanities to give the event as much credibility as possible in an institution where people had never before been able to get degrees in dance. Crossing over into the humanities led to more crossovers. Imagining a confluence of academics and practitioners, we scheduled Foothills and Footsteps to coincide with the High Performance Rodeo festival and exposed performers to the gentle scrutiny of a theatre full of conference goers. Imagining the exchange between students and the visiting academics, we created an undergraduate course around the conference paper sessions and exposed many students to dance outside of a studio setting.

The research network and conference were both interested in looking at the in-between spaces or intersecting terrain where dance and culture, theory and practice, professors and students, study and play, scholars and artists, academe and community, mountains and prairie, and Canada and America meet. We tried to spend time in the potentially awkward spaces between clear categories to see what it feels like to live with the discomfort of leaving home territory and not knowing exactly where you will wind up. Dance majors met theatre majors, English majors, and women's studies majors; the conference presenters, session chairs, and delegates came from a wide range of disciplines, including dance, English, French literature, performance studies, sport history, anthropology, and women's studies, as well as from the dance community.

Early in the process, we identified the need to have Aboriginal dance represented in the research network and conference, but this was easier said than done. The conference itself included a day trip to Head-Smashed-In Buffalo Jump, where we had arranged for an interpretive tour as well as a performance. Including this touristic event in the conference was easy. We had a more difficult time finding an Aboriginal scholar writing about dance and basically abandoned the search once the early grant applications were submitted. Later in the organizing process, Lisa Doolittle met with Marrie Mumford, artistic director of the Aboriginal Dance Program at The Banff Centre, and arranged for Marrie and Jerry Longboat (independent dancer and Aboriginal Dance Program participant) to be guests at the conference.

Because of a major snowstorm in the Canadian and American northeast, Marrie and Jerry did give a presentation at the conference after all. Tommy DeFrantz was snowbound in Rochester, so Marrie and Jerry took his place during an afternoon session. They gave a talk about the Aboriginal Dance Program in Banff and showed videos of performances. The students had lots of questions and it turned out to be a great session. We still feel regret when we realize how wrong we were not to formally invite Marrie and Jerry into the conference program. We take it as a gracious sign from nature that a snowstorm made it possible for Marrie and Jerry to speak. Our awkward experience with trying to include an Aboriginal presence in a very Euro-academic environment has been transformational, and we will know how to do it much better next time.

Daydreaming about the choreography of the research network in the very early days, we always imagined a mountain segment, a city segment, and a plains segment. We felt strongly that if we were going to organize an event in Calgary, it had to include taking people into the surrounding landscape so they could have a sensual experience of this place that was not just an urban one. In the middle of a city it can be difficult to tell where you are in relation to nature. We viewed the bus trip south as a part of the presentation of the paper "Dancing in the Wasteland" because we believe it helps to have sensual references to the big landscape where events took place. We wanted people to stand on the lookout at Head-Smashed-In Buffalo Jump and see the vast plains and distant mountains and feel the January fierceness at one of the windiest places in North America. We thought it would help clear our minds.

The commitment in publishing this book is to simply get dance scholarship out there in the liberal-arts mix so that it becomes totally commonplace for dance and other studies of the body to be included in the humanities and social sciences. We believe in dancing bodies living history and dancing bodies changing history. We believe that the body has been excluded from the academy for too long and hope that this collection will help in some way toward greater inclusion for dance and dance studies. Dance does matter to the study of history, and it is no longer revolutionary to expand from writing about dancing into writing dancing into history. In the last decade, we have welcomed a huge array of books and collections of papers on this subject into the dance-history canon.[i] Too often, current discussions of the body and its practices within and across disciplines are "incommensurate and mutually incomprehensible."[ii] Dance is one set of embodied practices that can expand from history, anthropology, women's studies, and sociology to include not just the static bodies of symbol and inscription, but the moving bodies of people dancing. This book, while its collected essays all start with dance, takes us from that point all over the disciplinary map. We hope that readers from any particular disciplinary standpoint or intellectual location may dance into another area.

The essays cover a wide range of topics because we invited people to present work on whatever topic in dance they were currently pursuing as part of their research agenda. Then we got together. Except for Cheryl Blood-Doore, Marrie Mumford, Thomas DeFrantz, and B. J. Wray, the writers in this collection met for two days in the Rocky Mountains, getting to know one another and discussing papers, discovering what everyone's agenda was for doing his or her work. We physically spent time together, sharing meals together, having long discussion sessions, and late-night visits in the hotel and sulphur hot springs. The bodies of most of these writers hung out together for six days in winter in the Canadian northwest.

We had to borrow warm coats and boots for the participants from warm climates. It was a really wonderful and special time that helped us to see the choreography of the conference ahead and our role as a pickup company in a dance that would last for six days. And then everyone went home. These are the essays they sent back.

Following the conference, several contributors extensively revised or rejected papers they had presented, seeking more relevant subject matter, methodologies, or presentational strategies. These re-creations reflect the influence of the research network interchanges, the response of the conference participants, and the geographical and cultural displacement experienced by contributors to this book. Instead of focusing on the handbag-as-object, why not follow the gesture that dances with the object? Instead of an exploration of American appropriation of Native dance imagery in the early twentieth century, why not engage here and now with contemporary Aboriginal dance in Canada? While M. J. Thompson re-choreographed her conference presentation, both Jacqueline Shea Murphy and Thomas DeFrantz wrote different essays for the book than the papers they prepared for the research network, seizing an opportunity to present more exploratory or foundational work. The network sessions revealed the variety of approaches to movement analysis as a tool in cultural critique. The use of dance and filmic analysis ("Blood Wedding") refracted against the analysis of dance and literary form ("Stepping Out of Attitude") to illuminate new possibilities for understanding the dance of identity and gender. We could begin to glimpse the strengths and inadequacies of theoretical and methodological strategies as we watched fellow scholars use them to grapple with questions of embodied life, and we could begin to imagine what new tools might be invented. In discussions about the performances we viewed as part of the conference, we speculated about how to close the gap between academic and artistic choreographies.

The inadvertently closed border we had created in the programming for the conference, which put academics on the podium to the exclusion of practitioners, proved to be particularly misguided vis-à-vis the presence of minority voices. Giving space for Aboriginal voices to speak for themselves became an urgent priority, and, as a result, we have included a photo essay about the Aboriginal Dance Program at The Banff Centre for the Arts, with comments by artistic director Marrie Mumford. We have chosen to reprint Cheryl Blood-Doore's evocative piece "They Were Singing and Dancing in the Mountains," to make a reference to *Chinook Winds: Aboriginal Dance Project* (Banff Centre Press and 7th Generation Books, 1997). This book is a collection of interviews with and articles by participants in the 1996 Aboriginal Dance Program, and it is a beautiful and innovative model for one way of documenting dance activity. Our reach across academic and other cultures sometimes exceeded our grasp. But a week is a short time, and the repercussions of a network like this are perhaps not always easily and quickly absorbed. In any case, the experiences during that week of meetings gave new clarity and purpose to our enterprise.

The essays remain largely exploratory and speculative. They deal with bodies as intriguing sites of memory, agency, and subjectivity, and with methodologies for reading the process of embodiment, inscription, and reinscription. Once we had a chance to see how the essays sat together, we worked to group them thematically, waiting for the choreography to reveal itself. We've chosen the following groupings to organize the book: Everyday Moving, Working Women Dancing, Innovating and Perpetuating, and Retrieving. These categories seem to capture the main agendas of the pieces.

The story of the evolution of the dance degree program at the University of Calgary is emblematic of the struggle of dance for legitimacy, and this chapter has a happy ending. The research network and conference were experiments in cross-disciplinary research on the body and embodiment. There we attempted to write new kinds of stories and to rehearse new versions of history. Supported by and mirroring the hopeful connections made in the place where it was incubated, this book reaches beyond the boundaries of genre in a similar spirit of inclusiveness and expansiveness.

notes

i We have the privilege of being able to draw on approaches of contemporary dance scholars such as Cynthia Cohen Bull (Cynthia Novack), Susan Leigh Foster, Susan Manning, Lena Hammergren, Ann Cooper Albright, and others who have given us new and effective ways of writing about dance, the body, and the politics of movement.

ii Kathleen Canning, "Reflections on the Place of the Body," *Gender and History*, 11, 3, 1999.

abstracts

everyday moving

M. J. Thompson's "The Pas de Deux of Women and Handbags" examines the history of women's handbags. Intrigued by the ordinariness of the bag, found everywhere, borne by many, Thompson identifies the conditions of both hegemony and anarchy in the common handbag. Evocative as much of space as of containment, this object offers a dialectic of the interior. Like the mouth, stomach, and genitalia, the handbag opens and closes, transgressing the boundary of the interior and exterior. In this way, the bag works as a model of transgression and intimacy. To the women who carry them, these are talismans that conjure private space through an unmarked pedestrian gesture that transcends corporate identity, gender politics, and the commodity exchange.

B. J. Wray, in "Choreographing Queer: Nationalism, Citizenship, and Lesbian Dance Clubs," takes Susan Leigh Foster's seminal dance studies essay "Choreographing History" as her point of departure to examine the complex nexus of identity, bodies, politics, and dance in Canadian queer culture. Whether in clubs, bars, parties, on stage, in literature, or on film, the corporeal meaning of queerness is often signified through dance. Or, as queer performance theorist Jose Munoz has said, "Dance sets politics in motion, bringing people together in rhythmic affinity where identification takes the form of histories written on the body through gesture."

working women dancing

Michelle Heffner Hayes, in "*Blood Wedding:* Tradition and Innovation in Contemporary Flamenco," deals with the history of flamenco dance as an art form and the ways in which the body of the female flamenco dancer serves as a site at which the tensions of class, race, gender, and national identity collide. The essay looks at Carlos Saura and Antonio Gades' *Bodas de Sangre* (1981) and focuses on choreographic conventions and moments from the embattled history of flamenco. Hayes examines the ways in which the director and choreographer construct a commentary on the future of flamenco as a living tradition. "Blood Wedding" received the Society of Dance History Scholars' Selma Jean Cohen award for best graduate student paper in 1997.

Kristin M. Harris, in "Gendered Movement in Romantic Ballet: An Analysis of Teresina in Bournonville's *Napoli,*" examines the nature of the Bournonville aesthetic to pursue the question of the female protagonist, with a primary focus on *Napoli* and the character of Teresina. Teresina's place within the narrative and the choreographic structure of the ballet is studied through an analysis of movement and feminist theory. Harris shows how the Bournonville aesthetic is manifest through his representation of gender and how his female characters epitomize the philosophy inherent in the Bournonville tradition.

Sarah Davies Cordova's "Stepping Out of Attitude: *La Fanfarlo* and Autobiography" reworks representations of the female dancer that reconstruct the Romantic stereotype of the ballet dancer, and to elaborate the contextualized identity of a woman-at-work during the nineteenth century. Part autobiographical voice, part reinterpretation, but also a cipher of archival fragments, this text generates an unfolding of the dancer's multiple identity positions.

innovating and perpetuating

Marrie Mumford, in "Reflections on the Aboriginal Dance Program," comments on four years of this groundbreaking project's activities from her perspective as artistic director. In a photo essay, the text dances with the images of the performances that took place at The Banff Centre and illuminates the issues, visions, and traditions that have motivated this remarkable body of Aboriginal dance.

Jacqueline Shea Murphy's "Lessons in Dance (as) History: Aboriginal Land Claims and Aboriginal Dance, circa 1999" interweaves discussion of recent Aboriginal land claims cases with discussion of the growing momentum of the Aboriginal Dance Program at The Banff Centre for the Arts, suggesting a relationship between these movements. Shea Murphy looks at how the work at the Aboriginal Dance Program in the summer of 1999 echoed and strengthened the relationship to Aboriginal land and celebrated the government's recognition of the land as Aboriginal. She intersperses her discussion of these issues with an examination of the act of watching and writing about Aboriginal culture.

retrieving

Cheryl Blood- (Rides-at-the-) Doore's "They Were Singing and Dancing in the Mountains" is both narrative and documentary, biography and geography. Olivia Tailfeathers, a Blood tribe singer and performer, and Cheryl Blood-Doore were brought together in Banff during the 1996 Aboriginal Dance Program. The fusion of new and old Aboriginal dance and music in the program inspired them to search together for their traditions. This essay presents their interviews with Elders who share their knowledge about drum, song, and dance traditions. It was first published in *Chinook Winds: Aboriginal Dance Project* (Banff Centre Press and 7th Generation Books, 1997).

Thomas F. DeFrantz's "Ballet in Black: Louis Johnson and African American Vernacular Humour in Ballet" explores the history of African American participation in classical ballet. Although the African American presence in classical ballet crystallized with the founding of the Dance Theatre of Harlem in 1969, general African American interest in the dance form grew more slowly alongside waxing American interest in theatrical stage dancing. The essay focuses on the work of Louis Johnson, a master choreographer whose ballets employ sparkling fragments of African American vernacular humour. DeFrantz proposes that although the African American presence in ballet has been circumscribed by ambiguous race relations in the United States, Africanist compositional strategies have had a dynamic impact on contemporary ballet choreography and are especially evident in Johnson's work.

Kate Ramsey, in "Melville Herskovits, Katherine Dunham, and the Politics of African Diasporic Dance Anthropology," poses the study of African diasporic dance as a key problem in the history of North American cultural anthropology. She focuses on its status in the field of "New World" Africanism pioneered and most closely associated with Melville J. Herskovits and argues that the development of an anthropology of African diasporic dance was a career long project for Herskovits. This is particularly illuminated by his professional relationship with Katherine Dunham, whose fieldwork he advised in 1935–6, when she travelled to the Caribbean to study dance cultures in Jamaica, Martinique, Trinidad, and Haiti.

Naomi M. Jackson, in "Dance and Intertextuality: Theoretical Reflections," explores questions of methodology for dance analysis. "Intertextuality" posits that a given work of art is a mosaic of quotations drawn either explicitly or implicitly from a variety of sources. These quotations mark the presence of different interpretive communities engaged in constructing notions of self and society through distinct practices and narratives. Jackson uses examples of intertextuality drawn from a variety of dance styles and refers to Jewish and modern dance texts in Sophie Maslow's *The Village I Knew* (1950).

Lisa Doolittle and Anne Flynn, in "Dancing in the Canadian Wasteland: A Post-Colonial Reading of Regionalism in the 1960s and 1970s," investigate two distinct artistic dance communities that danced out the divide between high-art/high-class/importation and low-art/low-class/local creation. Their separate trajectories helped choreograph the identity of the local region's current dance community, both past and present. The essay also comments on how the politics of whiteness, class, and gender form facets of Canadian regionalism and, in these two dance communities, it finds embodiment of national debates about decolonization and decentralization in the arts.

everyday moving

the pas de deux of women and handbags

m. j. thompson

everyday/extraordinary

The common handbag, with its long performance history, is at once a marker of gender, a commodity fetish, and a shopping tool essential to the consumer act. Recent feminist scholarship has shown the generative power of dressing up for women who seek to reinvent themselves in the public sphere. But how have the attendant gestural vocabularies — those associated with and produced in relation to objects of adornment — offered possibilities for transformation? While embracing the handbag and strolling in the public eye, women alter the presentation of their selves in everyday life, as well as rewrite the meaning and use-value of the commodity.

A curious doubling occurs: between the women and their bags, between the objects of purchase and their consumers. For if their display in public has conflated women with commodities, how might women's repositioning of a culturally loaded product like the handbag take on greater implications? Could it be that the magic of such a doubling lies in the movement? It was this possibility that I set out to investigate when, arriving in New York in 1997, I was first struck by the miniature handbags women carried and the kind of comportment they elicited.

The Kate Spade shop sits at the corner of Broome and Mercer in SoHo. It was in this neighbourhood that I first noticed handbags at all, and the mode of the day was unusual. With their short handles and extraordinarily tiny bodies, the bags were unsettling in their dysfunction. As carrying tools, their size alone was perverse. Worse still, the required gesture of carriage seemed awkward, even backward. Either affected in its daintiness or neurotic in its grasping nature, the handbag recalled a more confining era for women. The clutch and the clench, the fist and the fury: at first glance, the grip recalled the hysterical contraction of Charcot's clinic. And that such trifling objects should tie up hands that might otherwise be free to engage in more progressive or pleasurable activities bothered me, too; the very act of carrying restricted movement. Made full, kept busy, the hand was held hostage as if by handcuff. Why, if the pathological hunch was right, were the bags so popular?

The posture of the hysterical contraction prefigures the flexed bicep of the shopper.

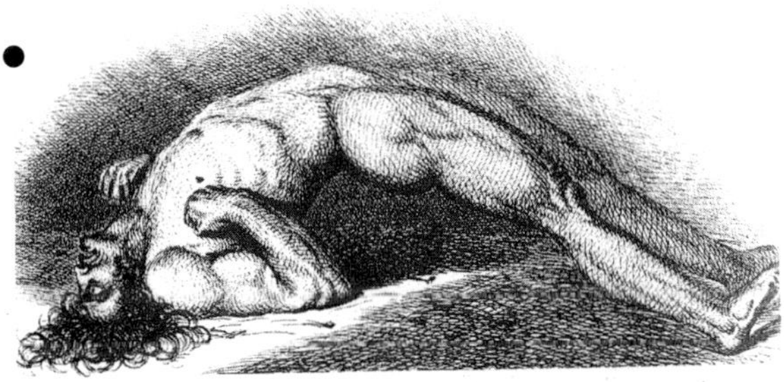

Handbag designer Nancy Garcia's pose echoes the hysterical contraction, but her attitude moves away from pathology.

I centred my research on the Kate Spade bag, because it was Spade's collection, launched in New York in 1993, that restored the top-handled miniature to prominence. I studied the shop as a site of collection and display, visiting it each week over the course of four months in the spring of 1998. My aim was to understand how the bag functioned first as a commodity within a collection, before following it out of the shop, into the street, carried independently, worn on the body. As a portable cabinet of curiosities, the bag's power lay as much in the meaning of its contents as in the meaning of its gesture. To determine how the bag got used and by whom,

I interviewed and photographed the women carrying the model and restricted my inquiry to this gender and to the neighbourhood of SoHo.

SoHo is the moniker for the neighbourhood south of Houston Street in Lower Manhattan.[1] During the nineteenth century, its buildings and streets were home to the working classes. Described by one New York City guidebook as a place for "light industry,"[2] SoHo housed the production of fashionable domestic goods, such as textiles, laces, china, and glass. Gentrification began in the mid-1970s, with artists moving into its large warehouse spaces in defiance of zoning laws. Today, the neighbourhood's avant-garde past serves as a scenic backdrop for the purchase and display of numerous consumer products that enact higher class: couture, art, makeup, high-end design goods, elaborate toys and novelties, Spade handbags.

Within these perimeters of class and tourist space, I set to work, intent on finding the fantasmata of the bag, as well as the lived experience. What sort of promise does the handbag make to the woman who carries it? How is that promise transformed by her use of the bag? How does pedestrian gesture figure in the equation? Rather than cinching a diagnosis of hysteria, the associated movement vocabulary proved ambiguous. Whether firmly grasped in the fist or held gingerly between the fingers; whether hooked over an elbow, bicep flexed, or drifting passively on the forearm, the motions conjure strength as much as anxiety. What, finally, might the Spade phenomenon reveal about the often unseen potential of everyday body techniques?

To have, or to hold.
To buy, or to be bought.
The Pouch Bag, a faux-drawstring made out of satin-like nylon, recalls the glamour and freedom of the flappers, revelling in the 1920s on the heels of World War I and the achievements of the Suffragettes.

hard bodies, serious anatomy

Kate Spade moved to New York from Kansas City in 1987. With a degree in journalism, she found work at *Mademoiselle* magazine, where she was an accessories editor. Six years later she quit the job to launch her own company with a handful of designs made out of construction paper. As she explains, "My goal was to create bags that I could never find anywhere as an editor, bags that were somewhere between L. L. Bean and Prada in both design and price."[3]

Her product gained immediate attention from the journalists, designers, and buyers who produce fashion trends: "the tools of their trade — Polaroid cameras, Filofaxes, and sketchbooks — fit neatly into the carryalls, the minimalist designs were perfect for their minimal outfits and, of course, the price was right."[4] Style writers later observed that the bags were "cheap but chic," "streamlined," and "compact, efficient, utilitarian."[5] The lines were clean and spare, the surfaces smooth: there were no obvious zippers, buckles, tags, or tassels. Instead, there were taut, muscled shapes in neutral colours built from industrial or unusual fabrics, using heavy interfacing. The designer's inspiration lay in the profane carrying gear of the past: coach bags and postal bags, shaving kits and water canteens.[6] Contrasting the retro design was the high-tech, water-resistant, and impenetrable nylon. The bags came in a range of sizes and cost under US $150.

Somewhere between L. L. Bean and Prada is like being somewhere between Lake Wobegon and New York City. Between the mail-order accessibility of the former and the boutique elitism of the latter, there is a lot of distance. In 1998, Spade's company realized US $28 million in sales; in 1999, it sold fifty-six per cent of its shares to Neiman Marcus, one of the oldest and most stable retailers in the United States. By 2003, forty new Spade shops will sprawl across the United States, and international sales, particularly in Japan and Europe, continue to grow. All bags are made locally, with much of the work done by hand, in five small factories in the city. Again the gap between corporate fictions and lived experience is vast. The factory I visited was run by independent contractor Veje Leather. The company makes Spade bags exclusively and was, until recently, across the hall from the glamorous Spade headquarters on the edge of Chelsea. But Veje Leather is currently involved in a labour dispute: with poor working conditions and wages of between US $5.15 and $9 per hour, workers attempted to unionize and were subsequently dismissed.[7]

The chasm is further mirrored in the difference between what the company and the mainstream media say about the product and what it in fact is. For instance, the architecture of the bag is transparent — its seams of construction often forming the only detail on its surface — but incredibly sophisticated. Spade designer Muriel Favaro observes "these bags are super-constructed and we use a lot of heavy interfacing and felt. They are built to stand up really well."[8] What counts as inexpensive are prices between US $22 and $500, with the most popular miniature designs costing from US $150 to $230.

Spade's use of fabric began as a strategy for keeping prices down. The choices are unusual: canvas, burlap, wicker, terry cloth, melton cloth, Irish tweeds, Liberty cottons, nylon, some leather, and suede. Nor are the patterns in any way typical: the stripe of Daddy's suit, the chintz of Grandma's curtains, summer ginghams, nautical stripes, Liberty florals. In general, the colour palette is muted: black, brown, navy, beige. Favaro describes the bags as "altered classics": inspired by traditional shapes, rendered in unconventional materials, in a scale that was radical to the fashion moment in which it arose.

A Kate Spade miniature presents a hard body: surface cut, skin firm, seams recalling the extreme musculature of a Streb dancer. These bags are pumped: they require no support structure and are made to stand independently. "We spend a lot of time thinking about how they look, how they're going to look after wearing, how they look on the shelf, in the store," says Favaro. The handles, meanwhile, offer provocation. Sturdy, erect, they extend an invitation: "Pick me up, take me home," said one woman I spoke to on the subject of the bag's lure. And they are small. A miniature drawstring bag referred to as the Pouch measures 16 cm in diameter and stands 6 cm tall, with handles that are 7.5 cm from the main body to the farthest point in their arc. The smallest version of the Basket design is 8.5 cm long, 5.5 cm wide, and 2.75 cm deep. Meanwhile, the hardy Mini-canteen is 7 cm long, 5.5 cm wide, and 3.5 cm deep.

The Spade label is articulate in its discretion and powerful in its ability to convey insider status. The designer affixes the monikers externally to some, internally to others; for instance, the nylon staple wears the label outside, while the evening bags — particularly those in the display case — bear their marks internally. The label is a small black rectangle of fabric, on which its makers inscribe "kate spade, New York" in white thread. Stitched to the bag near its top edge, centred between the handles, the label is discreet, its type barely discernible. Instead, the black square acts alone as the signifier: in this instance, it doesn't matter if you read it, only that you get it.

The allure of a Spade handbag is the allure of an intact body: well built, compact, improved by technology, beyond damage, immaculate. Her bags mirror our own desires for a constant body, and, in their very minutiae, this effect is heightened by the pronounced detail unavailable at different scales. Such detail condenses and expands our experience of the object, creating a simultaneous sense of wonder and control. Recalling his own experience of miniature, Gaston Bachelard observes that the device "sincerely detaches me from the surrounding world, and helps me to resist dissolution of the surrounding atmosphere. Miniature is an exercise that has metaphysical freshness: it allows us to be world conscious at slight risk."[9] Like the dancer who remakes her body with extreme attention to isolated bodily parts, Spade's bags deliver a unified whole, crafted from shards of material, design, and history.

To thirst, or to be sated,
To drink, and to want more.
The Canteen Bag repeats, in miniature, the shape and authority of the doctor's bag used to make house-calls when house-calls happened and before women had their own medical practices.

souvenirs of the body

Colloquial language identifies the association of the handbag with a woman's body: your box, your booty, your purse, your snatch. The sexual puns are endless. If you sleep around, you're a douche bag. When you can't give it up any longer, you're an old bag. Psychoanalysis supports this vernacular understanding. In 1905, Freud located the handbag as a stand-in for the girl's sex. In *Dora: An Analysis of a Case of Hysteria,* after urging his patient to admit to masturbation, he notes the following behaviour:

> Several days later, she did something which I could not help regarding as a further step towards the confession. For on that day she wore at her waist — a thing she never did on any other occasion before or after — a small reticule of a shape which had just come into fashion; and, as she lay on the sofa and talked, she kept playing with it — opening it, putting a finger into it, shutting it again, and so on. I looked on for some time, and then explained to her the nature of a symptomatic act . . . Dora's reticule, which came apart at the top in the usual way, was nothing but a representing of the genitals.[10]

Freud's analysis makes metaphorical a connection that in the nineteenth century was literal. In the 1850s, medical implements used to treat hysteria centred on the vagina and uterus as the site of the pathology, and their designs mirrored the shape of women's reproductive organs. Meanwhile, the design of handbags echoes these shapes, and designers are hip to the bodily connection. "The bag is this piece of you that's outside of you," says Favaro, motioning to her solar plexus as she says this. "The small bag, well, it's belonging to you."

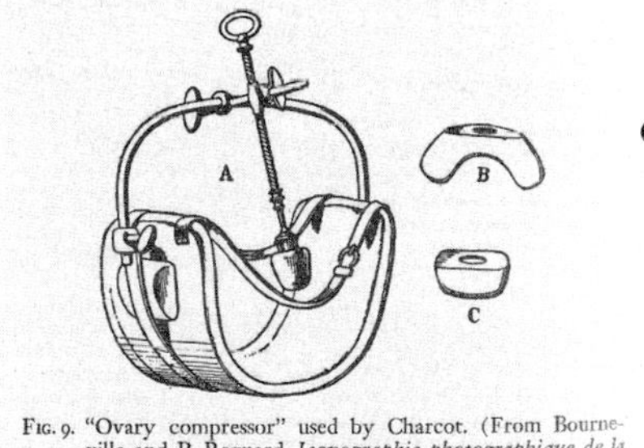

Fig. 9. "Ovary compressor" used by Charcot. (From Bourneville and P. Regnard, *Iconographie photographique de la Salpêtrière* [Paris: Progrès Médical, 1878].)

● *Ovary compressor, used by Charcot*

● *Handbags, 1950–70*

Before they were called handbags, they were called purses. Before that, pocketbooks. Fade to seventeenth-century pockets. Move back in time to baskets. Although the history of the container is its own massive project, as is the history of representations of women as containers, my interest returns to the object in the hand: the miniature handbag, affixed to the body, as an item conveying status, invoking leisure for upper-class women beginning around the sixteenth century. As fashion evolved, pockets for men remained on the body, while women's detached from the frame. The implications of this excision could mean only one thing: return to first impressions. See pathology, anxiety, limitation. Do not pass go.

Because handbags need not meet any particular size or shape requirements, as historian Vanda Foster notes, their "adaptability makes them particularly expressive of the needs and tastes of their time."[11] Her text tracks the presence of the bag from the sixteenth century onward and alludes to its social and political implications in various incarnations: for example, increased access to education led to the design of women's book bags; expanded rail systems resulted in expanded travel and coach bags; and, finally, increased opportunities for women to earn money were expressed by the business-centred pocketbook.

Pockets for men remained sewn into their breeches and various clothing items from the seventeenth century on, the constancy of the hidden orifice appearing like so much womb envy. Yet makers of clothing envisioned women's pockets — whether tie pockets, chatelaines, reticules — as distinct entities, discrete from the body and hidden under skirts and petticoats. By 1675, women of the elite classes in France, Britain, and Germany were wearing tie pockets outside the petticoat, with an apron over them so that they were partially visible. Always miniature in scale, they served a variety of functions: to carry coins, toiletries, talismans, and writing implements. The flat-bottomed gaming bag held coins and gambling ephemera; sweet bags carried odour-masking essences. Beautifully elaborate objects, they were hand-rendered by women in beading, embroidery, needlework, and lace. With the development of mechanical reproduction, women of the leisure class in Europe were encouraged to participate in the decorative arts; the handmade designs they produced exist today as an intriguing counterpoint to the homogeneity of mass-produced objects.

Aptly, bags also functioned as souvenirs. As commemorative objects, they served as elegant containers for mandatory New Year's gifts to the monarchy (seventeenth century); as markers of historic events, such as royal visits and the first hot-air balloon flight (eighteenth century); and finally as gifts of love, embellished with Limoges portraits and exchanged between lovers or between groom and bride as a symbol of material wealth.[12] The miniature inspired incredible detail, and ideas for shapes and patterns came from the natural world, as well as from the historical and political issues of the day.

In his book *The Tourist: A New Theory of the Leisure Class,* Dean MacCannell defines souvenirs as "spurious elements that have come out of the closet, occupying visible places in the domestic environment."[13] Furthermore, he locates the significance of the memento in its power to remind us of "the availability of authentic experiences at other times and in other places."[14] Back at the Spade galaxy, handbags recall a utopian moment in a vague past. As souvenirs, they conjure the better times afforded by historical distance: for instance, the happier times associated rightly or wrongly with Kennedy's presidency. But although MacCannell understands the process by which the monumental shrinks and is embodied by the miniature, he ignores the latter's potential to absorb the conceptual. The power of the souvenir lies in its ability to give presence to the unseen.

To run like Tom,
To dress like Sam.
Sam likes geometry: its body a rectangle, its sides two triangles, its strap-handles two lines of fabric arching 180 degrees from edge to edge. In name and style, the bag conjures tomboy childhoods and the omnipotence and style of Elizabeth Montgomery's post-sixties heroine in the TV show Bewitched.

real goods: welcome to planet spade

In his book *Cultural Excursions,* Neil Harris provides a vocabulary for how one might understand the Spade shop: "public absorption with mementos of a past that is continually recorded and yet recedes into memory as styles change can be satisfied ultimately only by total environment."[15] Through its exhaustive attention to detail and presentation, the total environment constructs an immersive space in which visitor experience is directed toward a particular ideological end. A key strategy for building such environments came out of early collaborations between designers of museums, department stores, and theatres, whose sites of work often overlapped. Harris builds a compelling historical argument for how museum culture borrowed from merchandising techniques in the 1930s and 1940s to reinvent space as the cure for dwindling audiences. Further, he suggests that the gap between exhibition design and the performing arts is eroding, a process anticipated by set designer Lee Simonson, writing in 1927: "The business of a museum is not to chronicle art as a fact but to enact it as an event and to dramatize its function. Its role is not as custodian but as showman."[16]

Spade closes that gap further, marketing her handbags through a performance of authenticity fashioned out of a stunningly coherent universe — a total environment made using display techniques cribbed from the public art museum. With its pristine white space, high ceilings, and minimalist aesthetic, the shop houses its collection of bags within a gallery that reinvents the debased handbag as precious work of art. In so doing, Spade offers customers a fantastic image of themselves as figures of elevated class and culture, and promises restoration amid a fragmented world.

Enter 454 Broome and check out its central display. Visible from street level and lit dramatically to continue its effect into the night, Spade's key exhibit comprises sixteen white cubes stacked in rows of four, each forming a perfect square foot. Single halogen spots light each cube from precisely above centre. Each cube houses either miniature Spade bags or "found objects": a mini-globe in faded earthen tones; an aphorism — "A Friend in Need Is a Friend Indeed" — rendered in pencil on cheap paper in a child's neat handwriting and pressed between Plexi; a trio of tiny glass bottles embossed with the words "Denzotine, Philadelphia," each bearing a solitary fresh daisy, without water. Follow the display's strategic use of books: one case holds a black-and-white houndstooth cosmetic bag, while beside it stands an elegant, worn paperback in red, white, and black titled *Poker: The Nation's Most Fascinating Card Game.* A white, satin-finish drawstring bag sits beside *Bunkelbüch,* with its fanciful Miro-esque design in mauve, leaf green, pale yellow, and cream. The presentation is modern, spare, with elements of wonder and nostalgia.

Examine the antique museum case that serves as the sales counter. Under its glass lies a selection of Spade wallets, Beatrix Potter books, airmail writing paper, and children's rulers in bright primary colours. All objects are laid out singly and flat, mutely facing the observer like so many relics. Visit the shop's small but gracious sitting area and recline on deep brown canvas chairs, armless and chic, poised on short wooden legs. Sit for a spell and enjoy the natural light that pours in through the large windows that line the shop's front and sides. Contrasting this light source are ten bare light bulbs that dangle from the ceiling on black wires. Notice the fierce detail and extreme lack of clutter. Beneath the window a concrete shelf traces the window's base. On it stands a wooden shadow box, *Her Dream Is in the Bag,* an artwork by Marc Gagnon. Beside it, the bags: bodies straight, standing alone, placed with exactitude. Wait for the counterpoints: a glass vase holding a single branch with tiny white flowers ready to bud, a beautiful book of black-and-white landscape photographs, *Intimate Portraits: Photos by Eliot Porter.*

Let your eyes wander. See how three heavy antique tables fill out the main floor space, each set with a small cluster of bags. Set apart by an independent wall, the rear of the shop houses the staple nylon collection arranged on plank shelves of "100-year-old yellow pine found in a lumber-yard."[17] Consider the literary references. Do you read me? Listen to the soundtrack of singers Nat King Cole, Peggy Lee, Harry Connick Jr. Can you hear me? In its clean lines and spare aesthetic, the shop speaks to enduring quality and common sense. The economic group? Old money. The year? Pick a boom decade: 1920s, 1950s, 1980s. Anything but the present. This is the old world, modified by technological advancements: "altered classics."

The store and the collection it encases display a carefully constructed utopian past. The definitive Spade bag — the top-handled miniature — recalls the nineteenth-century coach bag that appeared as a fashion novelty during a period of increased opportunities for women to travel and receive education. And it evokes the classic bags of the 1950s and early 1960s, a time of economic abundance, expanding civil rights, and the invention of the Pill. Whereas the promise of the feminist movement has always been of a transformed future, the Spade environment revisits feminist moments within a transformed past.

At the same time, Spade's world reiterates the client's membership in an elite class, and the security and safety such economics provide, by means of the careful use of language. For instance, manager Kolbrener's use of the term "found object" to refer to artifacts like the miniglobe is significant and affirms the self-conscious nature of this intent. Using the professional vocabulary of the curator and art historian, staff confer the status of art onto the range of everyday objects used in display; in turn, these words reposition the shop as museum, the bags as items in a precious collection.

L'objet trouvé is associated with the work of the Dadaists, the pre–World War I European avant-garde that sought rupture through the elevation of profane objects to the stature of art, purely through declaration of intent and mode of display. While key figures like Hans Arp and Kurt Schwitters worked with raw materials, debris, and refuse, Marcel Duchamp recast mass-produced goods as ready-mades, offering perhaps a closer comparison to Spade. But whereas these artists used the term as a strategy to undermine bourgeois values and the preciousness of the art object in general, Spade uses the phrase to seduce a bourgeois clientele and imbue the bags with added value through the power of naming.

The elegantly designed books that figure prominently in the shop create context and meanings for a given bag: for instance, Doris Lessing's *The Habit of Loving* stands beside a black nylon, fur-topped mini-Pouch with handle. Instant glamour, money, ennui. Or a purple shantung mini-Basket stands beside *John F. Kennedy, President.* Power, history, better times. Do you read me? Like the label in the museum, these words "exert strong cognitive control over the objects, asserting the power of classification and arrangement to order large numbers of artifacts."[18]

Borrowing from the historical avant-garde's strategy of collage and juxtaposition, found objects and books that function as didactics interpret the meaning of Spade for us through the power of association. Their unexpected appearance within the store effectively turns handbags into texts, available for reading and promoting the corporate message. In tandem with the total environment, they anchor the Spade handbag within a coherent, superior past and transform multiples into a single totality: the collection, with its mission to preserve and conserve. But this time out, the collection is offered up to the individual in the act of consumer exchange. In Spade's world, the shopper and the museum collector merge.

If history has undervalued women's work and play, then the debasement of shopping, which operates in both the aforementioned spheres, comes as no surprise. To sell her product, Spade's store elevates the act of shopping with a recuperation of its key tool, the change purse. But the fantasy cannot sustain itself outside the store's realm. The gap between the designer's "dream in the bag" and the everyday reality of women's lives rushes in as soon as the purchase is made and the client leaves the shop. Nevertheless, in the hands of girls and women, altered through the mechanics of domestic labour and leisure, a radically different kind of performance begins.

To dream, and to wake up.
To be violent, or to be violated.
Violet, a black canvas shopper with gingham lining and silk flowers by its handle, has the handmade whimsy of your mother's sewing basket, the elegance of Hepburn's bicycle panier, and the comfort of 1950s economic abundance.

performing the pas de deux

The women I met in SoHo that spring carried their bags in a variety of ways: grasped in the fist, dangling over curled fingers, balanced on an upturned wrist, sliding over an upturned forearm, pumped between the bicep and forearm, placed inside another, larger bag. One woman described the pleasure of the flexed arm; another assured me that, properly weighted, the handbag serves as a weapon of self-defence. "I just like carrying it: something about the grip makes me feel confident, like I feel my body and I'm in control," said another. Associated adjectives included funny, flirty, goofy, sexy. The nouns? Home, business, security, life. Throughout my conversations, there was a tremendous sense of irony and play. What remained consistent throughout was the grip — these women held on.

The day I encountered Nancy Garcia, a handbag designer who works for Vivienne Tam and Betsey Johnson, she was carrying a small, top-handled coach-style bag she had found at a market in Mexico City. It was held loosely between hooked fingers, the other arm swinging freely. Made of tan leather, with a painting on its side of a horse in a pasture, the bag contained a "Filofax, cell phone, some pens, and makeup." She says she carries nothing of "sentimental or fetishistic" value: "I keep my business in it — women have busy lives, they carry a lot of things, and that's why bags are great. It's like my security; it's my home."

As far as houses go, this isn't exactly the mansion on the hill. Or is it? When it comes to the miniature bag, the question of functionality arises again and again. Limited use-value marks the divide between craft and art; in rendering them small, the designer reiterates their status as art objects. Store manager Kolbrener says the bags are deceiving. "The smallest bags can fit a lot more than you might think. And people want to scale down. A lot of people want to carry less: they come in and say 'Okay, if I get a smaller bag I'm going to use it and I won't carry as much.'" Designer Muriel Favaro agrees: "You have your everyday bag for the absolute needs like your wallet and makeup, and you carry a separate one for your lunch and magazine and what-have-you." The miniature is essential, the larger bags contingent.

These words evoke the presence of the so-called bag lady, the homeless woman who carries her kitchen, clothing, necessities, and treasures with her in a sack. For her, the bag literally is home, providing some sense of security and privacy, however limited. Her image refracts here on privileged women of leisure, who share the same streets but for radically different reasons. Both use their bags to carry the essentials, but what gets deemed essential shifts dramatically. The smaller the bag, the higher the economic stature. Unlike the older technologies, things like cars and TVs, which enlarge to indicate status, the Spade miniature follows new technologies in the relationship between scale and status. In both cases, however, the bag acts as a support apparatus, a body extension that provides agency in varying degrees to its bearer. The value of this agency, finally, can be explained by the bearer alone, in relation to what these bags enact on the public stage.

In her review of the Brooklyn Museum of Arts 1997 exhibit "From Pockets to Pouches: Three Centuries of Handbags," Patricia Volk praises the handbag for what it reveals "about what we took with us and why."[19] When I asked people about what they carried in their bags, the responses came immediately, without hesitation. "Cigarettes, wallet, keys, makeup," says Stacey. "Keys, wallet, Chap Stick, shopping list," says Kimchi, who carries a transparent miniature. "Cigarettes, keys, wallet," says Cindy, holding a vinyl bowling-bag miniature. "That's the really sick thing," says Heather, laughing. "I've got another little bag inside, that holds the money and ID, and the Filofax and keys are loose." Keys, makeup, wallet. Rewind. Repeat. The perfume and the pills, the condoms and the curios slipped from sight. Finally, I began to see that the story of the handbag has less to do with what we take with us than with how we take things along and come out unscathed.

In the end, their private collections remained private, at once on display and out of sight. As only its bearer holds the legitimate power to open a bag, the object is impermeable; it can be looked at, but not into. Bachelard, writing about the importance of secret spaces, observes the following: "Wardrobes with their shelves, desks with their drawers, and chests with their false bottoms are veritable organs of the secret psychological life. Indeed, without these . . . our intimate life would lack a model of intimacy."[20] The handbag can be read as a compartment with talisman-like powers to protect privacy within the public sphere, where traditionally such interiority has been denied to women. But a dialectic is at work here; like the genitals themselves, a handbag opens and closes. Boundaries of interior and exterior, container and contained are not fixed.

Spade's miniature bag exists to contain and transport the significant documents and ephemera of the bearer. Yet its very size and detail — which promise access to the viewer — challenge perceptions about what and how containership works: we imagine its contents can't have import, but the hold on the handle suggests otherwise. Discovering the secret of the bag becomes less important than acknowledging its presence. In the action of carrying a handbag, a woman performs an age-old sleight-of-hand trick. Activating the metaphor of bag as body, the woman externalizes her body, places her physique on display, according to her own intentions. In doing so, she diverts the gaze while magnifying her claim over space.

Walter Benjamin has written that "ownership is the most intimate relationship that one can have to objects. Not that they come alive in him; it is he who lives in them."[21] Here, he implies a creative relation between our psychic and physical lives and the objects that surround us. Once held, the bag is transformed. Under the operation and control of the individual, the bag becomes both instrument and emblem of the bearer's values. Beyond serving metonymically for a woman's body and psyche, the bag in transit literally transforms the body and its psychology.

In Benjamin's essay on the work of art in the age of mechanical reproduction, he makes way for an understanding of the link between gestural practice and psychic states. Discussing the effects of slow-motion technique in film, he notes:

> Even if one has a general knowledge of the way people walk, one knows nothing of a person's posture during the fractional second of a stride. The act of reaching for a lighter or a spoon is familiar routine, yet we hardly know what really goes on between hand and metal, not to mention how this fluctuates with our moods.[22]

I want to argue that gestural practices performed by women with their handbags directly alter their perceptions of self, beyond any impressions such behaviour may have on the passersby who watch them. As much a site of possibility as of pathology, the relation is unstable and productive. More than simply echoing physical and psychological states, techniques of the body here break apart the corporate fantasy of Kate Spade and, as stated, directly alter the consciousness of the bearer. In a dance born of movement vocabularies compelled in relation to a charged object, women quietly conduct perceptual repair work to remake bodies — their own, and those of commodities that mirror them — before the public eye.

Perceptual repair work.

notes

1 "The overcrowded area caught fire so frequently it was dubbed 'Hell's Hundred Acres'; as late as 1962 a City Club of New York study called it 'commercial slum number one.' Today, the smallish walkable neighborhood (which encompasses only forty blocks from Houston Street south to Canal Street and from Lafayette Street west to Sixth Avenue) is the epitome of postmodern chic. An amalgam of black-clad art dealers, models, artists, celebrities and other Beautiful People rush in and out of galleries, bistros and boutiques all day long. Some New Yorkers have lately taken to referring to the area as being like a shopping mall." From *Fodor's Berkeley Budget Guide, New York City '97,* Jennifer Brewer (ed.) (New York: Fodor's Travel Publications, 1997), 95–8.

2 Ibid., 95.

3 Ibid., 114.

4 Pamela Lopez, *Vogue Magazine,* February 1996, 114.

5 In order, the three quotations are from *The New York Times,* 14 November 1995, Sec. B, 12; *The New York Times,* 29 February 1996, Sec. A, 16; *Vogue Magazine,* February 1996, 110–4.

6 Lopez, *Vogue Magazine,* February 1996, 114.

7 See Vivan Toy, "Behind High-End Bags, a Low-End Labor Fight," *The New York Times,* 22 September 1999, Sec. B, 1.

8 From an interview with Muriel Favaro, April 1998.

9 Gaston Bachelard, *The Poetics of Space* (Boston: Beacon Press, 1969), 161.

10 Sigmund Freud, *Dora: An Analysis of a Case of Hysteria* (New York: Touchstone Books, 1997), 68–9.

11 Vanda Foster, *Bags and Purses* (London: BT Batsford, 1982), 6.

12 See Foster for detailed history.

13 Dean MacCannell, *The Tourist: A New Theory of the Leisure Class* (New York: Schocken Books, 1976), 149.

14 Ibid., 148.

15 Neil Harris, *Cultural Excursions: Marketing Appetites and Cultural Tastes in Modern America* (Chicago: University of Chicago Press, 1990).

16 Ibid., 75. Or see Lee Simonson, "Skyscrapers for Art Museums," *American Mercury* 10, August 1927, 401.

17 Monica Geran, "It's in the Bag," *Interior Design,* April 1997, 194.

18 Barbara Kirshenblatt-Gimblett, "Objects of Ethnography," in *Destination Culture: Tourism, Museums, and Heritage* (Berkeley and Los Angeles: University of California Press, 1998), 21.

19 Patricia Volk, "For Ducats . . ." *The New York Times,* 6 April 1997, Sec. B, 43.

20 Gaston Bachelard, *The Poetics of Space* (Boston: Beacon Press, 1969), 78.

21 Walter, Benjamin, "Unpacking My Library," in *Illuminations* (New York: Schocken Books, 1968), 67.

22 Walter Benjamin, "The Work of Art in the Age of Mechanical Reproduction," in *Reflections* (New York: Schocken Books, 1978), 237.

bibliography

Bachelard, Gaston. *The Poetics of Space.* Boston: Beacon Press, 1969.

Benjamin, Walter. "Unpacking My Library." In *Illuminations.* New York: Schocken Books, 1968.

—"The Work of Art in the Age of Mechanical Reproduction." In *Reflections.* New York: Schocken Books, 1978.

Foster, Vanda. *Bags and Purses.* London: BT Batsford, 1982.

Freud, Sigmund. *Dora: An Analysis of a Case of Hysteria.* New York: Touchstone Books, 1997.

Geran, Monica. "It's in the Bag." *Interior Design,* April 1997.

Harris, Neil. *Cultural Excursions: Marketing Appetites and Cultural Tastes in Modern America.* Chicago: University of Chicago Press, 1990.

Kirshenblatt-Gimblett. Barbara, "Objects of Ethnography." In *Destination Culture: Tourism, Museums, and Heritage.* Berkeley and Los Angeles: University of California Press, 1998.

Lopez, Pamela. "Mixed Bag." *Vogue Magazine,* February 1996.

MacCannell, Dean. *The Tourist: A New Theory of the Leisure Class.* New York: Schocken Books, 1976.

Various articles from *The New York Times:*

Bumiller, Elizabeth. "A Cautious Rise . . ." 12 March 1999, Sec. B, 2.

Henderson, Steven. "A Diaper Bag that . . ." 30 March 1997, Sec. A, 27.

"New Yorkers and Co.," 14 July 1996, Sec. 13, 4.

Schiro, Anne-Marie. "By Design," 20 February 1996, Sec. A, 16.

—"Hands-On Handbags," 26 August 1997, Sec. A, 19.

Spindler, Amy, "Designers Discover Small . . ." 10 September 1996, Sec. B, 6.

Toy, Vivian S. "Behind High-End Bags, a Low-End Labor Fight," 22 September 1999, Sec. B, 1.

Volk, Patricia, "For Ducats, Billet-Doux and Tokens," 6 April 1997, Sec. B2, 43.

White, Constance. "New Wave of Designers . . ." 2 September 1997, Sec. A, 19.

—"Patterns," 24 December 1996, Sec B, 6.

—"Young American . . ." 31 December 1996, Sec. B, 7.

choreographing queer:

nationalism, citizenship, and lesbian dance clubs

b. j. wray

A body whether sitting writing or standing thinking or walking talking or running screaming, is a bodily writing. Its habits and stances, gestures and demonstrations, every action of its various regions, areas, and parts — all these emerge out of cultural practices, verbal or not, that construct corporeal meaning.
— Susan Leigh Foster, "Choreographing History," 1998

Well, let me tell you something. When I first came to Montreal, the words they say here in English are "FREAK OUT!" I went to my first gay bar, Baby Face, . . . and I walk in there and, bingo, I see all these women and I freak out again. And I say wooooo . . . WOMEN, WOMEN, WOMEN!
– Nairobi, *Forbidden Love*, 1995

decade of the dyke[1]

Never one to skip a current trend, I am compelled to begin this chapter in the spirit of millennial recaps. The final decade of the twentieth century has yielded an impressive array of lesbian images, and I ask for your indulgence as I wax fondly on a few of these milestones: the covers of *Newsweek* (21 January 1993) and *Vanity Fair* (August 1993); the media flurry surrounding Ellen's coming out;[2] the sudden mainstream visibility of more lesbian musicians than I could possibly enumerate. And my retrospective would be horribly incomplete without Nicole Conn's *Claire of the Moon* (1992), Rose Troche's *Go Fish* (1994), Lauran Hoffman's *Bar Girls* (1995), Maria Maggenti's *The Incredibly True Adventures of Two Girls in Love* (1995), Patricia Rozema's *When Night Is Falling* (1995), Andy Wachowski's *Bound* (1996), Emma-Kate Croghan's *Love and Other Catastrophes* (1997), Alex

Sichel's *All Over Me* (1997), Cheryl Dunye's *The Watermelon Woman* (1997), Lisa Cholodenko's *High Art* (1998) and Anne Wheeler's *Better Than Chocolate* (1999).

In these late-twentieth-century moments, it appears that the state of the (predominately white, upper-middle-class, skinny, and stylin') lesbian nation has never been more prominent, nor more fashionable. Our heady fifteen minutes of fame will undoubtedly be recorded in the annals of various rights organizations as a watershed along the trajectory of lesbian liberation.

Indeed, liberationist movements have always sought to flood the cultural mainstream with positive images in the hopes of displacing the pathological legacy of lesbian deviance, perversion, and unnaturalness. As Arlene Stein reminds us, "Lesbian life is indistinguishable from our images of it."[3] Remaining loyal to the power wielded by the visible realm, Pride discourses of all sorts wholeheartedly embrace a representational logic that promotes the political effectiveness of identity counter-images.

We are not surprised, then, that the celebrity status of the aforementioned lesbian icons is reinforced by gay and lesbian rights organizations desiring to solidify a queer presence within popular culture and, by extension, within society at large.[4] The use of these figures as counter images is, of course, intimately linked to the stereotypes they are meant to oppose. In fact, as the case of Ellen DeGeneres' sitcom character Ellen Morgan illustrates, the acceptability of a leading lesbian on prime-time television hinges upon the explicit rejection of deviance in favour of an almost hyperbolized normativity.[5] Passing as normal *enough* within the visible realm requires, then, that a priori dichotomies of deviance and naturalness not only remain intact but are incessantly reinforced by the image at hand.

This reinforcement has been soundly critiqued by queer cultural theorists such as Judith Butler, Sally Munt, Peggy Phelan, and Eve Kosofsky Sedgwick since the early 1990s.[6] These critics, often drawing on the lessons of psychoanalysis, point toward the vast array of limitations that are always already embedded within the visible realm. Performance theorist Peggy Phelan (via Lacan) comments on these restrictions: "Visibility is a trap; it summons surveillance and the law; it provokes voyeurism, fetishism, the colonialist/imperialist appetite for possession. Yet it retains a certain political appeal."[7] As this quotation indicates, Phelan foregrounds the apparent conundrum that visibility poses for activists and theorists alike.

A liberationist reliance on strategies of visibility opens myriad representational traps and inhibits the effectiveness of counter-images. And yet, in the face of numerous intense, articulate, and vigilant critiques of a visibility politic, I am left to wonder why its appeal still holds. Are there no other viable means through which a more diverse cultural imaginary may be fostered? Even the apparently disparate views held by various lesbian communities concerning the types of representational strategies that we should employ are surprisingly alike in their unwavering faith in their ability to manipulate and control the visible realm:

> Some believe we should create only "positive images," which are most palatable to the mainstream. Some think we should represent the full spectrum of our lives — warts and all. Others contend that we should create an alternative lesbian culture that can stand completely outside the mainstream, while others assert that we should struggle to make inroads into mainstream film, music, and the like.[8]

None of these tactics pose any challenge to the system of representation itself, nor do they critically assess their own complicity within that system, whether as assimilationists or opponents. The question remains: Given the significant costs of unproblematically taking up the visible, what goal could possibly be worth the risk of activating these traps?

the right to be . . . citizens

The risky politics of visibility still retain their currency primarily because an overreliance on the visible realm characterizes both a Western democratic tradition of "rights discourse" and, more importantly, the attendant notion of full and equal citizenship. It is to this notion of citizenship, a concept that has permeated to the core of lesbian political organizing, that I would like to direct my inquiry. More specifically, I'm interested in the ever-shifting paradigms of citizenship that are performed, parodied, and regulated within the spaces of lesbian bars and dance clubs. Historically, these two locations have served as crucial sites for lesbian community-making, their walls tentatively demarcating a nightly lesbian nation, and their dance floors usurping the serious reality of everyday life with bodily pleasures and playful socialization. The mythologization of the club in lesbian popular culture and lesbian theory ensures that this space remains fundamental to a collective narrative of lesbian identity.[9]

I am interested, then, in the nexus of space, dance, and citizenship that the club and its representations afford. This nexus prompts an interrogation of the relationship between social dancing and political citizenship. As dance theorist Jane Desmond asserts: "Looking at dance . . . demands that we theorize the relationships between the public display of bodily motion and the articulation of social categories of identity, of their transmission, transformation, perception, and enactment."[10]

How then might dance signify *sexual* identity claims? In what ways are (hetero) normative discourses of sexed bodies challenged on the dance floor? How are bodies marked by the space of the club? And, most importantly, to what extent are conventional notions of nation-making reiterated, or perhaps re-imagined, in this nexus of space, dance, and citizenship? Before I turn my attention to the clubs themselves, I want to contextualize my inquiry within an overview of the ways in which citizenship tends to be articulated in mainstream gay and lesbian political organizing. A significant critique of these citizenship politics arises out of current queer studies and provides a point of departure for my foray onto the dance floor of the lesbian club.

Citizenship and rights discourse[11] exist in a reciprocal relationship to each other; to attain citizenship means that one has a specific claim to certain inalienable rights under national laws, wheras only when one is marked as a citizen are there rights conferred. What I am driving at here is that a liberationist insistence on visibility is very much tied to an insatiable longing for one's rightful *place* within the national body, one's citizenship papers, and the only way in which that territory may be delineated is by marking and re-marking one's claim to certain rights. As Alan Sinfield explains, the agency assumed by rights advocates is inherently problematic: "For it is not that existing categories of gay men and lesbians have come forward to claim their rights, but that we have become constituted *as gay* in terms of a discourse of ethnicity and rights."[12] A rights discourse works to the extent that it both constitutes *and* articulates the existence of an identifiable, marginalized group of people.

The multiple traps accompanying heightened visibility are intimately bound to the foundational paradox inherent in rights claims: one becomes a citizen equal to other citizens under national law at the moment one's position of otherness is marked within the body politic. This conception of citizenship hinges on the simultaneous declaration and display of difference and sameness. In other words, to be constituted as a group in need of rights protection and, therefore, entitled to full benefits under the law, the group must prove its disadvantaged or stigmatized status — that it is the same but not treated the same. Gays and lesbians cannot be naturalized as citizens until our relatively "unnatural" status is reconfirmed through what the conservative Right in North America has termed "special rights."

Similarly, a liberationist appeal to rights legislation often overlooks the ways in which the power attached to a normative conception of citizenship is unwittingly reinforced by these rights claims. Borrowing from Judith Butler's arguments concerning the process of identity formation, it becomes tenable that the unmarked norms that regulate the very concept of citizenship (white, heterosexual, male, and so on) require the boundary-shoring actions of a constitutive outside to conceal their own non-originary, inauthentic status. Butler remarks: "This exclusionary matrix by which subjects are formed thus requires the simultaneous production of a domain of abject beings, those who are not yet 'subjects,' but who form the constitutive outside to the domain of the subject."[13] The "not yet" status of these subjects must be reiterated over and over again to stabilize and delineate the domain of subjectivity. At this point, Sinfield's insistence on the *illusory* nature of gay and lesbian agency within a rights discourse rings true indeed.

The late-twentieth-century employment of a rights discourse reiterates a normative citizen through a tacit reinforcement of the margin/centre dichotomy that stresses the "not yet" citizen-status of homosexuals and, inadvertently, reproduces a domain of abject beings. More often than not, attempts to overcome this abject positioning involve, as I have suggested, the reassertion of normalcy through a distinct valorization both of mainstream gay and lesbian celebrities, as well as of the notion of nationhood itself. In writing on her experiences in the New York chapter of Queer Nation, Sarah Schulman astutely discerns this compulsion:

> *Queer* did get old very fast, nowadays only academics take it seriously. But *Nation* managed to live on in many fond conversations. Transgender Nation, Alien Nation, Reincar Nation. And all along the line no one noticed how much that word echoed with the secret store of nostalgic desire for normalcy, normalcy, normalcy.[14]

Even the so called radical facets within liberationist organizing have frequently clung to the stability and privilege that discourses of national citizenship provide. Schulman makes her readers aware of the fact that organizations seeking a recognition of difference and diversity are unable and unwilling to critique the operations of national discourse, precisely because those operations hold the promise of sameness and equality for a community in need of validation.

The "nostalgic desire for normalcy" bespeaks an investment in the psychic maintenance of traditional narratives of belonging and placement, and gestures toward the ways in which liberationist discourses of all kinds are haunted by the spectre of their own outsider positioning. A rights discourse, seeking to produce a domain of intelligible and, therefore, legitimate homosexual bodies, tends to replicate the mechanisms of exclusion by which the subject/citizen is formed. Again, in the words of Butler: "every oppositional discourse will produce its outside."[15] The result is a cyclical replaying of how normative categorizations are constructed, rather than the intended expansion of what full and equal citizenship might mean.

Creating our own rules for citizenship — as emblematized in the call for distinct geographical locations, or in the uncritical engagement with a rights discourse — falsely ascribes liberatory power to "outsider" positioning. Although useful to visions of a lesbian utopia in which safety and community are secured through real or imaginary sites, the notion of "outsiderness" remains bound up with dominant discursive constructions of proper placement. The transformation of citizenship, then, requires that we are highly cognizant of "the exclusions by which we proceed."[16] The politics espoused by a rights discourse are most frequently *additive* rather than transformative of the categories at hand.

image(a)nation

The potential for transformation is not to be found within a full-scale abandonment or disavowal of our apparently overwhelming desire to secure a territory of our own within a national body politic. Indeed, as I have alluded to, the longing for full citizenship, and the stabilization of identity that it affords, is most often figured as an acute longing for place. In their introduction to the recent *Queers in Space* anthology, Gordon Brent Ingram, Anne-Marie Bouthillette, and Yolanda Retter remark on the crucial role that space-making plays in minority communities: "Although in the late twentieth century space has become recognized as a signifier of a group's status in society, this realization has not yet transformed society or yielded real inclusion."[17] In a similar vein, Sally Munt observes that "the lesbian's movement through time and space is an act of her professed belief in an imagined community, one in which there is full *citizenship* for her"[18] (emphasis added).

This place may be conceptualized as an actual geographical location in which our own rules of citizenship apply (lesbian bars/clubs, lesbian urban ghettos, lesbian separatist land, and so on), or place may be understood, more abstractly, as recognizable sites within the cultural, social, and political imaginary (lesbian films/books/plays/performances, lesbian politicians, lesbian mothers, and so on). Whether conceptualized as literal or abstract or more accurately as both, place-making and space-taking are fundamental to the making of lesbian identity itself. In fact, as the quotation from Munt suggests, it is an almost seamless relationship between the quotidian and the imaginary that defines the parameters of lesbian existence.

Much of the recent queer commentary on this interlining of the "real" and the imaginary in place-making, citizenship, and identity politics is indebted to Benedict Anderson's seminal text, *Imagined Communities:*

Reflections on the Origin and Spread of Nationalism. Although, as the editors of *Nationalisms and Sexualities* note, Anderson does not address sexuality in any detail, his writing "furnishes a series of terms that have proven exceedingly useful for us."[19] Among those terms is of course the notion of the imaginary status of the nation. According to Anderson, the nation is imagined "because the members of even the smallest nation will never know most of their fellow-members, meet them, or even hear of them, yet in the minds of each lives the image of their communion."[20]

Anderson's description, then, powerfully resonates with Munt's aforementioned articulations of the "lesbian belief in an *imagined community.*" As a queer culture we are not rooted in a particular geographical location, nor can we lay claim to territorial borders or other conventional markers of nation-status. These conditions require that our paradigms of citizenship seriously account for the complicated and wonderfully playful operations of the imagination in queer community-making. Similarly, the constraints that a heterocentric culture places on daily living can, in many ways, be countered only through a recourse to the imagination: "The imagination is of paramount importance in a heterosexual world which effaces our experience, by rendering us absent."[21] Anderson's musings on the foundational role of the imagination in the constitution of *all* nations provides an obvious theoretical framework for queer speculations on community and citizenship.

Our models of belonging (national or otherwise) must, however, foreground *more* than the use-value of the imagination as an identity-constituting force. In addition, an attentiveness to the *inseparability* of the actual and the imagined will be necessary to highlight both the historically grounded power of discourse to materialize identities and the bodies attached to those identities, as well as the influence wielded over social and political realms by a cultural imaginary. In his recent essay "Queer Space," Jean-Ulrick Desert insists that, "Queer space is in large part the function of wishful thinking or desires that become solidified."[22] Desert's description of queer space resists the impulse to stabilize boundaries or to concretize the abstractness attached to such a definition. In this way, a much more fluid, provisional, and nuanced version of space, and, by extension, the citizens producing and produced by that space is made possible.

Anderson's notion, then, of the very real, yet very precarious, foundation of the nation, coupled with current examinations of the tenuousness of queer space, may serve as a rich paradigm for restrategizing the ways in which lesbian citizenship is pursued. Instead of relying on the inherently unreliable structures of visibility politics and rights discourses to make the lesbian subject culturally intelligible, a conception of citizenship that locates its existence somewhere in the *interstice* of reality and imagination potentially engenders a more critical engagement with some of the foundational binaries of sexual identity: centre/margin, homosexual/heterosexual, and normal/deviant.

out of the novel and into the bar

Perhaps no other space figures as prominently or as frequently in the collective lesbian cultural imaginary than the lesbian bar or dance club. The very germination of contemporary gay and lesbian activism in America is consistently represented as the 1969 uprising against New York City police by the dykes and drag queens of a Greenwich Village bar, the Stonewall Inn. And it is against the backdrop of bar stools, pool cues, strobe lights, and pulsating beats that the historical shifts in representations of lesbian citizenship have been played out; from butch and femme to androgynous lesbian feminist to gender-fuck queer to transgendered drag king, all of these identity offerings have called the club their home. The bar still tends to function today, both in lesbian popular culture and on seedy streets across North America, as the first realization of lesbian community for many women. Indeed, where would the "coming out" narrative find its triumphant culmination without the ubiquitous lesbian club as the site of our heroine's homecoming? The idealization of this homecoming in representational forms, ranging from the pulp fiction novels of the 1950s and 1960s to the spate of mainstream lesbian films in the 1990s, establishes the club as a stable marker of one's participation in the lesbian nation.

Aerlyn Weissman and Lynne Fernie's 1995 National Film Board of Canada documentary, *Forbidden Love: The Unashamed Stories of Lesbian*

Lives, wonderfully encapsulates the anticipation, the terror, and the excitement of discovering one's first lesbian club. *Forbidden Love* is a campy cross-genre blend of pulp-fiction representations of lesbian clubs and interview footage of Canadian lesbians retelling their bar and club experiences of the 1950s and 1960s. *Forbidden Love* functions as the title for both the film itself and the lesbian pulp novel that the film dramatizes through the story of Laura and Mitch. Intermittently appearing between the interviews, the fictional characters of *Forbidden Love,* the novel, literally come to life as an anonymous hand opens the paperback displayed on the screen and a narrator's voice reads the exposed text of this pulp fiction. Laura and Mitch play out the scene as it is narrated, and as each episode of this drama comes to a close, the actors' poses are captured in a freeze-frame. This static moment gradually transforms on the screen into the stylized artist's rendering that was often found on the covers of 1950s pulp fiction novels. Fernie and Wiessman then seamlessly slide back into the documentary format and continue with their interviews.

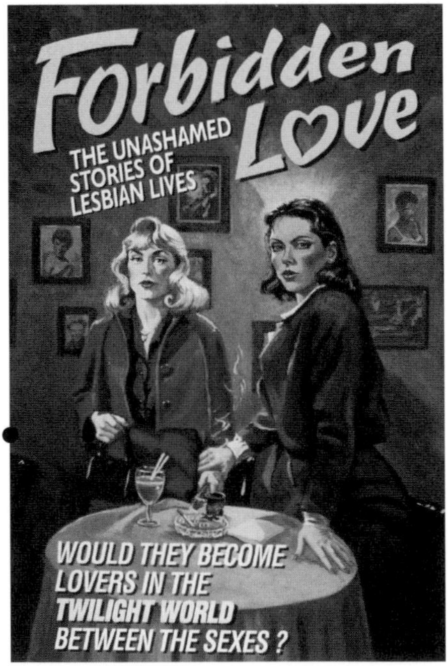

Laura and Mitch: blending documentary and pulp fiction in Forbidden Love.

This combination of "fact" and "fiction" enacts within the film a literal embodiment of the reciprocal relation between popular representational forms and the material experiences of the women interviewed. Reva Hutkins, a interviewee from Victoria, British Columbia, hilariously describes this relationship: "At one point we thought all the lesbians obviously live in New York, in Greenwich Village. At least the books said that's where they all lived. We decided we had to go and find *the lesbians* . . . off we went to Greenwich Village to look for the lesbians." Even though they never did find "the lesbians," Reva Hutkins fondly recalls her trek decades later as a key moment in her identificatory process.

Certainly, the *Bildungsroman* format of the pulp-fiction paperbacks narrates lesbian life as journey in which the heroine's entry into recognizably lesbian sites, in particular, the lesbian bar, provides a climactic moment of identify affirmation. When chapter two of *Forbidden Love* opens onscreen, we see Laura poised at the threshold of a lesbian bar pondering the enormity of the simple act she is about to undertake: "Laura's heart was pounding. She'd heard these places could be dangerous but her need to be with other women who were like her, like *that,* was stronger than her fear. Well, she was here and she might as well go in. She'd have just one drink." As these words are read, Laura steps from the shadows of the back alley into the light of the bar, and her journey begins. Looking very awkward and very alone, she sits at an unoccupied table. True to the pulp-fiction formula, Laura is immediately sized up by Mitch, the ubiquitous bar-butch posed by the jukebox. In an obviously well-practised gesture, Mitch motions to the bartender. Mitch arrives at Laura's table soon after the mint julep, and the seduction of Laura into a "lesbian lifestyle" begins in earnest.

Not surprisingly, the real-life experiences of the lesbians who are interviewed tend to reinstate the club as the culmination of their search for recognition and acceptance. One interviewee, Nairobi, explains: "You just glimpse across the room and you see somebody and you say, 'That's the one I want.' And you send them a drink. Then the flower lady walks in and you buy her a flower, a rose, and she gets it." The obvious interplay between representations and experiences in *Forbidden Love* reveals the extent to which these categories collude in the making of a lesbian cultural imaginary. Indeed, the film itself provides yet another level of representation wherein the signifying power of the lesbian club is amplified and rendered once again as a crucial site of identity stabilization and citizenship. Often, just knowing behind which unmarked door or down which darkened alley one may find this promised lotus land becomes the unofficial queer citizenship exam:

> So I used to go up and down all the bars on Granville Street [in Vancouver, British Columbia] because I didn't know where they were. I would go into a bar and have a beer and have my eyes peering around: "Are they in here? Are they in there?" [Stephanie Ozard, *Forbidden Love*]

Once found, the citizenship test in this imagined nation continues in earnest as the newcomer finds herself swiftly (if not humiliatingly) visually evaluated according to a historically — and geographically — specific set of *de rigueur* lesbian signifiers: clothing style, bodily stance, and, most importantly, haircut.

However, I am not interested in undertaking an ethnographic evaluation of the restrictive operations of club citizenship. Undoubtedly, the fact that lesbian clubs tend to replicate some of the worst aspects of exclusive nationalism is a point well made by lesbian-feminist cultural critics. But such studies invariably conclude with both a bitter denouncement of patriarchy's influence over lesbian culture and a liberationist call to find alternative sites in which to embrace a more diverse lesbian community. My interrogation of lesbian clubs intends to unravel the complicated representational dynamic among space, dance, and citizenship, not as a means of rehearsing well-worn negative perceptions of bar-space, nor as simple reaffirmation of the club as a utopic site of nation-building. Rather, I am drawn inside the club by its potential as a site in which the inseparability of reality and imagination, of representation and the real, is abundantly manifest. As both a geographical location *and* a historically mythologized representational icon of lesbian identity narratives, the club straddles the borders of an imaginary lesbian citizenship and a literalized territorial occupation.

dancing matter(s)

Susan Leigh Foster's seminal essay, "Choreographing History," provides a theoretical base (and the basis of my essay's title) for understanding this interlined relationship between historically situated discursive production and corporeality. The transmission of representations across, in, and through bodies delimits corporeal movements and the meaning ascribed to those actions:

> To choreograph history, then, is first to grant that history is made by bodies . . . In the process of committing their actions to history, these past and present bodies transit to a mutually constructed semiosis. Together they configure a tradition of codes and conventions of bodily signification that allows bodies to represent and communicate to other bodies.[23]

The importance of Foster's argument in terms of representations of lesbian clubs is threefold. First, she implicates both past and present bodies in the construction of a collective narrative of meaning. This tactic ensures that the historian or filmmaker or novelist or theorist is recognized as always already enmeshed in the making of bodily signification. Second, Foster foregrounds a reciprocal relationship between discursivity and corporeality. The body does not stand outside of its representations, yet neither do those representations overpower material existence. Bodies do not disappear behind a curtain of discursivity but remain unalterably intertwined with the signification process. Finally, Foster's observations engender a critical paradigm for re-imagining a lesbian citizenry. Her model emphasizes a continual exchange between past and present, discourses and bodies, and representations and experiences. Such a model produces a recognizable, yet entirely tenuous, notion of collective identity in which the conventions of bodily signification are irrevocably linked to the representational discourses attached to those bodies.

Foster's argument resonates with current queer theoretical speculations on the performative nature of identity. Figures in the queer theoretical canon (Judith Butler, Michel Foucault, Elizabeth Grosz, and Eve Kosofsky Sedgwick, among others) are united in their explorations of the discursive materialization of bodies and in their refutation of "natural" status of identities. In the oft-quoted phrasing of Butler, "what constitutes the fixity of the body, its contours, its movements, will be fully material, but materiality will be rethought as the effect of power, as power's most productive effect."[24] Corporeality is, thus, not natural nor innate nor stable, but is *materialized* "within the domain of cultural intelligibility."[25] To speak of the performativity of identities is to acknowledge "the reiterative and citational practice by which discourse produces the effects that it names."[26]

Where Foster usefully departs from Butler's philosophical stance is in her determination to reintroduce flesh and bones into Butler's body-equals-performativity-plus-cultural-intelligibility equation. In Foster's account of bodily signification, corporeality is an intimate and inseparable combination of discourse and the very real material body engaged in a communal configuration of identities:

> Constructed from endless and repeated encounters with other bodies, each body's writing maintains a non-natural relation between its physicality and referentiality. Each body establishes this relation between physicality and meaning in concert with the physical actions and verbal descriptions of bodies that move alongside it.[27]

Foster's invocation of a corporeal collectivity calls up images of a crowded lesbian club dance floor, where bodies brushing, bumping, and grinding together participate in an ongoing configuration of bodily signification. These dancing bodies move within a recognizable lesbian cultural imaginary, their appearance and gestures performatively encoding and encoded by representations of lesbian sexuality.

Dance theorist Ted Polhemus explains the central role that dance holds in the constitution of social meaning: "While physical culture may be viewed as a crystallization — an embodiment — of the most deeply rooted and fundamental level of what it means to be a member of a particular society, dance might be seen as the second stage of this process — a schema, an abstraction or stylizing of physical culture."[28] However, lesbian social dance does not have the framework of "belonging" or the popular memory that historically transmitted dance steps, such as the tango, mambo, or rumba frequently endow upon ethnic-based social dance cultures. Lesbian social dance does not lend itself to easy specification; "It has no name, and even if it did such a name would gloss a variety of historically complex and improvisational movement styles."[29] As I pointed out earlier in this essay, the political attempt to slot lesbian identity into an ethnicity and rights discourse unwittingly reinforces an exclusionary notion of citizenship. So, too, adopting an ethnic model in the description of lesbian social dance risks re-inscribing notions of authenticity and inauthenticity, and does little in the way of dismantling such dichotomous thinking.

Historically, lesbian social dance has often re-marked citizenship claims through a re-territorialization of conventional signifiers of corporeality. Take for instance the butch/femme dance pairings of the 1950s and 1960s, and to some extent their 1990s representational reincarnation. These non-normative figures employ conventional heterosexual dance couplings to secure, by proxy, the signification of desire wielded by that traditional pairing. Jonathan Bollen, in his essay on Australian gay dance culture, comments that "[s]ocial dancing is often seen as a trivial or frivolous practice, but it is perhaps for this reason that pleasures taken on the dance floor can constitute a form of resistance, even if the effects of that resistance are denied."[30]

In an act of resistance, butch/femme dance partners infiltrate existing discourses on femininity, potentially offering a re-articulation of desire that reworks the (hetero) normative regulation of bodies. Or as Lois M. Stuart teasingly reminds viewers of *Forbidden Love:* "Well, if you're gonna lead a double life, then *lead* a double life. I had to dress nicely all my life at work so [for the bar] I dressed in black pants, a black cowboy shirt, sometimes cowboy boots, and a big thick belt around my waist with a knife on it." Stuart's preference for the outlaw look enacts a necessary (even if temporary) refusal of prevailing norms.

The frequent police raids on lesbian bars in the 1950s and 1960s documented in *Forbidden Love* also testify to the radical re-signification of sexual citizenship that these dance partners embody: two women dancing together were subject to criminal prosecution.[31] These raids reveal the centrality of social dance as a marker of normative identity and desire, and those who dare to transgress the codes of (hetero) social conduct solicit harsh and frequent punishment. Cynthia Novack further elaborates on the regulatory power of social dance: "A dance performance . . . is always a cultural performance as well . . . It may constitute part of our sense of time and space, our understanding of the construction and relationships of the body, mind, and person, or our ideas of what a man and a woman are."[32]

Butch/femme dance pairs shift these gender "ideas" and offer a new connection between "body, mind, and person" that can account for lesbian desire. Butch/femme social dance provides a site of cultural resistance because "culture is embodied . . . We perform movement, invent it, interpret it, and reinterpret it, on conscious and unconscious levels. In these actions, we participate in and reinforce culture, and we also create it."[33]

The police raids on lesbian clubs further signal a determination to contain and isolate lesbian bodies from one another. The social space of the club is the space of a *shared* body, "a body which transcends the ultimate boundary marking public from private: the boundary of the body's surface."[34] The lesbian club's dance floor reverberates with culturally coded visual performances of desire, and crosses the threshold of a hetero-normative visual logic in which lesbian bodies are conventionally made to disappear. Jonathan Bollen describes this potentially subversive corporeality:

> For as much as the body on the dance floor is a bodily surface, it is through the sharing of kinesthetic experiences — visualized across the surface of the body, but incorporated via the oscillation of performer/spectator relations in a socially interactive and repetitive/imitative movement practice — that a larger communal body emerges.[35]

This communal body threatens to disrupt traditional conceptions of corporeality and the regulation of desire attached to those conceptions. The dance floor, then, by rendering culturally intelligible a communal rather than an individual body, openly interrogates the ways in which bodies themselves are produced by certain regulatory norms.

Consolidation of a "communal body" typified the advent of a lesbian-feminist ideology in the 1970s. Its invocation of the "lesbian nation" marked a dramatic shift away from the dominance of butch/femme relations within the lesbian cultural imaginary. Not surprisingly, lesbian social dance embodied these changes. In an effort to create a distinctive lesbian culture, outside of hetero-patriarchal paradigms of desire, lesbian-feminist dance culture moved away from the primacy of dance couples to the seemingly more egalitarian stance of androgynous-appearing bodies dancing alone or in groups. In doing so, lesbian feminist social dance participated in the wider cultural milieu of the late 1960s and early 1970s:

> For more politically minded people, rock dance constituted a metaphor for political awareness. The extensive improvisation in rock dance enacted the rejection of explicit structures by New Left and feminist organizations . . . And the lack of differentiation between male and female movement symbolized a rebellion against American gender roles.[36]

Social dance quickly became a critical component in lesbian feminist organizing strategies. The "dance" not only provided a much-needed meeting place to consolidate newly claimed lesbian identities, it also gave shape to those identities through a movement style that challenged predetermined, partnered forms of dance. Social dance furthered the creation of a distinct lesbian community, as well as connections *between* otherwise disparate political movements:

> As explicit political phenomena, the student movement, the civil rights and the black liberation movements, the antiwar movement, and the women's movement found only tenuous moments of alliance with each other. But dancing, a multivocal and flexible sphere of social activity, could on occasion alleviate and even transcend political differences, emphasizing the shared ethos of these movements for social change.[37]

However, the utopian transcendence of political differences tended to reinforce a rather uncritical faith in the unmediated nature of corporeality; dance figures in lesbian-feminist pride-centred events as a liberatory activity in which bodies freely express their "outsider" status. Dance critic Janet Wolff forcefully notes that an emphasis on the liberatory power of dance "depends on a mistaken idea of dance as intuitive, non-verbal, 'natural,' and . . . it risks abandoning critical analysis for a vague and ill-conceived 'politics of the body.'"[38]

Within these social events, the representational cachet of dance works in tandem with a liberationist political ideology to substantiate a newly formed lesbian nation and, concurrently, to reconstitute lesbian corporeality as oppositional to dominant cultural ideals. To these ends, the site of dancing also shifts away from the profit-driven, non-lesbian-owned bar to the not-for-profit community hall, church, or school. This change of location spatially enacts a more seamless relationship between politics and social dancing. Flanked by tables of political literature, lesbian merchandise, and vegetarian food, the oversized designated dance areas of these venues are literally encased by the trappings of a protective, and often unwittingly regulatory, lesbian nation.[39] These collectively organized social dances offer a re-narration of lesbian corporeality and, once again, demonstrate that dance is not simply a *metaphor* for renegotiating identities but is, instead, a performative instance of the interlining of bodies and discourse. In the words of queer critic Jose Munoz, "the dance of identity suggests neither being nor even becoming, but a body in motion that breaks into meaning to the polyrhythmic beat of history."[40]

Dance clubs and community-centred dances, though politically, aesthetically, and historically specific, each function as a site of sexual citizenship in which the materialization of lesbian identities is made glaringly apparent. Again, to quote Munoz, "Dance sets politics in motion, bringing people together in rhythmic affinity where identification takes the form of histories written on the body through gesture."[41] Crucially, though, the ways in which cultural representations, histories, and bodies interact is never fully known nor easily contained. As Foster succinctly comments, "Not only is this relation between the physical and conceptual non-natural, it is also impermanent. It mutates, transforms, reinstantiates with each new encounter."[42] The impermanence Foster attaches to the relation between the physical and the conceptual resonates with the provisionality of club culture itself. "Last call" signals the end of this localized lesbian nation and gestures toward its status as an "imagined community." Indeed, even within the boundaries of time and space provided by the territory of the club, the citizenry of this temporary lesbian nation is difficult to regulate, and, as the recent boom in drag king culture demonstrates, sometimes this nation is impossible to identify.

Or impossible to locate, for as lesbian theorist Yolanda Retter has recently lamented, "contemporary public lesbian spaces still reflect a lack of physical 'territorializing.' Whether due to economic, pragmatic, or essentialist factors, lesbian public spaces are now more often signified by events and networks that represent a wide(r) variety of interests."[43] Rather than lament this nomadic trend, it seems crucial that we embrace this sea change in notions of lesbian citizenship. Roving clubs embody the ever-shifting, unpredictable narrativization of lesbian corporeality and identity. Citizenship for one night is, indeed, unsettling, and it is precisely this instability that engenders a more reflexive relationship to the imaginary status of lesbian community.

notes

1 Introductory sections of this essay also appear in my essay on Canadian performance artists Kiss and Tell (*Torquere: Journal of the Canadian Lesbian and Gay Studies Association* 1, 1999: 25–46). Kiss and Tell engage with the issues of nationalism and citizenship through their representations of lesbian desire in a Canadian context. Their work raises concerns similar to the ones I take up in this essay.

2 Both comic Ellen DeGeneres and the title character she played on the ABC prime-time sitcom *Ellen* publicly came out as lesbians in April 1997. The character of Ellen Morgan announced her sexuality in a special one-hour episode on 30 April 1997.

3 A. Stein (ed.), *Sisters, Sexperts, Queers: Beyond the Lesbian Nation* (New York: Plume/Penguin Books, 1993), 63.

4 The reliance on celebrity status as a means of garnering public support for gays and lesbians is exemplified by the appointment of Chastity Bono (daughter of Sonny and Cher) as the media relations coordinator for America's pre-eminent gay rights organization, the National Gay and Lesbian Task Force.

5 Ellen Morgan, an unassuming, white, middle-class, girl-next-door who happens to be a lesbian, fulfills enough of the conventional registers of normalcy to make her palatable to a "general" audience. The normalization of Morgan (and, by extension, DeGeneres) is most explicit in *Time* magazine's cover story on DeGeneres (14 April 1997). In addition, two excellent essays on the relationship between normativity and lesbian visibility in popular culture are Danae Clark's "Commodity Lesbianism" and Sasha Torres' "Television/Feminism: *Heartbeat* and Prime Time Lesbianism" both found in Abelove et al. (eds.), *The Lesbian and Gay Studies Reader* (New York: Routledge, 1993).

6 See, for instance, Butler's *Bodies That Matter*, Munt's *Heroic Desire: Lesbian Identity and Cultural Space*, Phelan's *Unmarked: The Politics of Performance*, and Sedgwick's *Tendencies*.

7 P. Phelan, *Unmarked: The Politics of Performance* (New York: Routledge, 1993), 6.

8 Stein, *Sisters, Sexperts, Queers: Beyond the Lesbian Nation*, 63–4.

9 The lesbian bar has been iconized in countless movies, books, and essays. A few recent examples include Leslie Feinberg's novel *Stone Butch Blues* (Ithaca, NY: Firebrand Books, 1993); Rose Troche's 1994 film *Go Fish;* Lauran Hoffman's 1995 film *Bar Girls;* Joan Nestle's text *A Restricted Country* (Ithaca, NY: Firebrand Books, 1987), and Sue-Ellen Case's essay "Making Butch: An Historical Memoir of the 1970s" in Sally Munt's anthology *butch/femme: Inside Lesbian Gender* (London: Cassell, 1998).

10 J. C. Desmond, "Embodying Difference: Issues in Dance and Cultural Studies," in Jane C. Desmond (ed.), *Meaning in Motion* (Durham, NC: Duke University Press, 1997), 3.

11 By "rights discourse" I mean an appeal to a system of governance based on the legal protection of its subjects from discrimination through a state-approved set of protected identity criteria such as religious beliefs, ethnicity, race, sex, and so on.

12 A. Sinfield, "Diaspora and Hybridity: Queer Identities and the Ethnicity Model," *Textual Practice* 10, 1996, 2: 271.

13 J. Butler, *Bodies That Matter* (New York: Routledge, 1993), 3.

14 S. Schulman, *Rat Bohemia* (New York: Dutton/Penguin Books, 1995), 111.

15 Butler, *Bodies That Matter*, 52.

16 Ibid., 53.

17 G. Ingram, "'Open' Space as Strategic Queer Sites," in G. Ingram, A. M. Bouthillette, and Y. Retter (eds.), *Queers in Space* (Seattle: Bay Press, 1997), 6.

18 S. Munt, *Heroic Desire: Lesbian Identity and Cultural Space* (New York: New York University Press, 1998), 173.

19 A. Parker, M. Russo, D. Sommer, and P. Yaeger (eds.), *Nationalisms and Sexualities* (New York: Routledge, 1992), 5.

20 B. Anderson, *Imagined Communities* (London: Verso, 1983), 15.

21 Munt, *Heroic Desire: Lesbian Identity and Cultural Space*, 174.

22 J. U. Desert, "Queer Space," in *Queers in Space*, 21.

23 S. Foster, "Choreographing History," in Alexandra Carter (ed.), *The Routledge Dance Studies Reader* (New York: Routledge, 1998), 188.

24 Butler, *Bodies That Matter*, 2.

25 Ibid.

26 Ibid.

27 S. Foster, "Choreographing History," in *The Routledge Dance Studies Reader*, 180.

28 T. Polhemus, "Dance, Gender and Culture," *The Routledge Dance Studies Reader*, 174.

29 J. Bollen, "Sexing the Dance at Sleaze Ball 1994," *The Drama Review* 40, 3, 1996: 173.

30 Ibid., 172.

31 Gary Kinsman's *The Regulation of Desire: Sexuality in Canada* (Montreal: Black Rose Books, 1987) provides historical accounts of some of the raids on lesbian bars in Canada in the 1950s as well as the use of raids as a policing tactic into the 1980s.

32 C. J. Novak, *Sharing the Dance: Contact Improvisation and American Culture* (Madison: University of Wisconsin Press, 1990), 14.

33 Ibid., 8.

34 Bollen, "Sexing the Dance at Sleaze Ball 1994," *The Drama Review* 40, 3, 1996: 175.

35 Ibid.

36 C. J. Novak, *Sharing the Dance: Contact Improvisation and American Culture,* 39, 42.

37 Ibid., 42.

38 Janet Wolff, "Dance Criticism: Feminism, Theory, and Choreography," in Thomas Carmichael and Martin Kreiswirth (eds.), *Constructive Criticism: The Human Sciences in the Age of Theory* (Toronto: University of Toronto Press, 1995), 148-66.

39 Feinberg's autobiographical novel *Stone Butch Blues* (Ithaca, NY: Firebrand Books, 1993) provides several accounts of the border-policing of gender and sexuality carried out at lesbian-feminist dances and in lesbian bars in the name of "pure" lesbian citizenship.

40 J. Munoz and Celeste Fraser Delgado, "Rebellions of Everynight Life," in Jose Esteban Munoz and Celeste Fraser Delgado (eds.), *Everynight Life: Culture and Dance in Latin/o America* (Durham, NC: Duke University Press, 1997), 14.

41 Ibid., 9.

42 S. Foster, "Choreographing History," in *The Routledge Dance Studies Reader,* 180.

43 Y. Retter, "Lesbian Spaces in Los Angeles, 1970–90," in *Queers in Space,* 335.

bibliography

Anderson, B. *Imagined Communities: Reflections on the Origin and Spread of Nationalism.* London: Verso, 1983.

Bell, D., and G. Valentine. "Introduction: Orientations." In D. Bell and G. Valentine (eds.), *Mapping Desire: Geographies of Sexualities.* New York: Routledge, 1995.

Berlant, L., and E. Freeman. "Queer Nationality." *boundary 2,* 19, 1992:149–80.

Bollen, J. "Sexing the Dance at Sleaze Ball 1994." *The Drama Review* 40, 3, 1996: 166–91.

Butler, J. *Bodies That Matter.* New York: Routledge, 1993.

Carter, Alexandra (ed.). *The Routledge Dance Studies Reader.* New York: Routledge, 1998.

Desmond, J. C. "Embodying Difference: Issues in Dance and Cultural Studies." In Jane C. Desmond (ed.), *Meaning in Motion.* Durham, NC: Duke University Press, 1997.

Grosz, E. *Space, Time, and Perversion.* New York: Routledge, 1995.

Ingram, G., A. M. Bouthillette, and Y. Retter (eds.). *Queers in Space.* Seattle: Bay Press, 1997.

Munoz, J. and Celeste Fraser Delgado. "Rebellions of Everynight Life." In Jose Esteban Munoz and Celeste Fraser Delgado (eds.), *Everynight Life: Culture and Dance in Latin/o America.* Durham, NC: Duke University Press, 1997.

Munt, S. (ed.). Afterword to *butch/femme: Inside Lesbian Gender.* London: Cassell, 1998.

—. *Heroic Desire: Lesbian Identity and Cultural Space.* New York: New York University Press, 1998.

Novack, C. J. *Sharing the Dance: Contact Improvisation and American Culture.* Madison: University of Wisconsin Press, 1990.

Parker, A., M. Russo, D. Sommer, and P. Yaeger (eds.). *Nationalisms and Sexualities.* New York: Routledge, 1992.

Phelan, P. *Unmarked: The Politics of Performance.* New York: Routledge, 1993.

Roof, J. *A Lure of Knowledge: Lesbian Sexuality and Theory.* New York: Columbia University Press, 1991.

Schulman, S. *Rat Bohemia.* New York: Dutton/Penguin Books, 1995.

Sinfield, A. "Diaspora and Hybridity: Queer Identities and the Ethnicity Model." *Textual Practice* 10, 2, 1996: 271–93.

Stein, A. (ed.). *Sisters, Sexperts, Queers: Beyond the Lesbian Nation.* New York: Plume/Penguin Books, 1993.

Wolff, Janet. "Dance Criticism: Feminism, Theory, and Choreography." In Thomas Carmichael and Martin Kreiswirth (eds.), *Constructive Criticism: The Human Sciences in the Age of Theory,* 148–66. Toronto: University of Toronto Press, 1995.

working women dancing

blood wedding:

tradition and innovation in contemporary flamenco

michelle heffner hayes

"The mention of Spanish dance perfumes the air with sensuous and exotic images . . ."[1] So spoke Celia Ipiotis, host and producer of the *Eye on Dance* television and video series, during the opening credits of a 1991 episode. With this sound byte she teases the viewers, convinces them to stay where they are — don't touch that dial! — and promises to deliver images borne upon air. Ipiotis directly addresses the underlying assumptions held by most spectators as they view Spanish and Gypsy dances. She invokes the image of Carmen, the flashing thighs that conceal a knife, flying dark hair, heavy lidded eyes, and the cloud of dust that rises from the flurry of her footwork. In my research, I focus on the stereotypical image of the Gypsy dancer, particularly the female flamenco dancer, and how her image reflects the tensions of class, race, gender, and national identity in Spanish history. I argue that the transformation of flamenco as a practice has paralleled the political and social changes in Spain, and the world, in the twentieth century.

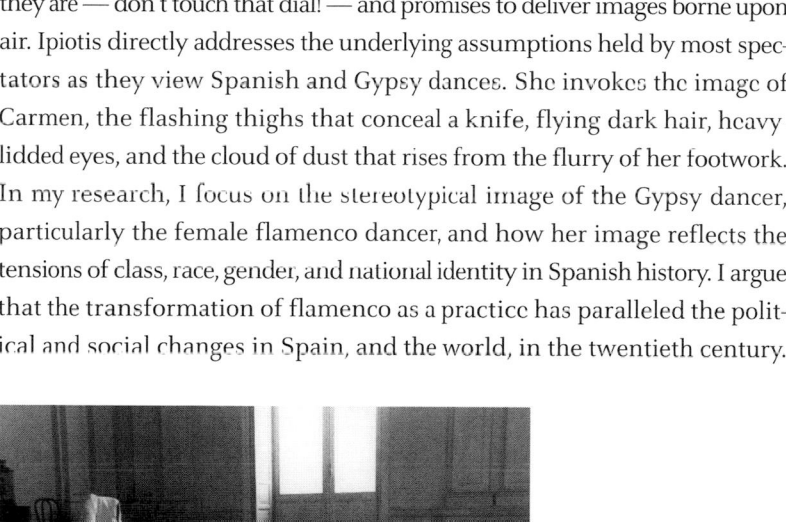

Understated masculine prowess and irreverent, fatal femininity share an illicit embrace in Carlos Saura's Bodas de Sangre *(1981).*

I would like to map out the historical landscape that has surrounded and produced the image of the flamenco dancer. This essay will focus on a close reading of *Bodas de Sangre,* a flamenco ballet on film, adapted from Federico García Lorca's 1933 play. I'm going to sketch out a timeline of events, including significant details about the performance of flamenco in different historical contexts.

The genre that most musicologists, flamencologists, aficionados, and practitioners recognize as flamenco song and dance emerged during the nineteenth century as a hybrid product of Andalusian and Gypsy cultures. At the turn of the century, lower-class Gypsy men and women performed for wealthy Spaniards and foreign travellers in the *cafés cantantes* (flamenco bars of Seville, Madrid, Granada, Cordoba, and Barcelona). Guitarists, singers, and dancers shared the stage, participating equally in the performance. Members of the *cuadro* accompanied one another as they took turns doing solos. Men performed phrases of rhythmic footwork, while women articulated spiralling shapes with their fingers, arms, and upper torsos.

In the years before the Spanish Civil War, poet and playwright Federico García Lorca animated his works, which dealt with the oppression of Gypsies and lower-class Andalusians, with the image of the dancing Gypsy girl. Her sinuous arms traced hypnotic paths, echoing the landscape of southern Spain. During Franco's fascist regime, flamencos performed around the world, garnering the attention of international audiences and Hollywood filmmakers. Large flamenco companies presented chorus revues featuring dancers in bright costumes who incorporated acrobatic leaps and turns into the "traditional" vocabulary.

Following a series of United Nations negotiations with the Franco government, the United States established military bases in Spain. Soldiers and tourists alike fuelled the immense popularity of the *tablaos* (flamenco nightclubs), which advertised flamenco dance as the symbol of progressive Spain and provided a highly lucrative commodity during an economic depression. The dance element of flamenco came to the forefront of these burlesque productions, pushing the guitar and song components into the background. The commodification of flamenco performance corresponded with a growing association between prostitution and female flamenco dancers.

In response to the effects of commercialism during the 1970s, institutions such as the National Ballet of Spain made an effort to rescue flamenco dance forms from the commercial arena and recuperate them as part of a "classical" dance tradition. To this end, professional schools were founded to train a population of young dancers committed to the purification and preservation of flamenco as a tradition.

The movement toward *flamenco puro* (pure flamenco) has characterized dance historical scholarship since the 1960s, particularly among American flamencophiles. The proponents of *flamenco puro* look back on history and imagine a period in which flamenco reflected the innocence of an untouched paradise. They rewrite the history of Andalusia, producing a portrait of a land and a people unspoiled by the political and economic realities of civil war, a fascist dictatorship, and international commercialism. Many practitioners and aficionados attempt to recapture the dance style of the Golden Age of the *cafés cantantes* (roughly, 1881–1900) in private, non-commercial, or professional concert settings. Traditional flamenco, as it has been reinvented since the 1950s, eschews the acrobatics and "vulgar" sexual display of commercial productions. Instead, the male dancer projects a severe columnar silhouette as his feet strike the floor in a building, rapid display of footwork. In contrast, the female dancer seems rooted to the ground as she arches her spine. Her fingers flutter and her arms are curved like half-moons.

Flamenco purists regard themselves as caretakers of a centuries-old tradition. Important to this tradition is the concept of an authentic dance, an essential style of movement that can be protected from outside contagion. For some aficionados, genuine flamenco can be performed only by pure-blooded Gypsies. For others, authentic flamenco performance occurs only in private settings in which the artist can invoke the *duende,* the spirit of inspiration. In the early part of the twentieth century, poet and playwright Federico García Lorca served as the oracle for the spirit of flamenco. He wrote two famous cycles of poetry devoted to Andalusian and Gypsy cultures: *Poema del Cante Jondo* (1921) and *Romancero Gitano* (1928). In these works, the image of the Gypsy dancer plays an important role, shattering the more accessible stereotypes circulated in commercial flamenco circles. According to flamenco scholar Félix Grande, the poems of García Lorca "did not narrate flamenco, they palpated it. They did not describe what could be seen, they translated what could be felt."[2] For García Lorca, the dancing Gypsy was not only a *bailaora* (flamenco dancer), she was the incarnation of the *duende*. In an essay entitled "Theory and Function of the Duende," he wrote:

> The duende works on the body of the dancer as the wind works on the sand. With magical power he changes a girl into a lunar paralytic, or fills with adolescent blushes the broken old man begging in the wineshop, or makes a woman's hair smell like a nocturnal port, and he works continuously on the arms with expressions that are the mothers of the dances of every age.[3]

Duende, more than any other component of flamenco, seems to be the key to "authentic" performance. Federico García Lorca is frequently invoked in traditional flamenco performances as the poet who became the artistic voice for the Gypsies of Andalusia, a vehicle for the *duende,* and a sponsor of flamenco during the first three decades of the twentieth century. His verses have been set to flamenco song, and his plays have been converted into flamenco ballets.

Perhaps the most famous of these productions is the collaborative film work, *Bodas de Sangre* (Blood Wedding), made in 1981 by director Carlos Saura and choreographer Antonio Gades. This production rests uneasily in the tension between commercial and traditional flamencos. Gades is a problematic figure for many flamencologists. A former director of the National Ballet of Spain, he incorporates mime, ballet, modern, and regional dance styles into his choreography. His productions "adulterate" traditional flamenco vocabulary through the introduction of these various dance styles, placing him outside the realm of *flamenco puro.* Even though Gades is recognized by purists as a talented and prolific choreographer, he is not generally regarded as a true flamenco artist. However, his work places him in constant dialogue with promoters of flamenco tradition through his use of Gypsy themes, fragments of "traditional" flamenco vocabulary, and particularly his adaptation of García Lorca's play, *Bodas de Sangre.*

The genre of film is uniquely difficult for supporters of *flamenco puro* to embrace. The performance, relentlessly rehearsed and staged for the benefit of the camera's eye, robs the spectator of the opportunity to witness the spontaneous arrival of the *duende*. Once captured on film, the event can be reproduced endlessly through mass-marketing techniques. This movement away from the "original" moment of performance plays into the anxiety of authenticity held by purists. Director Carlos Saura creates added tensions for the viewer who hopes to suture into the diegesis of the film and recapture the immediacy of live performance. He uses unconventional camera techniques to disrupt the seamless flow of the film's narrative, constantly reminding the viewer of the "production" of this flamenco production.

The image of the Gypsy dancer plays an important role in the epic flamenco film narratives created by director Carlos Saura and choreographer Antonio Gades. The two produced three collaborative film projects during the 1980s: *Bodas de Sangre* (1981), *Carmen* (1983), and *El Amor Brujo* (Love, the Magician) (1986). I will add, parenthetically, that Saura has gone on to produce two very different and important works in more recent years, *Sevillanas* (1992) and *Flamenco* (1996). However, in the "flamenco trilogy," a unifying element of all three films is the figure of the female flamenco dancer, who moves from the centre of each narrative. Her actions seem to determine the fate of the community — men die and women mourn as the result of her excessive passions. Her body serves as the site of racial conflict, class struggle, sexual tensions, and national identities. She metaphorically represents the embattled history of flamenco. In each instance she is invoked, conjured up like the spirit of the *duende,* and the continuing practice of flamenco dance is re-established in relationship to its past.

marked: the character of la novia in *blood wedding*

In *Blood Wedding,* the first film of the three-part series, director Carlos Saura and choreographer Antonio Gades reinterpret Federico García Lorca's play as a flamenco ballet. The ballet, staged as a dress rehearsal, serves as a *mise en scène* within the diegesis of the film. In the first half of the film, the camera follows members of the company as they arrive at the studio, don their costumes, apply makeup, and warm up for the dress rehearsal. The voice of the choreographer overlays this section. He tells the story of his beginnings, how he learned to dance, and how he eventually came to meet Vicente Escudero, a flamenco legend. It is a significant moment because Vicente Escudero was one of the most famous male flamenco dancers of the twentieth century. He toured internationally during the 1920s and 1930s, partnered the female flamenco stars La Argentina and Pastora Imperio, and published an autobiographical account of his life in flamenco in 1947, titled *Mi Baile.* But Escudero was also regarded as a rebel by flamenco purists. Though he was a dancer of great artistry, a performer of the difficult *jondo* dances as well as more popular forms, he often danced outside of the *compás,* the rhythmic structure of flamenco dance. To do away with the *compás* is to dismiss the skeletal structure of flamenco. When Gades aligns himself with the difficult figure of Escudero, he locates himself within a flamenco genealogy as a descendant of a proud but eccentric bloodline.

Working with Saura, Gades presents important problems for the continuing tradition of flamenco. For the purposes of this essay, I would like to specifically address the choreographic and filmic conventions that construct gendered bodies in *Blood Wedding,* and how these bodies signify within the space of the film and in flamenco dance history. Gades relies on the strict codes of masculinity and femininity from traditional flamenco technique to develop characters within the narrative. For those unfamiliar with García Lorca's play, I'll briefly explain the plot: A young Bride is betrothed to a Groom from a wealthy family. The Bride has a lover named Leonardo who is already married. During the wedding, the Bride escapes with Leonardo. The Groom hunts down the illicit lovers. The Groom and Leonardo fight a duel. Both men die, leaving the Bride and the rest of the community to mourn.

The first scene I would like to discuss is a short solo for Leonardo's wife. She performs a movement sequence that displays an almost excessive femininity. The Wife of Leonardo is seated on the floor, rocking an empty cradle. She raises her head and lifts her gaze from the cradle to the camera. She rises and frames her face with one curved arm, fingertips slightly undulating. She departs on the diagonal, away from the camera.

The camera tracks back, the mirrors are again visible, as well as the other company members, who are seated and watching. The Wife lunges and pulls her dress against her thighs. She reaches out with her arms crossed and then executes a series of turns to land facing the mirrors and the other company members. She looks beyond them for her absent husband, then returns to the cradle, performing the sequence in reverse.

I read this performance as excessively feminine because, though she employs spiralling fingers, curved arm movements, and manipulations of her skirt, the Wife exaggerates these traditional gestures by bringing them close to, and sometimes touching, her body. A traditional female flamenco dancer would usually maintain a certain distance between her hands and her body, lifting up through the elbows to execute arm movements.

In the next sequence, the Wife and Leonardo perform a duet. Here, the difference between the codes of masculinity and femininity are clear. The camera cuts to the Wife, framing her torso and head as her eyes trace the vertical line of her husband's body. The trajectory of her gaze propels her to standing. She wraps her hands around his face, brings her face close to his, eyes pleading. The camera cuts to a shot of her upturned face from a position above her husband's shoulder. Her eyes loom large, accentuated by heavy, orientalized makeup. He throws her hands away from him; she clings again, he moves away from her. She turns away from him, traces her hips and breasts with her hands and tapered, spiralling fingers. Her arms frame her face then reach out to him as she follows, arms extended toward him. With each gesture, he moves away, his arms slashing out in the space between them. Each time she manages to wrap her arms around him from behind, he throws her off, stamping a sharp, insistent rhythm on the floor.

They circle each other, duelling, spinning to face one another. She falls to the floor; he pirouettes along the diagonal to view the empty cradle. The camera cuts abruptly to her as she collapses in a heap on the floor. She slaps the floor with her palm, matching his denial with her demand. She grasps her skirts and stands. She runs along the diagonal to hold the cradle in her arms. Her eyes move up his body once again, accusingly, then she turns away.

As the Wife dances, her arms move in curved shapes toward her body, her fingers and wrists articulate serpentine shapes, and her upper back and torso arch. Leonardo, on the other hand, slices away from his body with angular arm movements. His hands move from flat, knife-like shapes into fists, and his body remains almost relentlessly vertical. At one point they execute the same choreography in unison, a variation of a *pasada* in back *attitude*. In this moment, the choreography of sexual difference is apparent in the arms and posture of each dancer.

The character of Leonardo is the only role that bears a name in the play and the ballet. Marked by the name of the Father, a proper name, he can be recognized as a figure of authority. It is not a surprising coincidence that Antonio Gades chooses to perform the principal role. As the choreographer, he is the most powerful member of the company. In the ballet, he dances with uncompromising virility, characterized by understatement and the display of technical control. His arms slice away from his body in angular shapes, his hands move from flat (knife-like) shapes into fists, and his body always remains erect. The qualities of masculinity and, therefore, dominance and authority are displayed in the solo that follows the duet between Leonardo and the Wife.

Standing, facing the diagonal, Leonardo's arms travel out away from his body, his hands move from flat to fisted, and his torso remains absolutely vertical. The camera shifts positions. It has framed his face and body from the diagonal, and now switches to a frontal position, echoing the structure of the proscenium arch. His legs extend in a lunge — he appears to grow still longer — but he never compromises the rigidity of his bodily posture. He moves backwards along the diagonal. The camera follows him, his whole body visible in its frame. He executes a slow turn on demi pointe, his arms travelling up to form a brief, elongated frame above his head. He repeats this sequence and executes another slow turn. The moment his arms reach the shape of framing, he rises with a leg extended behind, breaking the frame. He completes yet another slow turn. He sinks onto one leg and extends the other in a long straight line. His arms travel out and away from his body.

The clearly gendered choreography invokes a host of underlying associations that help to propel the narrative of the dance. Nowhere is the dichotomy of sexual difference and its effects more clearly visible than in the choreography for the Bride, whose performance carries both masculine and feminine qualities. Her movements disrupt the traditional codes of gendered bodies, setting her apart as a dangerous and aberrant character. While the Wife defines abundant curves on and around her body, the Bride flattens the curves of her arms to a position that is defiantly vertical, a quality associated with the male role. The choreography in her solo includes a significant amount of zapateado. At the same time, the Bride performs some of the feminine vocabulary as well. She lunges deeply into the horizontal plane, baring her thighs. Her arms move through the framing patterns around her face and torso, but they are more angular than curved. The Bride represents a woman dangerous not in her excessive femininity, like the desperate Wife, but in her taking on of masculine, as well as feminine, qualities.

In her extended solo, the Bride performs more abstract, as opposed to pantomimic, movements. At this point in the film, the female characters perform more discursive movements, as can be seen in the choreography for the Wife, who searches for her husband, reaches out to him, clings to him, and achieves only a single moment of percussive sound as she slaps an ineffectual hand against the wooden floor. The Bride performs a solo that is more analogous to the masculine solo by Leonardo, which is a display of mastery through technique. Yet the sequence contains moments of passionate expression similar to the Wife's choreography. The choice to represent the female body as a transparent vessel for the tides of emotion and the masculine body as a differentiated instrument for technical display marks the separate and hierarchized spheres of activity assigned to the feminine and masculine roles. The Bride's transgression of these distinct realms reveals her dangerous and unruly nature as a femme fatale.

The Bride's performance resists the codes of desirable femininity, just as she resists the marriage contract and her role as an object of exchange between Father and Husband, or Lover and Bridegroom. The moment when this aspect of her performance is most visible occurs in the framing of her body between the bodies of two men as they sing "Awaken, Bride, on the day of your wedding." She moves between and around them, in front of and behind them, continually escaping the framing of her body between the two singers. This framing echoes and then disrupts the historical representations of the female flamenco dancer as a commodity of exchange between tourists and commercial producers of flamenco. Saura and Gades invoke the conflicted history of international tourism in which the female body serves as a site of confrontation in a masculine order of power. The female dancer as commodity of exchange serves as a fetish for the hierarchical relationships between Spaniards and tourists in the flamenco industry, Gypsies and landowners in the poetry of Federico García Lorca, and purists and tourists in flamenco histories. All of these tensions accompany the image of the female flamenco dancer in performance, enabling her body to signify within the structure of both the choreography and the film. The construction of the Bride's character suggests the possibility for resistance and intervention within these orders of meaning and power.

Again, the ghost of Merimée's Carmen invades the scene. A Gypsy seductress, she represents the qualities of resistance and seduction often attributed to the female flamenco dancer in performance. A femme fatale, she causes the misery and downfall of the men who love her. The Bride in *Bodas de Sangre* performs these dangerous qualities as well, but, significantly, she does not have to die to ensure narrative resolution in this film. Instead, the two men perform a violent and erotic duet, which culminates in their mutual penetration as they fatally stab each other.

The duet begins as the Groom spots the two lovers fleeing on horseback. The camera focuses first on the Groom's face and then frames the two lovers. The men lock gazes, and from this point on they never glance at the Bride. They stand shoulder to shoulder and advance forward in a competition of zapateado. The camera cuts to different angles during their exchange, always including the bodies of the two men in a single frame. They mirror one another as they remove their coats and draw their knives. The Bride is visible in the background, reaching her arms out to them, then covering her face.

At the moment the knives are drawn, the company gasps and the two men move in slow motion as they spar. They connect in a circle of tension formed by torsos, arms, and legs. As they pass each other, their bodies overlap.

Leonardo and the Groom coupled in the homoerotic battle over the Bride.

The camera circles the men, joins their bodies in its frame, and positions the Bride in the background, in between them. They move in slow motion, their heavy breathing the only sound that breaks the tension of the silence. Slowly, painfully, Leonardo slashes toward the Groom with his knife. He misses and the Groom lunges toward Leonardo.

As they struggle, the Bride slowly performs a series of gestures between and behind the outline of their bodies. She clutches at her head, hides her eyes, and reaches out toward the couple. The camera focuses on their feet, advancing and retreating, interrupted by a pair of white heels. The camera continues to circle. The breathing of the two men is heavier and their faces shine with sweat. Their bodies clasp as if joined. The Bride continues to watch, then hides her face behind her hands. The circle traced by the camera tightens and the company begins *palmas,* a low, contrapuntal clapping. Leonardo stabs/penetrates the Groom in the side and the tempo of the clapping increases, punctuated by shouts and grunts from the company. The Groom throws back his head as he stabs/penetrates Leonardo. The Groom sinks to the ground and Leonardo falls slowly after him. The clapping increases in volume and speed as the camera traces the limbs of the two men as they make contact with the floor: thigh, waist, wrist, elbow, back, face. The Groom is dead.

The camera cuts to the face of Leonardo, lying motionless on the floor. The clapping and shouting stops abruptly. Again, the company sings, "Awaken, Bride, on the day of your wedding." The Bride walks between the bodies of the fallen men, her face cast downward.

The Bride resists the economy of exchange between lover and bridegroom, emerging as an aberrant femme fatale who survives the resolution of the narrative.

She walks toward the mirrors; her hands trace her breasts. She drags her hands down her bodice, leaving bloody prints on her dress. She looks to her own face in the mirror. The bodies of the murdered men lie in the background, elegantly folded in death. The credits run over the marked body of the Bride/La Novia.

The audience is left with the lingering image of La Novia in her stained bodice. What kind of femme fatale is this? The self-reflexive marking of the female flamenco dancer as the site at which the tensions of tradition, nation, and race collide differs from the portrayal of an exotic whose titillating or transportive performance draws attention away from conflicts of hierarchy and power. This play of signifiers addresses the ways in which the female flamenco body has been constructed in the twentieth century. Even though the choreography and framing within this piece depart from representations of "traditional" flamenco, the intelligibility of the narrative depends on the standards for male and female roles in performance. The plot for this production is based on a play written by one of flamenco's most important artistic voices, and the image of the dangerous, unruly woman evokes one of the most enduring and problematic stereotypes of the Spanish south.

The analysis of the collaborative works by Carlos Saura and Antonio Gades poses important questions for dance scholars. Saura and Gades do not fit into the convenient divide between commercial and traditional flamenco. Instead, their work demands a recognition of the complex political and social history of the art form, and perhaps an examination of how practitioners and aficionados define the concept of "tradition." So, again, we return to the idea of authenticity within a tradition. And, within flamenco, the notion of the *duende* seems to be inextricably linked to the authenticity of the dance. Because the *duende* is a notoriously slippery and capricious character, it would make sense that it would not appear where you look for it. The practice of "traditional" dance involves an attentiveness to the intended effects of a performance as well as a respect for the choreographic structures of the form. I would assert that the maintenance of a tradition involves the continuous reconstruction and reinvention of dance forms from the past. Rather than aiming for an exact duplication of dance vocabulary as it was performed at some "originary" moment, contemporary artists invoke, represent, and manipulate traditional dance forms from the past. Flamenco dance is then perpetuated as a living tradition capable of assimilating innovation by its practitioners, instead of a museum piece that must be protected from contamination. The commitment to keep flamenco alive, infused with meaning, is a passionate decision. It marks the dance with a vibrancy and depth that betrays the arrival of the *duende,* the spirit of inspiration.

notes

1 *Eye on Dance: Spanish Dance.* Producers Celia Ipiotis and Jeff Bush. New York: ARC Videodance, 1991.

2 *Memoria del Flamenco II: Desde el Cafe Cantante a Nuestros Dias.* Madrid: Espasa-Calpe, S.A., 1979, 500. My translation.

3 J.L. Gili (ed.), *Selected Poems* (Harmondsworth: Penguin, 1960), 51.

bibliography

Saura, Carlos (director), and Antonio Gades (choreographer). *Bodas de Sangre.* Madrid: Emiliano Piedra, 1981.

gendered movement in romantic ballet:

an analysis of teresina in bournonville's *napoli*

kristin m. harris

In Denmark, the name Bournonville is practically synonymous with the ideal of ballet. Images of sylphs, trolls, and witches intermingle with those of folk and national dance. The lightness of the ballerinas and the strength and prominence of the male dancers culminate in a joyous aesthetic that is, in many ways, unique to the Danish style. August Bournonville was the instigator of the quintessential Danish Romantic style, and his legacy endures all over the world.

Feminist dance criticism has often focused on the ballet genre and the typical heterosexual power relations that it can connote. Many analyses have been conducted into various aspects of the era of the Romantic ballet, of which Bournonville was an integral part. Ann Daly, Judith Lynne Hanna, Susan Leigh Foster, and Susan Brownmiller have all presented important arguments dealing with movement and dance in terms of how it has regarded women. Furthermore, Laura Mulvey's discussions on issues relating to the gaze are also extremely relevant and applicable.[1]

The underlying message of all these scholars is similar. "Traditional" ballets are often seen as presenting an old-fashioned, patriarchal hierarchy that has forced women into particular iconographical stage roles and, off stage, has suppressed feminine creative and administrative talents. There have been few female ballet choreographers and artistic directors, and the female dancer typically portrays princesses and wronged lovers, relying (in both plot and choreography) on a man to arrive and support her. Although it is true that males historically dominated the dance world, this should not imply that all women were subservient, either as dancers or as characters. Teresina, as an example of a female Bournonville protagonist, stands outside many of these conventions.

Bournonville was born in a time when the ideal of the Romantic ballet was spreading across Europe. In 1832, Taglioni's *La Sylphide* initiated a great breakthrough in the idea of Romanticism in ballet. In his own version of the ballet, Bournonville not only further developed elements of the European Romantic genre, but also matured his own choreographic aesthetic and technique. In other words, August Bournonville "gave his ballet its individual style based on French Romanticism supported by his own school and his own repertoire."[2] Inspired by the French ballet style, Romanticism's Danish counterpart differed chiefly in narrative approach. "Danish romantics pursued the positive and optimistic. They believed in a world of meaning, beauty, and harmony."[3]

In Danish Romanticism, rather than having to come to terms with the harsh realities of the world, Bournonville's protagonists were able to overcome the conflict that had separated them from happiness. Bournonville's immersion into choreography was analogous with the growing exploration of the psyche during the Romantic era. In general, themes of Romantic ballets concurred with one another: good versus evil, dark versus light, and true love versus materialism and/or shallow eroticism.[4] However, Bournonville still preferred a more lighthearted finish. Rather than a story ending in tragedy, as seen in many ballets at the time, the Danish Romantic narrative often concluded on a positive note. This optimism is easily found in Bournonville's works.

One other inherent aspect of the Bournonville style is epitomized by his use of mime, aided in part by his penchant for narrative within choreography. This fondness for mime indicated that, "except for his divertissements, Bournonville works were narrative story-ballets, even dance-dramas. Drama was at the core of his concept of ballet."[5] This further developed his singular approach to dance and dancers, particularly his demand that dancers be equally expressive with their faces and hands as with their arms and feet. His mixture of dance and pantomime in the Romantic setting has aided in the development of the Bournonville style as possessing light, enchanting, and infectious dance, enhancing the storytelling qualities for dancers and audience.[6]

Bournonville always had high expectations of his dancers, demanding not only mastery of difficult steps and the ability to mime long sequences of dramatic gestures, but also a great sensitivity and awareness of emotion and its exploration through narrative dance. Erik Aschengreen states: "Bournonville is an eminent storyteller and precisely his ability to stage a dramatic-psychological story helped to cultivate the mime which is so characteristic of Danish dancers."[7] Bournonville believed that dancers should not indulge in what he referred to as showiness and technical effects in order to elevate their reputation and to cater to public desire. Although his ballets were indeed technically difficult, Bournonville took great pains to conceal the challenges behind his choreography.[8] This is in direct contrast to the virtuosic aspect of the Russian classical style, to which Bournonville was strongly opposed. Rather than valuing the dazzling and complicated, he felt that "the *beautiful* always retains the freshness of novelty. The *astonishing* soon grows tiresome."[9] Furthermore, the dancer should be able to attain a style that is synonymous with both suppleness and lightness, as well as balance and strength.[10] This ideal of dancing style and choreographic technique was the impetus behind the instigation and maturation of Danish Romanticism.

Thus, Bournonville ballets transcended into another level. Aschen green further states that for Bournonville, "ballet was not only neat dancing, entertainment and escapism into a theatrical world; on the contrary, it was a matter of artistic expression of existential problems."[11] This intellectual interest proliferated in his choreography, and it is obvious when viewing his dance pieces that he likened his creative forces to other art forms. "With Bournonville, prose never gained the upper hand over poetry. He preferred the naïve to the ruminating, the gestures of idyll and ideality to the poor manners of conflict."[12] His exploration into the motivations of characters and how they related to external forces became part of the signature style of a Bournonville piece.

In general, Bournonville demanded similar qualities equally from both his male and his female dancers. They were all expected to incorporate lightness, playfulness, and grace into their every movement and static pose. Erik Aschengreen's allusion to Bournonville's "infectious delight in dancing"[13] is evident in his choreography and was an absolute necessity for all his dancers to achieve.

Bournonville believed that dance was a "pure" form of art, and compared it to other art forms, particularly the plastic arts (sculpture) and poetry, in *My Theatre Life,* his autobiography. It is evident from his writings that Bournonville felt that dancing comes from the soul and that it should manifest itself in joyous expression of the body. This is reflected well in many of his pieces, where the choreography is light and energetic. It is also evident in the plots of his story-ballets, where any discord is resolved at the end, leaving the protagonist(s) happy, their burdens lifted. Bournonville also illuminated the importance of dance as a form of non-verbal communication in that it is able to express that which words cannot. All these elements combine, in Bournonville's perspective, to form a beautiful and touching art form to be enjoyed by all.

Several readings can be applied to *Napoli* to deconstruct various elements of its narrative and character structure. Some possible readings of *Napoli* include (but certainly are not limited to): love story, journey toward self-realization, a search for identity, cultural appropriation and fusion, reflection of a culture and time, and issues of femininity and masculinity and their interaction. A central element of the story is the collision between the earth and the spirit world, both the supernatural world of the Sea Spirits and that of Christianity. This angle allows the viewer to see the ballet not only as a simple love story, but as a morality tale dealing with both religious themes and male/female dynamics.

Teresina, as a female Bournonville protagonist, can be examined as a means to explore Bournonville's ideas. She not only typifies the female Bournonville character in both choreography and character, but stands outside many conventional analyses of the woman of the Romantic ballet. During the *mise en scène* of *Napoli,* Teresina undergoes numerous changes. The peasant girl leaves her home and enters the mysterious world of Golfo and the Sea Spirits. After her rescue, she is brought back and reunited with Gennaro, and the two are married. The character of Teresina evolves along with her adventures, as is evident in numerous visual indicators, including costume, choreography, narrative, and characterization. The shift in these elements is an interesting indicator of her status in the diametrically opposed worlds of the earthy and the spiritual. Teresina's journey is reflected throughout the three acts of the narrative.

In *Napoli,* Teresina is typically dressed in colours and styles that epitomize a feminine ideal. In the opening act, she is clothed in a costume that is part peasant dress, part romantic ballet dress. She is ensconced in a vibrant pink, knee-length skirt, which flares around her body as she jumps and runs. Her waist is cinched in a black, laced bodice that, along with a bloused top, accentuates her female form. Generally speaking, Teresina's costume blends in with those of the other women, with a few small exceptions. Aside from the colour of her dress, Teresina's other distinguishing costume feature is that she wears a blue scarf around her neck, coupled with a heavy chain bearing the likeness of the Virgin Mary. Her shoulders are bare and her hair is in a single braid down her back, both implying a girlish charm and demeanour. She wears pointe shoes.

As she enters the opening act, the stage is full of activity. Teresina is young and free-spirited as she flits girlishly around the stage. When Teresina and Gennaro dance together in short sequences, they dance in the middle of the corps. This establishes their place within the town, yet emphasizes their impending importance for the narrative. This scene relies heavily on mimed passages to situate various characters within the setting of the ballet.

Immediately before the pas de deux between Teresina and Gennaro, the corps dance together. Various sequences occur, indicating an equality in prominence between the men and women, and concomitantly, integrating all the characters with one another in the story. In terms of stage time and prominence, the traditional Bournonville disparity between men and women shines through. Although the men and women dance separately, the men demonstrate large, travelling jumps, and the women perform quick, small footwork with many directional changes.[14] However, this difference tends to disappear when they join forces in dancing as an ensemble. In this situation, the men and women perform the same steps, which are a cross between the delicate and intricate footwork of the women and the grandiose jumps of the men. Bournonville therefore has created a gender power balance that is not typical of most Romantic ballets.

As Teresina and Gennaro enter the spotlight to begin their pas de deux, the corps part from the front of the stage, allowing the audience focus to shift from the ensemble to the pair. They dance connected, holding hands, with Teresina dancing in front of Gennaro.[15] The two characters perform the same jeté sequence as they proceed to centre.

Teresina and Gennaro announce their engagement.

From there, the two separate, each dominating one side of the stage, just off centre. From this point, throughout the pas de deux, the two keep on this vertical median, crossing back and forth across its axis. This gives both characters equal stage prominence. Another important factor is that Teresina and Gennaro dance the same steps throughout the sequence, which is vastly different from the norm in most ballets.[16] The sameness of their choreography is indicative of two things: the equal importance that Bournonville placed on dancers of both sexes, and that their characters bear equal weight in narrative importance. This Bournonville element is beneficial for both the male and female dancer. The male dancer is allowed to display his talent in performing alongside the female dancer (rather than merely supporting her movements and dancing only on his own), and the female dancer is able to hold her own as both character and dancer, rather than appearing as frail and needing support from her male counterpart. Both characters (and dancers) illustrate an equal partnership that is not often found in the ballet genre.

The next scene takes place when Teresina encounters the supernatural world for the first time. Hesitant at first, she begins to dance with the Sea Spirits and becomes more comfortable in her new setting. She receives her new clothing, a crown, and is welcomed into their world. As Jack Anderson has written, "The Naiads appear to live in a subjective state of pure sensation unrelated to the outer world. If they experience no pain, neither do they seem to possess deep feelings or high aspirations. They are, in effect, drugged."[17] The Naiads' costumes are gauzy, glittery, and blue, reminiscent of the depths of the water, and in harmony with the typical uniform of the spirits of the Romantic ballet genre.[18] In contrast, Teresina's solid pink dress emphasizes her outsider status. Golfo's subsequent arrival and conventionally masculine movements indicate his power in this world.[19] However, he retains some similarity in costume to the female spirits — his unitard is the same colour, and his supernatural potential is conveyed through his gauzy cape, made of the same material as the women's dresses. Although they are obviously part of Golfo's entourage, "their role is more atmospheric than dangerous."[20] As the corps dance, the accompanying music is light, matching their delicate arabesques and *posés,* broken only at Teresina's awakening and fear. As Teresina and Golfo meet, Teresina's dress is transformed into that of the rest of the female Naiads. Her hair is let down, thereby creating a softer, more flowing effect in line with her new role. Her actions become more confident and comfortable, and the music adjusts to suit the new mood as well.

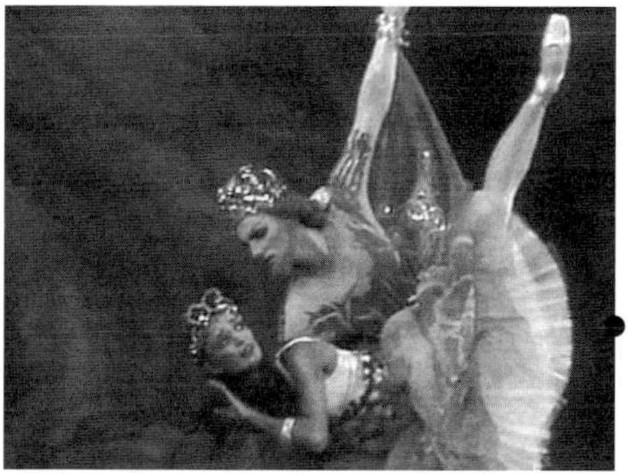

Teresina dances with Golfo in the underworld.

Immediately before Teresina's solo, the corps line up along either side of the stage. Two Naiads flank Teresina and then part to allow her to become the focal point of the stage. Therefore, Teresina has almost the entire stage upon which to dance. She begins in centre stage, then walks alongside the dancers lining the right side of the stage. They further part and Teresina is left almost entirely by herself. This is definitely her moment. She takes a few steps, then turns in arabesque (on pointe) with a partner. Although this might initially seem like a typical balletic movement, there is a twist. Teresina dances with one of the female Sea Spirits. She supports

Teresina's small sequence in the same way as a male dancer would. The choice for a female to support Teresina's otherwise traditional pas de deux movement, rather than a male character, indicates Teresina's equivalent relationship with the other Naiads. She is now one of them.

Teresina's solo again begins from upstage left, and she traverses across a diagonal axis, backtracks, then forges forward to centre stage. From there, she once again turns her directional focus to the horizontal axis. This segment contains more steps that are encompassed in the Romantic ballet genre, including bourrée, pirouette, arabesque, *penché,* and *soutenu* turns. However, there are also numerous quick footwork steps, such as chassé, glissade, jeté, and other jumps. There are a number of stops in this sequence. Teresina does not completely stop her movement flow but does pause between steps and poses. This is an element that is familiar to most balletomanes and seems to typify this sequence to the ballet genre.[21] However, it is important to note that Teresina in fact dances by herself this entire segment. Although she is now confident as part of this unusual spiritual world, she still stands out as independent from it.

Teresina dances with the Naiads.

The final excerpt is from the final act, at Teresina and Gennaro's wedding. This scene is constructed in a fashion similar to the first, in that there is a combination of solo, pas de deux, small groups, and corps work. The air of solemnity and drama that was found in the world of Golfo and the Naiads is now gone, and the joy and fun from the first act have returned. Teresina and Gennaro take turns dancing individually and as a couple. She has returned from her journey and is reunited with her love.

Throughout this act, Teresina and Gennaro are welcomed back into the arms of their village. Although they are part of the action, they are often singled out. They are still in the spotlight, despite the fact that they are dancing with everyone else. At the same time, it is important to note that neither main character has long solos.[22] In fact, Teresina and Gennaro are assigned solo dancing passages of approximately the same length and difficulty as other principal dancers in this act. The third act of *Napoli* is renowned for its tarantella sequence, which comprises most of the dancing in this final act. This predominance of folk dance within the choreographic structure can be regarded as a Bournonville convention, in that many of his ballets weave folk or national dance into the more strictly balletic choreography. Additionally, by incorporating the tarantella into the third act, he is not only allowing the corps more stage time, but is further allowing both men and women equal time on stage with equally challenging choreography.

This third act can be seen as one of "showcasing" talent; that is, there is far more dance in this section than in previous acts (where there was a larger amount of mime), and there are more solos and small groups dancing, rather than everyone as a whole.[23] All the solos are performed by men, whereas all the group dancing is performed by either an all-female group or a mixed (male and female) group. Thus, Bournonville's prominent male dancers once again emerge. Throughout these small divertissements, several commonalities can be observed. Although all the women wear pointe shoes, the choreography is designed so that the women dance a great deal on either flat foot or demi pointe.[24] The plié in second and a flat foot pas de bourrée are also recurring themes with both male and female dancers in this section.

This final act, Teresina and Gennaro's wedding, presents an interesting mélange of the two previous costuming choices. The opening moments see all the characters dressed in identical drab beige robes. This sameness suddenly ends as everyone disrobes, revealing a spectacle of a bright array of colours and costumes. Teresina is dressed once again in pink; however, this time, it is a softer shade, intermingled with white. The material of the costume is also a light and gauzy material, more similar to that of the Sea Spirits than of the hearty peasant stock seen at the outset of the narrative. She still wears a fitted and bloused bodice, but it is no longer laced at the front. Her hair is worn up and covered with roses, signifying her entrance into the adult world.

Immediately preceding Teresina's solo, Gennaro performs on stage. His solo consists of numerous grandiose turns and leap combinations. He covers a large area, uses many directional changes, and seems to dominate the entire stage with his very presence. This is markedly different from the precise and almost prim solo that follows.

Teresina and Gennaro briefly touch hands as he exits the spotlight, and she finds her place on stage. In contrast to previous sections, Teresina begins this solo at centre stage, slightly off to the side. She begins dancing on this very strong spot and remains in its vicinity for the entirety of her segment. Teresina dances essentially in place, with small variations to one side of the stage or the other, and occasionally she ventures farther upstage or downstage from her starting point. This particular sequence seems to be more performative, in that Teresina is clearly dancing for her family and friends. This is particularly evident through her small pauses between movement phrases, where she poses for a moment before resuming her dancing. She begins with small, lilting phrases and a little quick footwork.

Teresina's solo.

The second part of her solo changes and consists almost exclusively of footwork, particularly numerous combinations of pas de bourrées, entrechats, chassés, *changements,* and more. There is a combination of both demi pointe, full pointe, and flat footwork in this section. This visual realization of Teresina's spiritual journey is shown through her choreography, evident in both the first sequence (that of a simple, naive peasant girl) and the second sequence (as a Naiad). This transformation and integration of elements is apparent throughout.

The Romantic ballet has often been highly criticized in terms of its gender inequality. In this examination of *Napoli,* as an example of a typical Bournonville ballet, Teresina fares quite well under this particular microscope. Daly suggests:

> Dance classicism is an ideology devoted to tradition, chivalry, and to hierarchy of all kinds — gender, performer's rank, the distinction between types of roles, spectator's placement, stage organization, the canon. Romanticism's emphasis on personal expression also relies on the theatricalized dichotomy of feminine and masculine temperaments.[25]

Indeed, *Napoli*'s structure is in accordance with many of these elements in that it follows a certain hierarchical pattern with which ballet audiences can identify. For example, there is a distinction made among corps dancers, soloists, and principals. Throughout the piece, dancers in each category are allotted a certain amount of dancing time in various patterns. *Napoli,* like many other Bournonville ballets, incorporates copious amounts of mime, which allows various dancers to shine in an often-overlooked aspect of ballet. There is also a smaller distinction between soloist and principal dancers, as many scenes require a large amount of dancing from all characters concerned. It truly requires a more collaborative effort from dancers than many other ballets. *Napoli* does correspond, in certain respects, to Romantic ballet conventions; however, it by no means rigidly adheres to all of Romanticism's common elements.

It is also true that there are differences between male and female forms of dance. This is particularly evident when examining which steps are allotted to various dancers in the ballet. The pas de deux receives particular scrutiny. In her article "Classical Ballet: A Discourse of Difference," Daly discusses Romantic ballet's fondness for the grace and beauty of its dancers, particularly as required in female dancers.[26] Bournonville's male dancers are often predominant on the stage, particularly because Bournonville is renowned for reinstating the importance of the male dancer. However, *Napoli*'s correspondence with this description ends here. As illuminated in the analysis, Bournonville has chosen, in this piece, to provide a different but egalitarian approach to his characters and, thus, to the dancers as well. This intention is illustrated through the equality in dancing prominence between Teresina and Gennaro in Acts 1 and 3, and the interesting moment of pas de deux between Teresina and the female Naiad in Act 2. This egalitarian approach raises interesting issues related to the gaze, usually designated as that of the male spectator (active) on the female object (passive).[27] The commonality of prominence reflects not only an equal gaze on both male and female, but also designates a balance in power relationship between male and female dancers.

Daly argues that stage dynamics in Romantic ballets consist of males denoting power and females denoting fragility. This dynamic leads to an asymmetry, the two polarities creating the balance in the male/female relationship on stage.[28] Hanna also raises the notion of the pas de deux as the penultimate representation of heterosexuality in dance. Furthermore, it reinforces two ideas: sexual proximity and tension between the two dancers and, a more contemporary reading, a metaphor for the idea of romantic love.[29] The structure of the choreography of the pas de deux conforms to our prescribed notions of male/female relationships.

In her article entitled "The Ballerina's Phallic Pointe," Susan Foster asserts that all bodies in dance are gendered, through their costuming as well as their choreography. She argues that the common dynamic on the stage is for the female to be presented to the audience by her male counterpart. "*He* and *she* do not participate equally in their choreographic coming together. *She* and *he* do not carry equal valence. *She* is persistently put forward, the object of his adoration."[30] Although this is the norm in the ballet genre as a whole, *Napoli* and other Bournonville ballets are an exception.

In my analysis of *Napoli,* Teresina and Gennaro are indeed different, but Teresina expresses strength in dancing as much as Gennaro. Their pas de deux segments are not traditional in that Gennaro is not solely Teresina's support; rather, they dance as equal partners, neither upstaging the other. This is in direct contradiction to the typical ballet pas de deux, in which certain conventions, particularly those concerning support, balance, and strength, are not broken.[31] However, Teresina's and Gennaro's movements are not entirely described by these conventions. Yes, Gennaro does perform the large jump and turn sequences, for which the Bournonville men are so famous. Teresina also performs smaller, seemingly more feminine steps. Whether this was Bournonville's choice of aesthetic or the dancers' physical capabilities (likely a combination of both) is open for speculation. However, both characters exert moments of greater and lesser prominence. The gaze and the power is shared between both, and they dance, for the most part, as equal partners.

Apart from the immediate sentiment that one experiences with Bournonville, there is also the underlying meaning to his works. While Bournonville's ballets often consist of cheerful plots, there is always a message. Although heroes may face danger and adversity, they always finish their journey, wiser and happier for the experience. Bournonville allowed for a greater expression of character and plot, both of which were greatly enhanced by his fondness for choreographing mimed passages throughout his ballets. The example of Bournonville through *Napoli* illustrates that one genre does not produce a uniform result. Although *Napoli* does conform to many images associated with Romantic ballet, a close reading of the ballet reveals that it also defies many of these conventional elements. This defiance can be attributed to a number of reasons. Perhaps national differences, both in Denmark itself and in Danish artistic sensibilities, account for each culture bringing its own interpretation to any work of art, thereby subverting any universality that may be assumed to exist. It may be that the unique Bournonville perspective, through both story and dance style, has enabled it to remain one of the most beautiful and enduring dance forms, still speaking to modern sensibilities while retaining its timeless appeal.

notes

1 Mulvey's writings deal with the visual and are often used to discuss film and visual arts. To fully appreciate her arguments, it is useful to be familiar with Lacan's theories on the gaze.

2 Ebbe Mørk, "The Royal Danish Ballet: The World's Oldest Ballet Tradition," *Danish Journal Special Issue on The Royal Danish Ballet and Bournonville* (Copenhagen: Ministry of Foreign Affairs, 1979), 10.

3 Erik Aschengreen, "The Royal Danish Ballet," in John R. Johnson (ed.), *Dance in Tivoli* (Denmark: Borgen Publishers, 1983), 72.

4 Ibid., 71.

5 Walter Terry, *The King's Ballet Master* (New York: Dodd, Mead, and Co., 1979), 118.

6 Erik Aschengreen, "August Bournonville and the Royal Danish Ballet," in Erik Aschengreen, Ebbe Mørk, and Ole Kjaer Madsen (eds.), in *Dance in Denmark* (Copenhagen: Royal Danish Ministry of Foreign Affairs, 1991), 12.

7 Ibid., 5.

8 Walter Terry, *The King's Ballet Master,* 106.

9 Ulla Skow, *August Bournonville Etudes Choréographiques* (Copenhagen: Rhodos, 1983), 19.

10 Ibid., 73.

11 Aschengreen, "The Royal Danish Ballet," in *Dance in Tivoli,* 71.

12 Niels Birger Wamberg, "Bournonville's Romantic Vocation," in Ebbe Mørk (ed.), *Salut for Bournonville* (København: Statens Museum for Kunst, 1979), 94.

13 Aschengreen, "August Bournonville and the Royal Danish Ballet," in *Dance in Denmark,* 5.

14 Beats, bourrées, and so on.

15 I would assert that this is more a spacing determination (because the female dancer is shorter than the male) than a power statement.

16 Quite often, pas de deux present the male and female dancers in different ways. The woman is supported by the man, who does little other than serve as a support for the ballerina's pirouettes and lifts.

17 Jack Anderson, "Bournonville: The Sequel," *Dance Chronicle* 15, 1992: 337.

18 I am reminded here, in particular, of the Sylphs in *La Sylphide* and the Wilis in *Giselle.*

19 Golfo connotes strength with large and bold movements, chiefly in mime, that indicate his power over the Naiads.

20 Selma Landen Odom, "Napoli," *Dance Magazine,* March 1982: 46.

21 It is also a convention for audiences to applaud at various points during a ballet. This is usually done at the end of an act, when a curtain opens to reveal particularly attractive scenery, or after a difficult solo passage.

22 Clive Barnes, "Napoli," in *Dance and Dancers,* October 1954: 16.

23 This section encompasses every combination imaginable, for example, solo, pas de deux, pas de trois (female), pas de quatre (mixed), and pas de six (four women, two men).

24 This is likely in keeping with the technical advancement of the pointe shoe. In Bournonville's time, dancers could not stay up on pointe for more than a few moments at a time.

25 Ann Daly, "Classical Ballet; A Discourse of Difference," *Women and Performance* 3, 2, 1978–88: 58.

26 Ibid., 59.

27 Laura Mulvey, "Visual Pleasure and Narrative Cinema," *Screen* 16, 3, 176.

28 Daly, "Classical Ballet; A Discourse of Difference," *Women and Performance*: 60–1.

29 Judith Lynne Hanna, *Dance, Sex, and Gender* (Chicago and London: University of Chicago Press, 1988), 166.

30 Susan Leigh Foster, *Corporealities: Dancing, Knowledge, Culture and Power* (London and New York: Routledge, 1996), 1.

31 Susan Brownmiller, *Femininity* (New York: Linden Press, 1984), 182.

stepping out of attitude:

la fanfarlo and autobiography

sarah davies cordova

Do you imagine in reading my books that I am drawing my portrait? Patience: it is only my model.[1]

What parts are "remembered" and which ones are invented is quite a difficult thing to discern, particularly when the "memory" serves as a basis for a work.[2]

attitude: (at ' ə · to͞od)
1 *Position/step in ballet.*
2 *State of mind or conduct, as indicating opinion.*

Conventional figurations of female nineteenth-century ballet dancers register indices of evanescence, canvases of desirous appropriation, and phallogomorphic romantic plots. They adhere to the period's socio-political requisites and effectively reiterate the stereotype of the dancer as illicit, dissolute woman. The practice of "overreading"[3] representations of and by the female dancer constructs an infraction to this attitude, to the intransitiveness of her stereotype. Memoirs, newspaper articles, letters, contracts, documentation on salaries and pensions, "realist" fiction, historical and medical texts, and guidebooks register the gaps in stereotypical depictions of nineteenth-century dancers. The lacunae that transpire from the clichéd evanescence of dance and the monoscopic visualization of the dancing body convey the absence of women's experience of the dance as spectat*rices* and professional performers.

A relation of these artifacts inflects an intratextual practice of interpretation that takes the corporeal, the textual, and the visual together in their status as socio-cultural records to examine the double binds of the nineteenth-century dancer. Without privileging autobiography, biography, or fiction, the composite of corporeality viewed and written with the body-at-dance and at-work graphs a complex of a self who danced and experienced the nineteenth century as a working woman. Such a representation situates her identity as inherently fractured and multiple. In biography, the necessity of remaining with the facts proscribes going where fact leaves off, even though truth demands further questing.[4] In autobiography, performativity distends those severe limitations. Autobiography draws upon the notion of fiction for its generation. But it does not embrace the imaginary, invented aspects of literature.[5] Rather, it turns to the etymology of "fiction," wherein *fictio* denotes shaping, to point to form.[6] Each inscription approximates using details, makes adjustments, and emphasizes an arrangement of truths.

The adherence of fact to *fictio* in dealing with such a cultural icon as the ballerina affiliates two types of texts: those she actually danced in, which I view as biographical, and the (life) self of the dancer, which I would term "autégraphy."[7] Both attempt to rescue from historical oblivion that which has not been depicted and which has been written out. With the palimpsest as its paradigm, this "ghost writing"[8] features collage as its design form. The resulting collection of multifarious "self" portraits works in a curious, alluring space between fact and fiction to denote metatextually the activity and process of constructing a subject on the page, of "autobiographing."

ballet's figures

After the revolution of 1789 and the demise of the Napoleonic empire, theatrical dance responded to the prevalent sense of socio-cultural estrangement. Ballet, like social dancing, no longer contributed to a performative sociability, to the creation of a decorous social intercourse.[9] Instead it represented in story form life-stories, (auto)biographies in which the period's dilemmas about self, gender, class, and nationalism played themselves out. With the expulsion of meaning from the body's physicality, dancing lost its discursive status and no longer synthesized perfectly painting and poetry.[10] To the change in aesthetic climate from a painted expression of human society to the self-presentation of individuated experience, dance responded with ballets that integrated virtuosity, drama, and spectacle.

The derivation of much of ballet's storylines from literature — many of the libretti were authored by the period's *littérateurs* — engenders a different relationship between the story and the dancing from earlier theatre dance. Despite the Romantic and symbolist poets' vision of the dancer's metaphoric correspondence to dance, ballet disaggregates the two. In its enactment of its character's role, the material body of the ballet dancer presents itself to the audience as it embodies a trans-position of what the libretto can only say. The dancer is not simply sylph, wili, or pigeon, she performs a role within a narrative. The complement of pointe work with the augmentation of technical feats produced a lexicon and syntax of steps, which together with the different performance settings, effectively supplanted antecedent dance spectacles. Ballet calls upon mime for its discursive passages, makes its impact with its accumulation of pas de deux and solos, and emphasizes its hybridity with its incorporation of local and ethnic dances and its synthesis of pantomimic and classical vocabularies. Seventeenth- and eighteenth-century classical myths and fables, which frequently inspired eighteenth-century ballets, are reworked to incorporate new performance criteria.[11] The arrogation of the fantastic of classical, oriental, and medieval myths does not restore meaning to the deposed *ballet d'action*'s tableaux; they add narrative density to plot.

Ballet of the nineteenth century represents evanescence in the unfolding of its plot lines as it enacts its own disappearance at each performance. The period's writings about dance affirm the ephemerality of its form and recognize in that very evanescence a metaphor for the times. Hence, they poeticize dance as the perfect trope for capturing the essence of "*l'indicible,*" of the Ideal or the Absolute.[12] Situating dance in the absence that metaphor creates through substitution, the texts in effect efface the dancer. Yet ballet, as a type of dance, challenges the artistic notion of the work of art as a unity of form and content because it tells a story sequentially over time. Its topic is not its evanescence but the aspirations and desires of the characters. Ballet tenders, like romantico-realist literature, fragmentary representation — biographies.

Ballet obfuscates genre categorizations. It marks the dissolution of the boundaries between the arts by proposing the interchangeability of the verbal and the visual in the presentation of stories. As it advances further the plasticity of dance into the territory of the rhetorical arts, it crosses aesthetic limits of visual representation with those of literary narrative. Ballet disrupts the law and order of the arts by crossing between or grafting different modes together. As such, ballet materializes allegory. Allegory, like ballet, concerns itself with the projection — spatial, temporal, or both — of structure as sequence. It is traditionally defined, following Quintilian, as a single metaphor introduced in a continuous series, as a rebus, and thus participates in both form and content. The association of story and mode of representation in ballet is allegorical.[13] Like allegory, whose etymology *(allo agoreuei)* indicates that it makes public something other than itself, ballet signifies or signs something other, rather than mirroring form in content.[14]

Continuing to refer to itself as an artistic event, ballet also alludes to the social, cultural, and political realities of which it is a part. Even as ballet appeals to bourgeois audiences, it presents the period's instability in the very form and the content of the performances. Often transposed to locations outside of France — exotic and/or orientalist — or fantastic, the ballets attend to bourgeois ideology as they narrate and as that ideology is conveyed by the body as signifying practice.[15] Like mid-nineteenth-century painting, which can be treated as political allegory,[16] ballet allegorizes the culturally significant.

As with most signifying practices that shape us, be they political, social, linguistic, or balletic, their duality is less a confrontation of different elements and more an expression of indifference toward the other. The dualisms of male/female, mind/body, conscious/unconscious, good/ bad, same/other, enacted in ballet and in writing about dance and dancers are products of one side of the duality: male, mind, conscious, good, sameness. The other side participates only to support the dominant side. The side of the other or Woman is necessarily silent, denied a voice in language, dance, and politics.[17]

what happens when the silent one speaks, writes, or moves?

Ghost writing or autobiographing crosses back and forth between established verities and constructed notions of self, as individual and social entity. At the beginning of the nineteenth century, the autobiographic "genre," as two female authors, George Sand and Daniel Stern, penned it out, was marked as masculine and inflected by the confessional mode of their eighteenth-century predecessor Jean-Jacques Rousseau. Indeed, the lexeme "autobiography" only came into use at the beginning of the nineteenth century. Romantic male authors repeated Rousseau's paradigmatic gestures, writing *in* others, usually women, as they watched and saw them, to explicate their inability to consolidate an identity worthy of their aspirations. Moving away from an ocular economy — from "oculocentrism," which views according to phallomorphic standards[18] — Sand and Stern, after Staël, devise a diverse and disjunctive subjectivity traced from the embodiment of their actions and feelings.

Whether fictionalized or "real" autobiographies, retrospective novelistic narratives such as Staël's *Corinne ou l'Italie* frequently resemble the Romantic ballets' scenarios. Recurrently, the ballets' diegeses stage analogous versions of the Romantic trope of the young male hero who has lost his true path because of a woman. Women in these stories appear unreliable because of their flightiness, their vaporous nature, their ungroundedness. Each scenario asks the female protagonist the love question: "Would you die for me?" and pushes her to prove her answer. The question subtends the spectator's desire. Often, as in Staël's novel, the female protagonist must die for the male to fulfill the patriarchal social agenda. As with Corinne, in ballet, which culturally overdetermines and over-marks the female dancer as object of the desiring gaze, the women characters rarely escape the determination of their social role. Yet they embody for a scene or an act, usually in a non-Parisian location, roles that do not cohere with the heavily promulgated bourgeois codified comportment and agenda for private and public spaces.[19] Although the end message of any particular ballet may be read as a lesson to wayward women, the alternative behaviour that the unfolding of the plot presents opens up possibilities if not for emulation at least for envisioning other social interactions and configurations.

Reading, opening up, touching, turning over, folding again influence my writing. Fiction, librettos, journalistic accounts, letters, decrees, pictures merge into an autobiography. I fill an image of a moment with memories drawn from others. These representations are my access to the life of a dancer of the nineteenth century. They are entrances into haunting memories. Images, movements, constructions — remains at the "archeological" site — surface, sometimes compellingly vivid, other times frustratingly opaque and distorted. They encourage and deter from a reconstruction of a society operating according to binarisms and polarisms, for they do not fit neatly into such categorizations. Women have varied histories of mobility and habitus and they spatialize the century as a site differently.

"Overreading" Charles Baudelaire's *La Fanfarlo* returns one entry about nineteenth-century dancers. Although the novella has been understood as an early rewriting of the Salomé story,[20] and acknowledged as the fictionalized autobiography of the author, I read it from the perspective of the period's culture, as a socio-cultural reflection on women dancers. Flaubertian in its scathing assessment of bourgeois mediocrity, the novella points to theatrical dance's presence in bourgeois culture and fashion as it elaborates an image of the dancer's life that extends beyond her commodification.

First published in 1847, but probably composed in 1845,[21] the story harks back to Jean de la Fontaine's seventeenth-century fable "Les Deux pigeons," whose affirmation of the value of marital love and fidelity acts, at the very least, as a motif throughout the nineteenth century. Its elaboration structures the third section of Honoré de Balzac's *Béatrix* (1839–44), at the end of which the loving wife who has succeeded in recovering her husband claims that "nous avons joué la fable des deux pigeons."[22] Alex Privat d'Anglemont's 1842 "Une Grande coquette," published in *La Patrie* and which became the basis for Baudelaire's version, adheres to the scenario. Later, for the 1886 ballet *Les Deux pigeons,* which Stéphane Mallarmé analyzes in "Crayonné au théâtre," Henry Regnier and Louis Mérante indicate their La Fontainian source on the cover of their *livret.* Their plot draws on *Béatrix* to include another female character, the daughter's mother, in the stage production. As in Balzac's novel, she helps reunite the "pigeons." Of course, the "pigeon" and her rival, "the Gypsy," dance marvellously well, and their duets with the male character are further enhanced for the men in the audience because a woman performs his role *en travesti.*

The major transformation between d'Anglemont's and Baudelaire's versions of the short story appear in the development of the dancer's character. The mistress is clearly a dancer in d'Anglemont's version and is characteristically deprecated by the lovelorn wife, the countess Blanche de Kermadec. According to Blanche, dancers of the "choeurs de l'Opéra" are "apprenties sauteuses."[23] Even though she admits that the ill will she bears "figurantes"[24] may only really result from her resentment, she nevertheless places herself above them. Because the dancer "chaque soir montre ses jambes à un parterre composé de mille visages nouveaux"[25] [every night shows her legs to the pit's thousand new faces], she is unworthy of the countess's jealousy. The only other indications the reader culls from "Une Grande coquette" about the dancer in question, Madame Anastasie de St-Valery,[26] is that she lives at #8, rue Neuve-Béda, where there is a porter; that she has a chambermaid, Juliette, and space enough in her apartment to practise with a ballet master; and that she can write. As the male go-between character exclaims, her handwriting is a horrible scrawl and she is too beautiful to know how to spell. The plot to Baudelaire's novella bears uncanny resemblances to Anglemont's text,[27] yet the characters' extensive portraiture transforms the narratological development: unlike *La Fanfarlo*'s male protagonist, Paul de Plouermel in *La Grande cocotte* is not the dupe of the two female characters.

La Fanfarlo's oft-repeated characterization as the author's fictionalized autobiography stands out for its initial resemblances to the nineteenth-century autobiographic paradigm.[28] It is affirmed to be a true story: "Quelques lecteurs scrupuleux et amoureux de la vérité vraisemblable trouveront sans doute beaucoup à redire à cette histoire, où pourtant je n'ai eu d'autre besogne à faire que de changer les noms et d'accentuer les détails"[29] [No doubt a few scrupulous readers desirous of verisimilitude will find fault with this story, even though I have only had to change the names and to emphasize the details] — even as it is recounted in a narrative *dedoublement* by a third-person narrator.[30] This arrangement situates Samuel Cramer as the poet's alter ego, whom the narrator treats with indulgent irony, intruding into the text as an "I" to comment and address the reader. Samuel's situation mirrors the Romantic poet's predicament and traces anxieties and aspirations as if it were a self-portrait of the youthful Baudelaire.[31]

Expressing a malaise about masculine identity, *La Fanfarlo* incorporates the poet's clichéd love of the unattainable — woman and poetry. The protagonist, Samuel Cramer, aspires to become a great poet but lacks the confidence and commitment to succeed. The first part of the story composes his portrait as a series of contradictions and oppositions, and dwells on his sentimental romantic nature, as well as on his reawakened love for his childhood sweetheart, Madame de Cosmelly. The rest of the novella veers off course and stages instead a narrative about the dancer referred to in the short story's eponymous title. Madame de Cosmelly directs the second part of the story. Upon meeting accidently with Cramer in the jardin du Luxembourg, several years after their adolescent romance in the countryside where they lived, she confides that her husband is having an affair with a dancer. She asks Cramer to have Fanfarlo fall in love with him so that she might regain the felicity of her first years of marriage. Cramer agrees to carry out Madame de Cosmelly's plan, believing that he might also realize his own wishes. Unable to distinguish between his role as pygmalionesque author and mere mortal, he casts himself as the "hero" of the adventure and falls prey to his own romanticism.

The focus on Fanfarlo as dancer and woman enables a parody of the romantic disposition that Cramer embodies. Although most ballet scenarios present the young male hero with a choice between two unmarried women, Cramer's belief that his help in realizing Cosmelly's plan will result in her undying love for him ironically references ballet plots in which the male character is incapable of differentiating between the supernatural and the real, or between figments of his imagination and reality. On the other hand, the extension of Anglemont's version articulates a representation of the period's dancer, which goes beyond the stage persona — the biography — to divulge the doubleness of her subjectivity — the autégraphy. Furthermore, the diegesis allegorizes the romantic ballet's story and genders Cramer according to the criteria that describe male dancers of the times. He signs his *Orfraies,* a volume of sonnets, as Manuela de Monteverde; the narrator describes him as having appeared to him as "le Dieu de l'impuissance — dieu moderne et hermaphrodite"[32] [God of impotence — modern god and hermaphrodite]. The allusions implicitly point to an effeminacy that repeatedly characterized the male dancer and problematized his position on the ballet stage. The two female protagonists ("la fleur qui s'est toujours gardée des passants dans les allées les plus obscures du jardin conjugal"[33] [the flower that has kept to herself, away from the passersby, in the most obscure alleys of the conjugal garden] and "la fleur que tout le monde a respirée"[34] [the flower that everyone has smelled]) embody the split between uplifting and seductive women that tears at the fabric of the male character's subjectivity. The themes determining the identity of each woman are in place: one is pure, the other femme fatale.

Their strength and consistency contrast with Cramer's equivocation. Even though their desires do not contest the limited choices available to women of their social classes, they nevertheless succeed in realizing their objectives without compromising their positions. As Madame de Cosmelly explains at length, and with the impressive straightforwardness of a virtuous and experienced woman, she would simply like to regain her husband's love. An amiable Elmire, "qui avait le coup d'oeil clair et prudent de la vertu,"[35] [whose glance was virtuously clear and prudent] she has Cramer promise to tear Fanfarlo away from Monsieur de Cosmelly. Fanfarlo, too, succeeds in her ambition. She sets up a household with Samuel Cramer, has twins, and working her contacts whom she continues to see, she aims to have him nominated to the Institut and awarded the "croix de la légion d'honneur" [legion of honour cross].[36]

The novella's physical, professional, and personal description of Fanfarlo recalls a number of dancers of the period: la Reine Pomaré, a dancing celebrity of the Parisian public balls; Marie Daubrun, who performed at the Théâtre-Montmartre;[37] Fanny Elssler, Marie Taglioni's rival;[38] Carlotta Grisi, who combined elements from Taglioni's and Elssler's dramatic repertoire; and Lola Montès, who was panned by most reviewers when she appeared in Paris, at the Opéra, for three nights in March 1844 and at the Théâtre de la Porte Saint-Martin a year later.[39] Fanfarlo dances in a theatre that could be the Théâtre de la Porte Saint-Martin. Although not as prominently written up as the Opéra, other theatres also boasted a "claque" and a number of critics who made or broke the various theatrical events and performers. Dancers such as Fanfarlo were known and assiduously followed by their admirers.

As Fanfarlo receives no one except her friends, Cramer decides to get her attention by panning her every Monday for three months in an important newspaper, even though he finds her "légère, magnifique, vigoureuse, pleine de goût pour ses accoutrements"[40] [fleet, splendid, vigorous, and with a good sense of dress]. Unable to find fault with her physique, he attacks her sense of taste and accuses her of sullying French concert space with her use of foreign articles of clothing and matching movements: "elle fut . . . brutale, commune, dénuée de goût, de vouloir importer sur le théâtre des habitudes d'outre-Rhin et d'outre-Pyrénées, des castagnettes, des éperons, des talons de bottes . . ."[41] [she was . . . brutish, vulgar, devoid of taste, wanting to import to the theatre customs from beyond the Rhine and the Pyrenees, castanets, spurs, and boot heels].

Even though Fanfarlo dances in ballet-pantomimes, Cramer compares her unfavourably to the Opéra dancers of the "ballets blancs":

> On lui opposait, avec cette tactique particulière aux journalistes, qui consiste à comparer des choses dissemblables, une danseuse éthérée, toujours habillée de blanc, et dont les chastes mouvements laissaient toutes les consciences en repos.[42]
>
> [According to those tactics particular to journalists, which consist in comparing dissimilar things, she was put up against an ethereal dancer, always dressed in white, and whose chaste movements left everyone's conscience at peace.]

The ballet-pantomimes devolved from the *harlequinade* tradition elaborated in the eighteenth century and illustrated by, among others, Watteau.[43] Fanfarlo dances in the role of Colombine, whose stock character traits stereotype the lively witty lady's maid seen in the plays of Molière, Marivaux, and Beaumarchais. At her gala performance, Fanfarlo as Colombine incarnates in quick succession Marguerite, Elvire, and Zéphyrine and receives the attention of several generations of characters from a variety of literary texts and countries. Such a ballet requires a combination of pantomime and dance with a syntax of steps that indicates the corporeality and earthiness of the character: "La Fanfarlo fut tour à tour décente, féerique, folle, enjouée; elle fut sublime dans son art, autant comédienne par les jambes que danseuse par les yeux"[44] [La Fanfarlo was by turns modest, enchanting, frenzied, playful; she was sublime in her art, as much an actress with her legs as a dancer with her eyes]. The unexpected reversal of bodily parts to performance characteristics that ends the glowing review emphasizes her mastery of the ballet-pantomime and reiterates the genre's particular combination of eighteenth- and nineteenth-century dance conventions — physical eloquence and spectacular technique. Its choreography should not match the serene, evanescent, and tragic movement quality of a wili or sylph, as Cramer's negatively marked appreciation of one of her performances underlines:

> Quelquefois la Fanfarlo criait et riait très haut vers le parterre en achevant un bond sur la rampe; elle osait marcher en dansant. Jamais elle ne portait de ces insipides robes de gaze qui laissent tout voir et ne font rien deviner. Elle aimait les étoffes qui font du bruit, les jupes longues, craquantes, pailletées, ferblantées, qu'il faut soulever très haut d'un genou vigoureux, les corsages de saltimbanque; elle dansait, non pas avec des boucles, mais avec des pendants d'oreilles, j'oserais presque dire des lustres. Elle eût volontiers attaché au bas de ses jupes une foule de petites poupées bizarres, comme le font les vieilles bohémiennes qui vous disent la bonne aventure d'une manière menaçante, et qu'on rencontre en plein midi sous les arceaux des ruines romaines.[45]
>
> [Sometimes la Fanfarlo shouted and laughed very loudly toward the pit as she landed a leap up against the footlights; she dared to walk as she danced. Never did she wear those insipid gauze dresses that allow one to see everything and leave nothing to the imagination. She liked fabrics that rustled, long skirts, loud, spangled, tinny, that one has to lift very high with a vigorous knee, harlequin bodices; she danced, not with earrings, but with pendants, I would almost dare say chandeliers. To the bottom of her skirts, she would happily have attached a multitude of strange little dolls, like the old Gypsies who menacingly tell your fortune, and that one meets at midday, under the arches of Roman ruins.]

Implicitly, Fanfarlo is associated with the corrupting woman and placed at the opposite pole from the pure, virginal ballerina in her translucent white gauze.

A long commentary on the reception of dance in France, which marks the turning point in *La Fanfarlo*'s narrative development, returns to this opposition. Although it is unclear whether Cramer or the narrator is voicing the appraisal, it associates, as Théophile Gautier's reviews do, the sensuous with Terpsichore and the vaporous with northern European fairies:

> Terpsichore est une Muse du Midi; je présume qu'elle était très brune, et qu'elle a souvent agité ses pieds dans les blés dorés; ses mouvements, pleins d'une cadence précise, sont autant de divins

> motifs pour la statuaire. Mais Fanfarlo la catholique, non contente de rivaliser avec Terpsichore, appela à son secours tout l'art des divinités plus modernes. Les brouillards mêlent des formes de fées et d'ondines moins vaporeuses et moins nonchalantes. Elle fut à la fois un caprice de Shakespeare et une bouffonnerie italienne.[46]
>
> [Terpsichore is a southern; I presume she was very dark, and that she often tossed her feet in the golden corn; her movements, filled with a precise cadence, are as many divine designs for statuary. But Fanfarlo the Catholic, not content to rival Terpsichore, brought to her rescue all the art of the more modern divinities. The fogs mix the outlines of less vaporous and less nonchalant fairies and undines. She was at once a fantasia of Shakespeare and an Italian buffoonery.]

Like Carlotta Grisi, who, according to Gautier, embodies both Terpsichore's paganism and the sylph's Christian motifs, Fanfarlo draws upon the bodily shapes found in Grecian or Roman art and on the limpid lines of medieval and English fantastic beings.

Nevertheless, before this more accurate evaluation of her talent, not only is Fanfarlo's performance style attacked, but also her social persona. Cramer states that she is a drunkard and implies that she has perverse sexual preferences and is lesbian: "sans compter qu'elle buvait comme un grenadier, qu'elle aimait trop les petits chiens et la fille de sa portière"[47] [without taking into account that she drank like a trooper, that she was too fond of small dogs and of her doorkeeper's daughter]. The dancer and the woman coincide in Cramer's attacks as if he were comparing Fanfarlo with Madame de Cosmelly. He disparages her according to the images that society promulgates about the mores of women dancers, and into which Blanche of "Une Grande coquette" bought so readily.

The conflation of woman-at-life with woman-at-work and character within a newspaper dance review besieges performers. It inscribes the woman-at-dance in the regime of commodification to which they are encouraged to acquiesce if they want to succeed and last. As a result, dancers make a point of selling themselves to the critics. They often buy themselves laudatory review articles that comprise the requisite passage about their delicious physiognomy in order to stimulate male interest and desire.

Indeed Cramer's description of Fanfarlo in her dressing room replicates the favourable sort found in the period's press:

> La reine du lieu, au moment de quitter le théâtre, reprenait une toilette de simple mortelle, et, accroupie sur une chaise, chaussait sans pudeur sa jambe adorable; ses mains, grassement effilées, faisaient se jouer à travers les oeillets le lacet du brodequin comme une navette agile, sans songer au jupon qu'il fallait rabattre. Cette jambe était déjà, pour Samuel, l'objet d'un éternel désir. Longue, fine, forte, grasse et nerveuse à la fois, elle avait toute la correction du beau et l'attrait libertin du joli. Tranchée perpendiculairement à l'endroit le plus large, cette jambe eût donné une espèce de triangle dont le sommet eût été situé sur le tibia, et dont la ligne arrondie du mollet eût fourni la base convexe. Une vraie jambe d'homme est trop dure, les jambes de femmes crayonnées par Dévéria sont trop molles pour en donner une idée.[48]
>
> [The queen of the place, upon leaving the theatre, recovered the attire of a simple mortal and, squatting on a chair, dressed her adorable leg shamelessly; her plump tapering hands threaded the ankle-boot's lace through the eyelets like an agile shuttle, without dreaming of pulling down the petticoat. That leg was already, for Samuel, the object of an eternal desire. Long, delicate, strong, plump, and wiry at once, it had all the correctness of beauty and the wanton attraction of prettiness. Cut perpendicularly at its widest point, that leg would have given a kind of triangle whose summit would have been situated at the tibia, and the rounded line of the calf would have provided the convex base. A real man's leg is too hard, Dévéria's drawings of women's legs are too soft to give an idea of hers.]

The extended look and representation of what Cramer gazed upon celebrates her leg as the ideal model. Objectified and singularized as in many contemporary descriptions of dancers' physical attributes, the leg is almost drawn on the page. Perfectly geometric in its triangulation, it supersedes a man's leg and its perfection cannot even be imagined from looking at those pencilled by a contemporary artist.

> Dans cette agréable attitude, sa tête, inclinée vers son pied, étalait un cou de proconsul, large et fort, et laissait deviner l'ornière des omoplates, revêtues d'une chair brune et abondante. Les cheveux lourds et serrés retombaient en avant des deux côtés, lui chatouillaient le sein, et lui bouchaient les yeux, de sorte qu'à chaque instant il fallait les déranger et les rejeter en arrière.[49]
>
> [In that pleasing attitude, her head, inclined toward her foot, exposed a proconsul's neck, wide and strong, and let one imagine the furrow of the shoulder blades, covered in a dark and abundant flesh. Her heavy, thick hair fell forward on both sides, tickled her breast, and so blocked her view that she had to remove it and throw it back every instant.]

The stereotypic rapture of the female body — legs, hands, neck, upper back, and hair — parcelizes Fanfarlo fetishistically. Cramer's monoscopic visualization dismantles her body as a locus of action and reassembles it in a discontinuous series of gestures and poses. The synecdochal construction of her anatomy dissimulates her personhood and presents her body to the consuming look of the spectator/reader.[50]

Fanfarlo remains sanguine and realizes that the barrage of criticism is "une sorte particulière de bouquet hebdomadaire, ou la carte de visite d'un opiniâtre solliciteur"[51] [a peculiar sort of weekly bouquet, or the visiting card of a headstrong suitor]. Her elliptical commentary to Cramer when they do meet demonstrates that as performer she has internalized a gaze that goes beyond the public's constructed perception of dance and dancer: "vous êtes un monstre; cette tactique est abominable. — Pauvres filles que nous sommes! . . . dites-moi si vous m'avez trouvée bien ce soir?"[52] [you are a monster; these tactics are abominable. — What poor girls we are! . . . tell me if you liked me tonight?]. Her self-reflexivity allows her to see herself dancing and not just in the terms of the audience's appreciation or lack thereof.[53]

At least in Cramer's mind, it is as poet (Pierrot?) and dancer (Colombine?) that Fanfarlo and he leave together after her triumphant performance. A weather backdrop worthy of any "northern romantic" passionate scene, whether in poetry or on stage, accompanies them, and he stops an instant to open the window and savour his conquest. Like the lover on stage or the spectator at the theatre, Cramer is enchanted. Fanfarlo continues to incarnate his desire until she appears before him "dans la splendeur radieuse et sacrée de sa nudité"[54] [in the radiant and sacred splendour of her nudity]:

> Quel est l'homme qui ne voudrait, même au prix de la moitié de ses jours, voir son rêve, son vrai rêve poser sans voile devant lui, et le fantôme adoré de son imagination faire tomber un à un tous les vêtements destinés à protéger contre les yeux du vulgaire?[55]
>
> [What man would not want, even for the price of half his life, to see his dream, his real dream pose unveiled in front of him, and have the adored phantom of his imagination drop one by one all the clothing destined to protect it from the commoner's eyes?]

The realization in the flesh of desire — *l'attrait* — dissolves his fantasy. Seeing her without clothes is tantamount to allowing her to create herself, to assert her independent existence. She should have meaning only because the poet can reveal her. Clearly the scopic economy does not wish to see reality. Cramer desires the desire of the desire[56] and his monoscopic viewing excluded the material bodily presence of Fanfarlo as woman. He calls out for her disguise and her makeup, the artifice of the rouge:

> Il aimait un corps humain comme une harmonie matérielle, comme une belle architecture, plus le mouvement; et ce matérialisme absolu n'était pas loin de l'idéalisme le plus pur. Mais, comme dans le beau, qui est la cause de l'amour, il y avait selon lui deux éléments: la ligne et l'attrait, — et que tout ceci ne regarde que la ligne, — l'attrait pour lui, ce soir-là du moins, c'était le rouge.[57]
>
> [He loved a human body like a material harmony, like a beautiful architecture, with movement; this absolute materialism was not far from the purest idealism. But, as in beauty, which is the cause of love, there were according to him two elements: the line and the attraction — and that all this only has to do with the line — the attraction for him, that night at least, was the rouge.]

Fanfarlo views his desire as a capricious whim. Although she acquiesces, she sees her costumes as a professional pose, not an attitude to life[58], and as woman-at-life she entertains him with a private showing of woman-at-dance.

Fanfarlo abandons the adoring Monsieur de Cosmelly for Samuel Cramer's originality. Because of its novelty, his eccentricity appeals to her. She grows accustomed to him and decides he is worthy of her endearment. Sufficiently assured of her position at the theatre, she cancels a number of appearances, causing the suspension of performances, and neglects rehearsals. As "une danseuse magnifiquement appointée et entretenue"[59] [a lavishly appointed and kept dancer], she lives in a small house in a new and green neighbourhood. Her preference for intimate, cozy spaces over the expansive rooms of old châteaux is an extension of her personality. Similarly, her style in furniture dismisses large armchairs and impressive beds and turns to a cluttered look, strewn with lace and strongly coloured fabrics. A few paintings decorate the walls of her interior. She also affirms herself in culinary matters, favouring wines from Burgundy, Auvergne, Anjou, and the Midi as well as from Spain, Greece, and Germany over champagnes and Bordeaux. She likes her meats rare with sauces and spices from the world over and reveres truffles. Thus her autégraphy drafts a nineteenth-century working woman's pleasures.

Cramer and Fanfarlo continue to cohabitate and settle down. Fanfarlo gains weight ("elle est devenue une beauté grasse, lustrée et rosée"[60]) and gives birth to twins while Cramer writes four learned books. To try his hand at politics, he starts a socialist newspaper and Fanfarlo becomes a "lorette ministérielle"[61] — as enterprising as in her role as Colombine — in her effort to promote him. The narrator postulates that she may soon go to Communion and pay for the holy bread in kind to her parish. Should Cramer die, she may come to look like a canoness and turn a young heir's head. Together, as the narrator indicates, the couple comes to represent bourgeois aspirations at the eve of the 1848 revolution.

intentionally autobiographing blurs the diegetic lines of ballet libretti, fiction, and social history

The trio configuration of one male to two female dancers, found in *Giselle* or *La Sylphide,* participates in Baudelaire's narrative, but the novella complicates it by extending the story beyond the happily-ever-after ending of *Les Deux pigeons.* Typically, the Romantic poet cannot tell the dancer from the woman, nor dance from life. Dance, according to the narrator (or is it Cramer?), expresses mysteries. "La danse, c'est la poésie avec des bras et des jambes, c'est la matière, gracieuse et terrible, animée, embellie par le mouvement"[62] [dance, it is poetry with arms and legs, it is matter, graceful and terrible, animated, embellished by movement]. Fortunately, Cramer's romantic and poetic dreams evaporate as in a ballet scenario. Indeed "[la danse] a de plus le mérite d'être humaine et palpable"[63] [dance has the added merit of being human and palpable].

Although representation is generally on the side of the observer, Baudelaire's text in writing about one person — Cramer — talks of another, Fanfarlo. In talking about his own life, Baudelaire displaces the dichotomy of ideal/disparaged woman from poetics to the socio-cultural plane. Similarly, the rehearsal of the public relationship of poet to dancer as a material sign of his poetry shifts in the novella to represent the private (domestic) relationship between the dancer and the poet. The novella *La Fanfarlo,* as its title points up, in the end documents the life of a dancer and accentuates her subjectivity.

The writing *in* of the other reaffirms the norms of the period's autobiographical form. It also parallels the spectacularization of the female dancer in such ballets as *La Sylphide,* wherein the woman-at-dance presents her body in a direct and literal way. But the text of *La Fanfarlo* distinguishes the dancer from the dance. The dancer plays a role in a ballet. Fanfarlo's terpsichorean and *catholique* character entertains with biographical portrayals of Colombine, Marguerite, Elvire, and Zéphyrine. Her multiple roles also gesture allegorically toward various subject-positions that dancers as women of the nineteenth century could inhabit. The writing *in* also reveals the dancer as a woman-at-life within the period's socio-political structures.

Baudelaire calls *presque rien* the artifice that separates the courtesan (the body-at-dance?) from the *honnête femme* (the body-at-life?). "Ce presque rien, c'est presque tout, c'est la distinction."[64] The distinction inters attitudes about the dancer. This "almost nothing" twists his fictional autobiography to enable an autégraphy of a dancing woman in the nineteenth century.

notes

1 Colette's epigraph to *La Naissance du jour* reads in French as: "Imaginez-vous, à me lire, que je fais mon portrait? Patience: c'est seulement mon modèle." It is a reworking of Proust's "ce 'je' qui est moi et qui n'est peut-être pas moi" [This "I" who is me and who is perhaps not me] (see "notice" of *Colette Oeuvres III,* 1378). Colette, herself a music-hall dancer, portrays well her working life as a performer at the beginning of the twentieth century. All translations are mine.

2 Toni Morrison, "The Site of Memory," in William Zinsser (ed.), *Inventing the Truth* (Boston: Houghton Mifflin, 1987), 115.

3 The term is Nancy K. Miller's. The first foal of "overreading" is to unsettle the interpretive model, the paradigms [the male's look at the dancer] (Miller, *Subject to Change.* [New York: Columbia University Press, 1988], 83).

4 Jay Parini, "Delving into the World of Dreams by Blending Fact and Fiction," *The Chronicle of Higher Education,* 27 February 1988, B5.

5 This use of the term "autobiography" steps away from what Philippe Lejeune has called the autobiographical pact, according to which the "I" of the subject in the text and the "I" recounting would be one and the same person. Philippe Lejeune defined autobiography in *L'Autobiographie en France* as "the retrospective narrative in prose that someone makes of his existence, when he places the main emphasis on his individual life, especially on the history of his personality" (Paris: Armand Colin, 1971, 14).

6 Parini, "Delving into the World of Dreams," B4.

7 Although Leakthina Chau Pech Ollier does not use the term "autébiography" in her work on Yourcenar, she raised the issue of the problematic gender of autobiography in many discussions. Katherine Callen King suggested the transformation of the term "autobiography" to "autébiography." I use "autégraphy" to inflect the activity as feminine, and to express the corporality of self expression, whether it be through a pen/keyboard or through dance. The erasure of "bio" de-emphasizes the aspect of life-writing intrinsically associated with the lexeme "autébiography."

8 Lejeune calls Robert Phelps' autobiography of Colette ghost writing. In *Earthly Paradise,* Phelps "[strung] together moments in Colette's life with passages from her works in a thematic and roughly chronological continuum" (Nancy K. Miller, *Subject to Change,* 61).

9 Susan Leigh Foster, *Choreography and Narrative: Ballet's Staging of Story and Desire* (Bloomington: Indiana University Press, 1996), 253.

10 Ibid., 259.

11 Susan Leigh Foster's *Choreography and Narrative* details the extensive use of myths in eighteenth-century dance. For a succinct summary, see the conclusion (253).

12 This evanescence also constitutes Baudelaire's "modernité": "La modernité, c'est le transitoire, le fugitif, le contingent, la moitié de l'art, dont l'autre moitié est l'éternel et l'immuable" [Modernity, it is the transitory, the fleeting, the contingent, half of art, whose other half is the eternal, the immutable] ("Le Peintre de la vie moderne," *Oeuvres complètes II,* 695). Victor Hugo's poem "Fantomes" (*Les Orientales,* 171–3) is but one example of the poet's vision of dance and dancers — and the title is telling: Mon âme est une soeur pour ces

ombres si belles. / La vie et le tombeau pour nous n'ont plus de loi. / Tantôt j'aide leurs pas, tantôt je prends leurs ailes. / Vision ineffable où je suis mort comme elles, / Elles, vivantes comme moi! // Elles prêtent leur forme à toutes mes pensées. / Je les vois! je les vois! Elles me disent: viens! / Puis autour d'un tombeau dansent entrelacées; / Alors je songe et me souviens [My soul is a sister for these ever-so-beautiful shadows. / Life and the tomb no longer have any law for us. / Sometimes I help their steps, sometimes I take their wings. / Ineffable vision where I am dead like them, / They, living like me! // They lend their form to all my thoughts. / I see them! I see them! They tell me: come! / Then around a tomb they dance intertwined; / Then I dream and remember] (II, 173).

13 I am proposing that nineteenth-century ballet was allegorical and wish to acknowledge my debt to Craig Owens' work on allegory, a figure that Romantic art theory and Modernism attempted to do away with. (See Owens, *Beyond Recognition,* especially 48–59.) I rework his text extensively to apply it to ballet, and in particular I look for such elements as appropriation, site specificity, impermanence, accumulation, discursivity, and hybridization, which "form a whole when seen in relation to allegory" (Owens, *Beyond Recognition,* 58).

Allegory rescues from historical oblivion that which threatens to disappear (Owens, xii, quoting Walter Benjamin's theses on the philosophy of history) by laying claim to the culturally significant and and adding meaning that supplants its antecedent one. Allegory first emerged in response to a sense of estrangement from tradition (Owens, xii). Throughout its history it has functioned in the gap between a present and a past that, without allegorical reinterpretation, might have remained foreclosed. Synthetic, allegory crosses aesthetic boundaries and confuses genres (Owens, 53).

I hope to argue that ballet uses allegory differently from court dances of the Renaissance when the spectator sought allegorical significance in the movement itself because the choreographer translated world events into movement (Foster, *Reading Dancing,* n.1, 235).

14 Heidegger, "The Origin of the Work of Art" (quoted in Owens, 61): "The art work is, to be sure, a thing that is made, but it says something other than the mere thing itself is, *allo agoreuei.* The work makes public something other than itself; it manifests something other; it is an allegory."

15 Susan Leigh Foster, *Reading Dancing: Bodies and Subjects in Contemporary American Dance* (Berkeley: University of California Press, 1986), n.3, 259.

16 T. J. Clark treats mid-nineteenth-century painting as political allegory (Owens, 53).

17 I am drawing on Susan Kozel's work on mimesis and her analysis of Luce Irigaray's mimetic strategy (especially 101–2).

18 Jane Gallop's reading of Irigaray's assessment of Freud's point of view in *The Daughter's Seduction* as a phallomorphic ideological angle on the subject (Ithaca, NY: Cornell University Press, 1982, 58) is taken up in Miller's discussion of the gaze in Staël's *Corinne ou l'Italie,* wherein the protagonist's "performing gaze . . . unsettles [the] conflation of contemplation, theory, maleness, phallic authority by showing the political investments of spectating, the limits of vision from father to son, and by complicating the notion of spectacle. This double move in fact connects the two problematics: of woman's performance as theater — what she by *her* [*sic*] gaze might give to be seen, *otherwise* [*sic*]; and what it would take for it to be received" (Miller, *Subject to Change,* 179).

19 Sally Banes analyzes in *Dancing Women: Female Bodies on Stage* the response of mid-

nineteenth-century Romantic ballet in France to postrevolutionary anxieties about women and their social (public) and personal (private) desires. Her argument points out how, even though the libretti forward the socio-political and narrative plots of "compulsory heterosexuality," they nevertheless question the values of marriage and monogamy (5–7 and 12–41). Although Evan Alderson is addressing present-day ideological and aesthetic conditionings, he also works through the stereotypes that ballets enacted about dancers and/as women ("Ballet as Ideology: *Giselle,* Act 2," in Jane C. Desmond (ed.), *Meaning in Motion* [Durham: Duke University Press, 1997], especially 123–31).

20 Unlike Gustave Flaubert, who maintains the chronotope of the Salomé biblical story in *Hérodias,* Baudelaire would have, according to that interpretation, transported the story to nineteenth-century bourgeois Paris, substituting Madame de Cosmelly for Hérodias, her husband for Hérod, Fanfarlo for Salomé, and the poet for St. John the Baptist.

21 The compositional history of *La Fanfarlo* is unclear. Baudelaire may have started the novella as early as 1843 and have been working on certain parts of it as late as 1846 (Robb, Graham, "Lola Montès et la Fanfarlo," *Etudes Baudelairiennes* XII nouvelles séries IV, 1987, 55–60).

22 Honoré de Balzac, *Béatrix* (Paris: Pléiade Editions Gallimard, 1951), 620.

23 Alex Privat d'Anglemont, "Une Grande coquette," and "La Fanfarlo de Private d'Anglemont," in Willy Alante-Lima (ed.), *Bulletin Baudelairien* 28, 2, December 1993: 50. The double entendre of "sauteuse" is lost in translation. Blanche's allusion to young dancers learning how to jump also implies their promiscuous behaviour — jumping (into bed).

24 Ibid., 51.

25 Ibid., 52.

26 The spelling of her name varies throughout the text from Saint-Valery to St-Valéry to St-Valery.

27 Baudelaire's and d'Anglemont's lives crossed frequently during the 1840s. They both knew Jeanne Duval and Elise Sergent (*La Pomaré* was so named because of the current events having to do with the queen of Tahiti, Pomaré III). Anglemont published a poem that he dedicated to Sergent in October 1844. Baudelaire probably met her through Théodore de Banville, and she may have stayed at his Hotel Pimodon, where "il entretient plus qu'un simple badinage" [he did more than just dally] with her (Jean Ziegler, *Gautier Baudelaire un carré de femmes Pomaré, Marix, Bébé, Sisina* [Paris: A.-G. Nizet, 1978], 31). Furthermore, Privat d'Anglemont was from Martinique and was Creole, rather like Samuel Cramer. Recent biographical work also points to Jeanne Duval's Haitian, rather than Reunionian, identity.

28 Graham Robb's article emphasizes the autobiographical dimension of Baudelaire's novella in seeking to date its composition. Baudelaire, who was cognizant of Lola Montes' reputation as a dancer and notorious woman, as well as of her involvement in the famous Beauvallon lawsuit, may have modelled elements of Fanfarlo's physique on her. The usefulness of Robb's research to this project lies with his highlighting the realism of the socio-cultural and historical components of the text.

29 Baudelaire, *La Fanfarlo,* 39–40.

30 Bernard Howells, "Baudelaire: Portrait of the Artist in 1846," *French Studies* 37, 4, 1983: 429.

31 John Jeremy, "Samuel Cramer — Eclectic or Individualist?" *Nottingham French Studies* 20, 1, 1981: 10–1.

32 During the nineteenth century, the terms "hermaphrodite" and "androgyne" were often used interchangeably and inaccurately, as Kari Weil elaborates in *Androgyny and the Denial of Difference.*

33 Charles Baudelaire, *La Fanfarlo* (Paris: Le Castor Astral, 1990), 38.

34 Ibid.

35 Ibid., 41.

36 Fanfarlo could be recognized in Balzac's narrator's depiction of the second *sujet*: "— Voilà . . . une basse-taille et un *second premier sujet* de la danse. La basse-taille est un homme d'un immense talent, mais la basse-taille étant un accessoire dans les partitions, il gagne à peine ce que gagne la danseuse. Célèbre avant que la Taglioni et la Essler parussent, le *second sujet* a conservé chez nous la danse de caractère, la mimique; si les deux autres n'eussent révélé dans la danse une poésie inaperçue jusqu'alors, celle-ci serait un premier talent; mais elle est en seconde ligne aujourd'hui; néanmoins elle palpe ses trente mille francs, et a pour ami fidèle un pair de France très influent à la Chambre.

Tenez, voici la danseuse du troisième ordre, une danseuse qui n'existe que par la toute-puissance d'un journal. Si son engagement n'eut pas été renouvelé, le ministère eût eu sur le dos un ennemi de plus. Le corps de ballet est à l'Opéra la grande puissance aussi est-il de bien meilleur ton dans les hautes sphères du dandyisme et de la politique d'avoir des relations avec la Danse qu'avec le chant" (Balzac, Les *Comédiens sans le savoir (novembre 1845)* [Paris: Pléiade Editions Gallimard, 1955], 18–19).

[There's . . . a bass player and a *second first sujet.* The bass player is a man of immense talent, but since the bass is an accessory on partitions, he hardly earns what the dancer earns. Famous before the arrival of Taglioni and Essler on the scene, the *second sujet* has maintained character dancing and mime here in France; if the other two had not revealed a yet-unheard-of poetry in dance, the former would be a first-class talent; but she is in second position today; nevertheless she touches her thirty thousand francs, and has as a loyal friend a very influential French peer in the Chamber.

Look, there's a dancer of the third order, a dancer that exists only on the strength and power of a newspaper. If her contract were not to be renewed, the ministry would have another enemy on its back. The corps de ballet is the great power at the Opéra, and so it is in much better taste in the high circles of dandyism and of politics to have liaisons with dance than with song.]

37 Robb, "Lola Montés et la Fanfarlo," 56.

38 Ibid., 69.

39 Ibid., 61–8.

40 Baudelaire, *La Fanfarlo,* 42.

41 Ibid., 43.

42 Ibid.

43 Over the course of the nineteenth century, the *harlequinade* tradition contributed to the popularity of mime shows with such personalities as Debureau, who linked the character of Pierrot with the figure of the accursed poet. The characters of this heritage have their origins in the sixteenth-century Italian *commedia dell'arte.* Although audiences expected the well-

known personalities to reflect the period in which they appear and to pinpoint the impact of society's ideologies on everyday life as types, they nevertheless retained certain essential and recognizable character traits.

44 Baudelaire, *La Fanfarlo,* 47.

45 Ibid., 43–4.

46 Ibid., 48.

47 Ibid., 43.

48 Ibid., 45. Other contemporary descriptions of dancers in their dressing rooms include Maurice Magnier, *La Danseuse,* and Ludovic Halévy, *Les Petites Cardinal.*

49 Ibid., 45–6.

50 For an elaboration of this point, see "Fugitive Desires" in Susan Leigh Foster, *Choreography and Narrative,* especially 228–30.

51 Baudelaire, *La Fanfarlo,* 45.

52 Ibid., 45–6.

53 Felicia McCarren, "The Female Form: Gautier, Mallarmé and Celine Writing Dance," Diss., Stanford University, 1992, 57.

54 Baudelaire, *La Fanfarlo,* 52.

55 Ibid., 52.

56 One thread in Peggy Phelan's *Unmarked: The Politics of Performance* theorizes what is represented, or rather what is not really there, in the context of the inequality that shows up between self and other. See especially "Broken Symmetries," 1–27; "Developing the Negative," 34–70; and "The Golden Apple," 93–111.

57 Baudelaire, *La Fanfarlo,* 53.

58 Jeremy, "Samuel Cramer," 16.

59 Baudelaire, *La Fanfarlo,* 42.

60 Ibid., 57.

61 Ibid., 57. A lorette was a type of prostitute. As a lorette ministérielle, Fanfarlo solicited ministers in order to obtain the légion d'honneur for Samuel Cramer.

62 Ibid., 47–8.

63 Ibid., 48.

64 "This almost nothing is almost everything, it is (the) distinction" [between a courtesan and a gentle woman]. I have removed the parentheses that frame this "aside" in Baudelaire's text ("Les Femmes et les filles," in "Le Peintre de la vie moderne," in *Oeuvres complètes II* [Paris: Pléiade Editions Gallimard, 1976], 719). In *Distinction: A Social Critique of the Judgement of Taste,* Pierre Bourdieu links the bourgeoisie's normativizing preference for form and style and its distanciation from economic need to point out that these so-called internal aesthetic choices are produced and learned as artifice.

bibliography

Alderson, Evan. "Ballet as Ideology: *Giselle,* Act 2." In Jane C. Desmond (ed.), *Meaning in Motion.* Durham: Duke University Press, 1997.

Balzac, Honoré de. *Béatrix.* Paris: Pléiade Editions Gallimard, 1951.

—. *Les Comédiens sans le savoir (novembre 1845).* Paris: Pléiade Editions Gallimard, 1955.

Banes, Sally. *Dancing Women: Female Bodies on Stage.* London: Routledge, 1998.

Baudelaire, Charles. *La Fanfarlo.* Paris: Le Castor Astral, 1990.

—. "La Modernité." In "Le Peintre de la vie moderne," *Oeuvres complètes II.* Paris: Pléiade Editions Gallimard, 1976.

—. "Les Femmes et les filles." In "Le Peintre de la vie moderne," *Oeuvres complètes II.* Paris: Pléiade Editions Gallimard, 1976.

Bourdieu, Pierre. *Distinction: A Social Critique of the Judgement of Taste.* Cambridge: Harvard University Press, 1984.

Chakravorty Spivak, Gayatri. "Subaltern Studies: Deconstructing Historiography." In *Other Worlds: Essays in Cultural Politics,* 197–221, New York: Methuen, 1987.

Colette, Sidonie Gabrielle. "La Naissance du jour." In *Colette Oeuvres III.* Paris: Pléiade Editions Gallimard, 1991.

Foster, Susan Leigh. *Choreography and Narrative: Ballet's Staging of Story and Desire.* Bloomington: Indiana University Press, 1996.

—. *Reading Dancing: Bodies and Subjects in Contemporary American Dance.* Berkeley: University of California Press, 1986.

Halévy, Ludovic. *Les Petites Cardinal.* Paris: Calmann-Levy, 1880.

Hannoosh, Michèle. "The Function of Literature in Baudelaire's *La Fanfarlo.*" In *L'Esprit créateur* 28, 1, 1988: 42–55.

Howells, Bernard. "Baudelaire: Portrait of the Artist in 1846." *French Studies* 37, 4, 1983: 426–39.

Hugo, Victor. *Les Orientales.* Elizabeth Barineau (ed.). Paris: Librairie Marcel Didier, 1954.

Jeremy, John. "Samuel Cramer — Eclectic or Individualist?" *Nottingham French Studies* 20, 1, 1981: 10–21.

Kozel, Susan. "'The Story Is Told as a History of the Body': Strategies of Mimesis in the Work of Irigaray and Bausch." In Jane C. Desmond (ed.), *Meaning in Motion.* Durham: Duke University Press, 1997.

Lejeune, Philippe. *L'Autobiographie en France.* Paris: Armand Colin, 1971.

—. "Le Pacte autobiographique." *Poétique* 14, 1973: 137–62.

Magnier, Maurice. *La Danseuse.* Paris: Marpon & Flammarion, 1885.

Mallarmé, Stéphane. "Crayonné au théâtre: Ballets." Paris: Pléiade Editions Gallimard, 1945.

McCarren, Felicia. "The Female Form: Gautier, Mallarmé and Céline Writing Dance." Diss., Stanford University, 1992.

Miller, Nancy K. *Subject to Change: Reading Feminist Writing.* New York: Columbia University

Press, 1988.

Morrison, Toni. "The Site of Memory." In William Zinsser (ed.), *Inventing the Truth: The Art and Craft of Memoir.* Boston: Houghton Mifflin, 1987.

Ollier, Leakthina Chau-Pech. "Mirror of the Other: The Autobiographical Writing of Marguerite Yourcenar." Diss., UCLA, 1995.

Owens, Craig. *Beyond Recognition: Representation, Power, and Culture.* Scott Bryson, Barbara Kruger, Lynn Tillman and Jane Weistock (eds.). Intro. Simon Watney. Berkeley: University of California Press, 1992.

Parini, Jay. "Delving into the World of Dreams by Blending Fact and Fiction." *The Chronicle of Higher Education,* 27 February 1998, B4–B5.

Phelan, Peggy, *Unmarked: The Politics of Performance.* London: Routledge, 1993.

Privat d'Anglemont, Alex. "Une Grande coquette" and "'La Fanfarlo' de Privat d'Anglemont." In Willy Alante-Lima (ed.), *Bulletin Baudelairien* 28, 2, 1993: 47–60.

Robb, Graham. "Lola Montès et la Fanfarlo." *Etudes Baudelairiennes* XII nouvelles séries IV, 1987: 55–70.

Weil, Kari. *Androgyny and the Denial of Difference.* Charlottesville: University of Virginia Press, 1992.

Ziegler, Jean. *Gautier Baudelaire un carré de femmes Pomaré, Marix, Bébé, Sisina* Paris: A.-G. Nizet, 1978.

innovating and perpetuating

reflections on the aboriginal dance program

marrie mumford

Inspired by the traditions of Aboriginal culture and the boundaries of contemporary dance, twelve Aboriginal dancers and seven instructors with both traditional and contemporary dance experience created the Chinook Winds Aboriginal Dance Project in 1996. Since then the dance project has created a dynamic and powerful dance language to communicate tradition and culture.

— *Alberta Sweetgrass,* August 1999

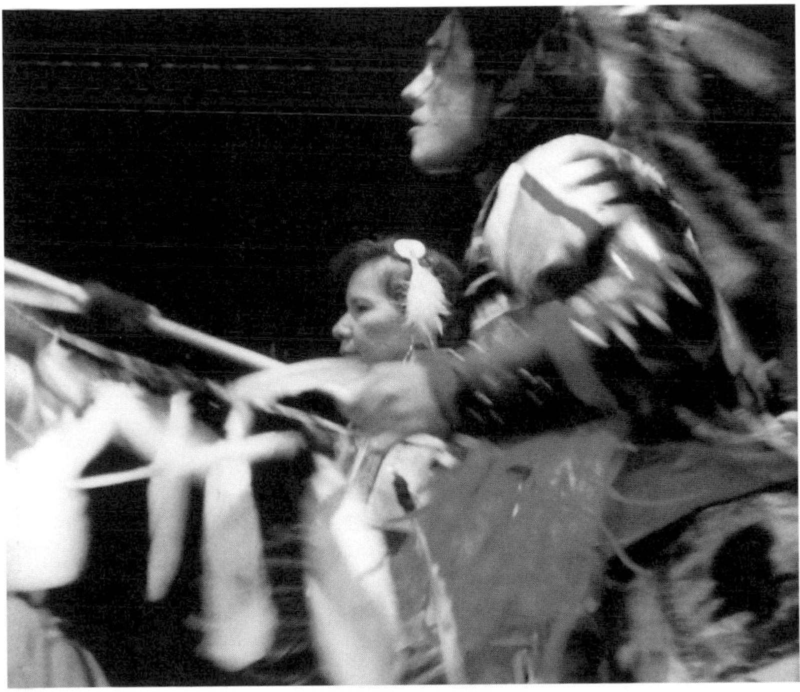

● Chinook Winds Aboriginal Dance Project 1996. *Grand Entry,* choreographed by Program Director Alejandro Ronceria with Dawn Ireland-Noganosh (Oneida), Daniel Secord (Anishnaabe).

marrie mumford

The Chinook Winds Aboriginal Dance Program at The Banff Centre for the Arts has become a unique gathering place for Aboriginal dancers and choreographers to practise, enrich, and expand their craft through intensive professional development residencies, workshops, creation of new works, and performances. The program has had a far-reaching effect on Aboriginal dance communities in Canada, inspiring Aboriginal dancers to further their careers elsewhere, encouraging new dance companies to form, and providing national and international exposure for Aboriginal dancers and choreographers.

The program provides professional development and performance opportunities for both emerging and established dancers and choreographers, as well as a whole community of workers who support this creative practice: in design, production, and program management. In this way, the program is developing an infrastructure to support the creation of dynamic and skilled Aboriginal dance communities across Canada.

One of the major challenges for the Aboriginal Arts Program is how to work within a process that affirms respect for difference — cultural differences, nation differences, and differences as a result of training, experience, and performance ideologies. This respect for difference builds solidarity within the program and establishes a safe creating place. A unique Aboriginal program, at The Banff Centre we recognize the strength of our own "difference" as well — the program has reaffirmed its original mandate to frame our activities within Indigenous world views, resisting pressures from dominant theories and cultures. Aboriginal cultures and ancient traditions provide the vision and methodologies to guide programming into the future. Our strength lies in affirming spirit as the inspiration for all aspects of the program, including dance training, cultural process, and performance.

The Aboriginal Arts Program was created to develop new forms of cultural practice within the principle of self-government in the arts. To create new forms without destroying the power of the old ways and to incorporate the old into the new without distorting the principles of ancient traditions is our challenge.

After concluding its fourth year, the Chinook Winds Aboriginal Dance Program began to find a balance between traditional principles and contemporary expressions — between research/process and performance, always with the goal of advancing contemporary Aboriginal dance in the context of respect for Aboriginal values, traditions, and music and dance forms. The program maintains a commitment to ensuring that Aboriginal methodologies for development and experimentation are not lost in the external pressures of production. The Aboriginal Dance Program ensures that the production becomes a vehicle promoting the building of Aboriginal communities by furthering the exploration of cultural processes.

We have faced insurmountable obstacles and now we are bringing forth with us those survival skills, refreshed and re-manifested in many ways. Our performance arts — songs and dance, we use to express our joy and celebration of life. A life that we enjoy, a sovereign life full of love, laughter and built-in hope.

— Sadie Buck, Chinook Winds Music and Cultural Director, 1999

● Closing Ceremonies. A round dance to celebrate the beginning of the partnership between the Aboriginal Film and Video Art Alliance and The Banff Centre for the Arts in 1993.

● The duplex tipi — a sign of the partnership.

Storytellers, artists, singers, and dancers — all have the power to move the souls and spirits of the people toward remembrance and recognition of who they are as a people. The Aboriginal Arts Program began in August 1993, when Aboriginal artists and storytellers gathered at Sleeping Buffalo Mountain and initiated a working partnership between the Aboriginal Film and Video Art Alliance and The Banff Centre for the Arts. This successful alliance, based on the principles of self-government in the arts, has evolved into a unique cultural partnership between a national council of Aboriginal artists from across Canada and The Banff Centre for the Arts. It is the only institution in Canada, perhaps in North America, that has created a partnership of this nature.

The theme which guides the Aboriginal Arts Program at Banff is the development of cultural forms that bridge traditional principles and contemporary expressions for the purpose of enhanced access, training and professional development in the arts for Aboriginal artists.

— Aboriginal Arts Program Strategic Plan, 1994

• • • • • • •

● Chinook Winds Aboriginal Dance Project 1996. *Four Directions,* choreographed by Program Director Alejandro Ronceria with Daniel Secord (Anishnaabe).

The Chinook Winds Aboriginal Dance Project was initiated by the Aboriginal Arts Program at The Banff Centre in 1996 as a pilot project. In the beginning, the focus of the Aboriginal dance classes and the choreographies created were the dances and music of the Plains nations as they have evolved into the dance styles of contemporary powwow. The dances and music of the Plains, one of the earth's oldest continuous cultures, was the starting place for our research to create a contemporary Aboriginal dance syllabus. The instructors for the Chinook Winds Aboriginal Dance classes were experienced powwow dancers who have been invited to participate in powwows across North America and are recognized dancers from Aboriginal communities. The program also brings in Aboriginal dance choreographers and instructors who are trained in ballet and modern dance. Classes in Eurocentric dance practice are also part of the program.

The Spirit of Powwow is to bring nations together . . . to gather Aboriginal people from across Turtle Island, to . . . allow participants the opportunity to renew ties with Indians from other nations to celebrate a common identity, and to display the distinctive qualities of their own identity, and its traditions . . . to promote a return to native social and cultural values . . . As long as people gather to celebrate the Indian way, there will be a future.

— Dennis Francis, *Supporting Native Dance in Canada,* Discussion Paper to the Canada Council for the Arts, 1992

● Chinook Winds Aboriginal Dance Project 1996. *Women's Traditional,* choreographed by Program Director Alejandro Ronceria with Siobhan Arnatsiaq-Murphy (Inuit), Alexandra Thomson (Metis), Dawn Ireland-Noganosh (Oneida), Sylvia Ipirautaq Cloutier (Inuit), Monique Diabo-John (Mohawk/Tiano), Sandra Laronde (Teme/Augama/Anishnaabe).

● Chinook Winds Aboriginal Dance Project 1996. *Four Directions,* choreographed by Program Director Alejandro Ronceria with Daniel Secord (Anishnaabe).

In the beginning, we studied dance histories and compared historical differences. In the late 1800s, while the great ballets of Europe were being created, Native people in Canada from many nations — from the east, from the north, and from the south — gathered in the Cypress Hills in southern Alberta. They sought a sanctuary, a last refuge for sovereignty for their families and for their nations to remain a "free" people. Treaties had just been signed and reserves set aside. In 1895, the Indian Act of Canada was amended to outlaw the Potlatch dances of the West Coast and dances of the Plains. Two years later, dancers from Aboriginal territories in northern Alberta challenged this law and danced. They were sent to prison.

In the first year of the Chinook Winds Aboriginal Dance Program, this was the starting point from where we began to tell our stories — to build our first choreographies. The first year of the program was a contemporary celebration of our music, dances, and songs. *Red Belt* was one of the choreographies created. During the chinook winds, the pine cones in the tops of trees turn red because of the warm wind, forming what is known as a "red belt." This belt has occurred as long as the mountains have been standing. It will always exist. We are like that red belt. In the words of Alejandro Ronceria, the program director and choreographer for Chinook Winds, "It is such a beautiful metaphor for Aboriginal peoples because, although we are still fighting for many things, we are still here." And in the words of Siobhan Arnatsiaq-Murphy, one of the Chinook Winds dancers, "and . . . we are still dancing."

Let no one say the past is dead, the past is all about us and within.

— Oodgeroo of the Noonuccal of Minjerriba, Australia

● Chinook Winds Aboriginal Dance Program 1997. *Seeing Voices,* choreographed by Jerry Longboat (Mohawk/Cayuga), duet with Geraldine Manossa (Cree) and George Leach (Stla'limx).

● Chinook Winds Aboriginal Dance Program 1998. *Shaping Worlds as Fire Burns,* choreographed by Gaetan Gingras (Mohawk), the 1998 recipient of the Clifford E. Lee Choreography Award, with Sylvia Ipirautaq Cloutier (Inuit), Andrameda Lutchman (Tagish/Tlingit/West Indian/Ukranian).

Each year, the Aboriginal Dance Program highlights an Indigenous culture. In the second year, the focus was on the stories and dances and music of the Inuit. The program explored Inuit and Inuvialuit cultures with dancers and instructors from Greenland and Canada's eastern and western Arctic, creating *Light and Shadow,* a new choreography inspired by Inuit art, mythologies, and landscapes. In the third year, the focus moved beyond Canadian borders to bring in an international component. It included dancers and choreographers of Mayan and Zapotec descent from Mexico, celebrating the dances, music, and stories from Chiapas to Inuvik. As a result of this project, the program has developed an ongoing international exchange with Fondo Nacional para la Cultura y las Artes (FONCA), bringing Indigenous dancers from Mexico to Chinook Winds each year.

Far from a mere display of ethnic dance, [Cultures Around the Fire . . . from the Mayan to the Inuit] *is a high-calibre theatrical production that effectively melds traditional influences with a contemporary aesthetic. A sophisticated blend of ancient and modern.*

— *Calgary Herald,* Summer 1998

● Top: Chinook Winds Aboriginal Dance Program 1998. *Shooting Stars,* choreographed by Georgina Martinez (Mexican/Zapotec) with Penny Couchie (Mohawk/Ojibway), Francisco Alvarez Quinones (Mayan), Jerry Longboat (Mohawk/Cayuga).

● Bottom: Chinook Winds Aboriginal Dance Program 1998. *Inuit Solo,* choreographed by Program Director Alejandro Ronceria with Phanuelie Palluq (Inuit).

• • • • • • •

Aboriginal dancers who come to the program come from many dance backgrounds. Some have studied at the National Ballet School; some have danced with Desrosiers Dance Theatre; some are Inuit drum dancers; some are powwow dancers; and some are both traditional and contemporary dancers. The program needs to respect each dancer's process and find a process by which the dancers and choreographers can work together. In the beginning, the Aboriginal dance classes and the classes in Eurocentric dance were very separate. In the evenings, we watched dance videos and discussed and compared differences in dance histories, ideologies, intention, process, methodologies, and movement — interweaving experiences that we could communally share. The program sought models of culture-specific learning systems in Aboriginal communities, recognizing the need for identifying and affirming Aboriginal collaborative systems by bringing in culturally strong instructors who could translate these systems to contemporary practices, both Aboriginal and European.

[Chinook Winds] is perhaps the most active and creative dance study and performance program for Natives in the hemisphere.

— *Indian Artist Magazine,* Sante Fe, New Mexico, Winter 1998

● Chinook Winds Aboriginal Dance Program 1997. *Light and Shadow;* Nostalgia, choreographed by Program Director Alejandro Ronceria with Christine Friday O'Leary (Teme-Augami/Anishnaabe).

● Chinook Winds Aboriginal Dance Program 1997. *Shaman's Journey*, choreographed by Raoul Trujillo (Apache/Mexican/French Canadian) with Santee Smith (Mohawk), Lizard.

● Chinook Winds Aboriginal Dance Program 1997. *Misabi,* choreographed by Christine Friday O'Leary (Teme-Augami/Anishnaabe) with Julia Jamieson (Mohawk/Cayuga).

Each of us who participates in the Aboriginal Dance Program may bring a different understanding of cultural process — we come from many nations and experiences. As we begin to work together, and honour difference, we also discover threads that we weave together as Indigenous people. We lead from relationships; not only our relationships with one another, ourselves, our families, our communities, our nations, but also our relationships to our ancestors and to the earth on which we live. In *Dwellings: A Spiritual History of the Living World,* Linda Hogan writes that we "share a common mission for survival" with the earth. As we hear the ancient stories we "learn of the infinite mystery and movement at work in the world." As we begin to create new stories that tell of our love for the earth . . . we imagine the continuation of the earth, creating a world for our children and future generations . . . in contrast to stories that foreshadow an apocalyptic end.

Aboriginal theatre echoes our past, reflects our present and imagines our future and by doing so affirms our unique identity as one of the ancient classical cultures of this earth.

— Lydia Miller, Artistic Director, The National Aboriginal and Torres Strait Islander Playwrights, Australia

● Chinook Winds Aboriginal Dance Program 1998. Dance Video, *Messengers,* choreographed by Program Director Alejandro Ronceria with Sylvia Ipirautaq Cloutier (Inuit) and Michelle Olson (Han/Irish/French).

lessons in dance (as) history:

aboriginal land claims and aboriginal dance, circa 1999

jacqueline shea murphy

From 1987 to 1991, the Gitxsan and Wet'suwet'en people presented their claim to more than 58,000 square kilometres of land in British Columbia to the Supreme Court of British Columbia. Arguing that they are descendants of people who have lived in the territory since time immemorial, and that their claim to the land has never been extinguished through treaty or warfare, the Gitxsan and Wet'suwet'en argued for legal recognition of their ownership and jurisdiction over the land and its resources. In support of their claim, Gitxsan and Wet'suwet'en Chiefs and Elders described and presented to the court not only totem poles, house crests, and regalia, but also oral histories: Gitxsan *adaawk* — sacred reminiscences about ancestors, histories, and territories — and Wet'suwet'en *kungax* — spiritual songs, dances, and performances about trials between territories, all tying them to the land.

According to anthropologist Dara Culhane's lengthy and incisive analysis of the *Delgamuukw* trial, the trial judge took exception to the material, particularly to witnesses singing in court. "'This is a trial,' he reproached an Elder at one point, 'not a performance,'" Culhane reports him saying.[1] In his ruling, the judge largely dismissed the material as evidence. "I am not able to accept *adaawk, kungax,* and oral traditions as reliable bases for detailed history," he wrote, admitting oral tradition only when used "'to fill in the gaps' left at the end of a purely scientific investigation."[2] Instead, the judge concluded, "The evidence suggests that the Indians of the territory were, by historical standards, a primitive people without any form of writing, horses, or wheeled wagons,"[3] and ruled in favour of the Crown. The case was appealed to the Court of Appeal of British Columbia, and then to the Supreme Court of Canada.

In declaring *kungax* to be antithetical to a trial, as a trial "is not a performance" (and *kungax* implicitly are), the judge rehearsed familiar attitudes about the relation between performances and legal enactments.

His annoyance with the Elders' "performance" in a courtroom trial, and subsequent dismissal of the performance material they presented as evidence, is based on his assumption that "performance" is in a different category from documents or declarations that carry legal weight or consequence. Unlike, say, a treaty, or a letter, or a bill of sale, a performance doesn't actually prove anything, make anything actual, or serve as an official record of having made anything actual in the past. It is just a performance, and by (his) definition, outside of what is legally admissible as factual. Although it may be interesting or amusing, it is superfluous and inappropriate to the decorum of a courtroom, where facts are adjudicated and a judge's trial pronouncements (because a trial is *not* a performance) create law and are reflected in documents, which then *do* carry the factual weight of official history and memory.

The conception of the lack of legal weight carried by *adaawk* and *kungax* performance echoes that of J. L. Austin's seminal proclamation, in *How to Do Things with Words,* about performative utterances. Austin writes that certain performative utterances do carry legal weight in a court of law or sanctioned legal setting, but when those same words are spoken as part of a stage performance, they do not. For example, according to Austin, when a heterosexual couple says "I do" and a justice of the peace declares them husband and wife, this creates them as such — but these same words are "in a peculiar way hollow or void if said by an actor on the stage."[4] Both Austin and this judge thus imply that a performance doesn't actually *do* anything, at least not in the way a bill of sale or a performative utterance does; it is a performance, an act — not a performative.

While *Delgamuukw* was under appeal, public Aboriginal song and dance performance continued to gain momentum in Canada. In 1993, Aboriginal artists and storytellers initiated a working partnership with The Banff Centre for the Arts in Alberta, Canada. This led to the creation of the Aboriginal Arts Program at Banff in 1994. In 1995, a residency for Aboriginal Women's Voices brought Aboriginal women together to share songs and create new works. In the summer of 1996, the Aboriginal Arts Program introduced a summer dance residency in conjunction with The Banff Arts Festival, which became the first annual Chinook Winds Aboriginal Dance Project. Also in 1993, the Parliament of Canada, the

Northwest Territories, and the Inuit of Nunavut signed the Nunavut Final Land Claim Agreement. The agreement established Inuit control of more than 350,000 square kilometres of land in northern Quebec, over a tenth of which includes mineral rights. The agreement followed over thirty years of Inuit organizing and study of unextinguished Inuit Aboriginal title in the Arctic.

Then, in December 1997 — after the Nunavut Agreement was underway, and while Aboriginal music and dance in Canada were gaining increasing support and visibility — the Supreme Court of Canada rejected the British Columbia judge's ruling in the *Delgamuukw* land claim case. This appellate judge argued that the earlier ruling was faulty due in large part to the first judge's rejection of oral tradition. "The Gitxsan Houses have an *adaawk* which is a collection of sacred oral tradition about their ancestors, histories, and territories. The Wet'suwet'en each have a *kungax* which is a spiritual song or dance or performance which ties them to their land. Both of these were entered as evidence on behalf of the appellants," the appellate judge noted.[5] "The oral histories were used in an attempt to establish occupation and use of the disputed territory which is an essential requirement for aboriginal title," he added. "Had the oral histories been correctly assessed, the conclusions on these issues of fact may have been very different."[6]

In coming to this decision, the Supreme Court of Canada ruling noted a 1996 commission report that states: "The Aboriginal historical tradition is an oral one, involving legends, stories, and accounts handed down through the generations in oral form. It is less focused on establishing objective truth and assumes that the teller of the story is so much a part of the event being described that it would be arrogant to presume to classify or categorize the event exactly or for all time."[7] It concludes, "The laws of evidence must be adapted in order that this type of evidence can be accommodated and placed on an equal footing with the types of historical evidence that courts are familiar with, which largely consists of historical documents."[8]

The Supreme Court found the lower courts' errors to be so "palpable and overriding" as to warrant a new trial, but advised instead that the issues of Aboriginal title be settled through negotiations and not future litigation. On the one hand, the decision was celebrated as a landmark victory that changed the legal landscape for Aboriginal title and rights litigation in Canada.[9] On the other, scholars have argued that the case was lost before the appeal decision because its terms had changed from the first case's claim for "ownership" of the territory and "jurisdiction" over it to the appeal case's claim for, instead, Aboriginal title and self-government.[10]

On 1 April 1999, Nunavut — "our land" in Inuktitut — was inaugurated, becoming the largest land claim settlement in Canada's history. In celebration, the Canadian government issued a new 1999 two-dollar "toonie" coin. As with previous toonies, one side of the coin carries Elizabeth II's profile, contained neatly in the gold-coloured circular centre, surrounded by a silver-coloured rim. Embossed on the other side, new to this edition, is the image of an Inuit drum dancer, inscribed over and extending past the inner gold circle that, on the other side, circumscribes the Crown.

When my plane touches down in Calgary on 2 January 1999, I don't know diddly-squat about any of this. I've been invited to "Foothills and Footsteps: New Writings in Dance Studies," a conference at the University of Calgary. I am to give a paper on how Ted Shawn, in his quest to legitimate dancing for men, used Native American dance material to negotiate issues of masculinity. I plan to argue that Shawn's use of this material, to address his needs, drained Native American dancing of its political vibrancy and cultural function for Native peoples — though perhaps not entirely, as his stage work has been viewed with interest by emerging Native choreographers. The bulk of my research has been done reading library books and watching videos, using the rhetorical analytical skills I've developed as a literary scholar to unpack Shaw's appropriation of the Hopi Eagle Dance and other Native dance practices for his own agenda. Mine is the only presentation on the schedule dealing with Native dance, and, when I arrive that day, passport in hand, this lurks in the back of my mind as an issue to be contended with. I've been paired on a panel with African American scholar Tommy DeFrantz, who will be presenting on "black dance" and the essentializing impulse. There'll be him and there'll be me — a non-Native scholar, flown in from California, presenting myself as an expert on issues in Native American dance. It is a problem. For the most part, though, I am much more worked up about finding an airport ATM that will give me Canadian currency, and meeting up with the people I am supposed to, and how that fur coat they are lending me will feel to wear.

Before the conference starts, they whisk us off to The Banff Centre, a stunning arts colony/professional development centre in the tourist resort town of Banff in the Canadian Rockies, for a few days of R&R. We soak in the hot springs and skate at Lake Louise and eat our meals together, staring out at stunning mountains and talking about desserts. Everyone talks about what aspect of dance studies they are working on and when I say my topic — the relation between Native American dance and modern dance history — the local people ask me, oh, do you know about the Aboriginal Dance Program here? You'll have to meet Marrie Mumford and Jerry Longboat. They're coming to the conference. I'll introduce you. I make a mental note of the names and go to buy the book *Chinook Winds: Aboriginal Dance Project* they said I could find at The Banff Centre café-store. After we marvel again at the mountains and catch up on the latest news (there is a snowstorm back east; Tommy hasn't arrived yet), we say good night. I stay up for hours, poring over *Chinook Winds.*

Back in Calgary, the conference room is full of excited students and there's a definite crackle in the air. I think how this is such a good idea, bringing a dozen of us here (and paying our way, and handing us spending cash!), having a winter session dance studies course built around our presentations, giving us a chance to hang out and get to know one another. It's the way conferences should be. I sit on the edge of my seat and crane my neck around, looking at everyone, catching the sense of expectancy that infects the room.

Marrie Mumford says "Oh" when Lisa Doolittle introduces me and tells her about the paper I'll be giving. Marrie is a big woman with big grey hair; she gives off a simultaneous sense of incisive outrage and warm generosity. She shakes my hand, taking in my blue eyes and fair skin, giving me that "What are *you* doing talking about Native culture?" look I've come to know so well. "Hello." She is not hostile, but there's a definite edge of cool in her response to me. I swallow hard and tell her how I've just read the *Chinook Winds* book, how excited I am to learn of all the Aboriginal arts work going on at Banff, and how I'd love to talk with her and Jerry Longboat about the work they've been doing. Jerry is there, too, and we shake hands, and they watch me as I talk, and when I'm done they nod and say, okay.

Over the course of the day, I start to sense some tension and hard feelings around the issue of why Jerry and Marrie are not involved more officially in the Foothills and Footsteps program. I get the sense that Marrie and Jerry have come, in part, to register their protest that Aboriginal dance isn't included on the program at this conference, even though the Aboriginal Dance Program is flourishing only an hour away. And now it turns out there's this white professor from California (uh, that would be me) talking about issues in Native dance. My stomach aches as my sense of all this grows. Then it gets worse: we hear that Tommy DeFrantz, my co-panelist, is still stuck in a snowstorm in New York and isn't coming to the conference at all. So it looks like it'll be just me up there on the panel. I start to wonder whether Jerry and Marrie could present with me, since Tommy couldn't come. I ask the people who've been around the area for longer than I have (which is to say, more than two days) about the idea, trying to feel out what the politics are of asking Marrie and Jerry to speak. Everyone thinks it might work.

Before the performance that night (every night we go to a performance), I scramble to find the conference organizers, Anne Flynn and Lisa Doolittle, to ask, if Tommy isn't coming, how about if Marrie and Jerry are on the panel with me instead? That way I don't have to be up there alone tomorrow. They say, would they want to be? I say, I don't know but I could ask. And Anne and Lisa say, hmm, yes, okay. But the show is starting so I have to sit down and I can't even seem to locate Marrie and Jerry in the audience, so I can catch them on the way out. But when we're leaving, I find Jerry and ask if he would be on the panel with me and talk about his work at Banff. And he says, hmm, yes, that sounds good, okay. But let's find Marrie. We start to look around — we need to catch her before she leaves — and then just as the place is clearing out and we think we've missed her, we catch sight of her grey hair by the box office and run over to ask, will you be on the panel? And she looks us both straight on and she says, "Yes, I will."

I am so happy and relieved I could jump in the streets. I'm excited to hear about the work Marrie and Jerry have been doing at Banff and what they have to say about Aboriginal dance today. And it's really important that they be included at this conference, that they tell their story — for the politics of the conference, for the students attending, for everyone. And now they will be and all that brewing conflict will be a chance for conversation instead. I am tickled and pleased with myself for having managed to bulldoze in past all the tension, like some oblivious outsider, and blithely get the Aboriginal dance folks on the program.

"I'm so glad this worked out," I say to Jerry. "And I know I'll get to hear you tomorrow, but I'd still love to talk to you more sometime, too — about your work as a dancer and the program at Banff — if you have any time these next few days." I'm still giddy and glad and riding high from feeling like I saved the day.

"Sure," he says. "How about now? Want to go get a drink?"

At a bar down the street, full of artists and actors and energy, we sip our beers and chit chat and then Jerry turns to me and says, "So. What are you doing writing about Aboriginal culture anyway?"

One thing the Supreme Court decision on *Delgamuukw* has done is open the way for oral histories to be admitted as evidence in Canadian courts, and not thrown out as "hearsay." In this court case, the oral histories considered included dance — recognized as part of the Wet'suwet'en *kungax* — and thus the court decision recognized dance as not only a central and legally valid form of Aboriginal culture, but also a type of historical document tying Aboriginal peoples to the land. In this sense, the court decision echoed understandings Aboriginal peoples have long held about dance as connected to their relationship to land. At the same time, the *Delgamuukw* decision signals how much official Canadian governmental attitudes on both land claims and Aboriginal dance have changed in the past century. Participating in Aboriginal cultural practices like potlatching[11] and sundancing and organizing for Aboriginal land titles were both outlawed and criminalized in 1884, according to Sections 140 and 141 of the Indian Act. In 1921, a letter from Indian Affairs Deputy Secretary General Duncan Campbell Scott decried Indian dancing as "excessive indulgence," resulting in neglect of farming responsibilities.[12] In 1951, the Indian Act was amended and both Section 140 (the anti-potlatch laws) and Section 141 (the ordinance against organizing for land claims) were dropped (though as Culhane notes, not repealed or acknowledged as wrong).[13] Yet, because they were added to the 1876 act together in 1884, and repealed at the same time in 1951, the Canadian government recognized and reinforced both a conceptual and a legal link between them — a recognition that Aboriginal peoples noted. "In Indian memories, section 141 is usually linked with the potlatch prohibition," Culhane writes.[14] In other words, there has long been both an Aboriginal assertion of the link between dancing and relationship to land and a Canadian legal and historical, as well as rhetorical, connection between Aboriginal feasts and dances and Aboriginal land claims.

But admitting Aboriginal dances, and other forms of oral history previously dismissed as "performance," into the courts as a form of historical document does more than just enter more evidence into legal consideration. It questions understandings that see "performance" as something with less "truth" and legal effect than, say, a written treatise or a courtroom trial. Admitting it into the halls of official memory forces a rethinking of how "performance" functions as "historical document" and suggests that performance such as dancing enacted, and continues to enact, an effect on the world.

This echoes what I understand of Native American and Aboriginal[15] conceptions of dance, even as these conceptions extend understandings of "enactment." "We dance to remember, we dance to remember all our beloved ones," reads the excerpt from Leslie Marmon Silko's *Almanac of the Dead* that I have hanging on my office door. "Through the expression of dance, especially in Aboriginal cultures, a step into the past may be retained, explored, revived, or created," writes Inuit-Irish dancer Siobhán Arnatsiaq-Murphy in *Chinook Winds.*[16] This relationship of dance and memory carries not only the physical sense of dance as something that is learned from others and held and remembered in one's body. It also carries a spiritual sense in which learning to dance, and the act of dancing, enacts a spiritual and physical connection to other beings, including those who have passed on (as the Silko quotation underscores), as well as to those who will come later.

Thus performance embodies not only relation to the past, as a letter or travel journal might, but also relation to the present and the future as illustrated in Arnatsiaq-Murphy's description of dance not only exploring a step into the past, but also reviving and creating it. This, in turn, raises questions for contemporary theorizings on "performance" as standing in for, and seeking in vain to replace, something that it is not — conceptions that harken back at least as far as the Platonic disdain for the arts as mimesis, or imitation.[17] Silko, in stating "we dance to remember all our beloved ones," understands dancing as enactment of memory in the present, a memory that recognizes the past, and connection to ancestors and to land, by embodying it.

I begin to get a sense of all this during the ten days I spend at the Aboriginal Dance Program in July 1999. The conference panel in January went great; our presentations worked well together and students had lots of questions and interest in what Jerry and Marrie had to say. Now, with Marrie's invitation, I am returning to see this season's Chinook Winds Aboriginal Dance Program performances, watch videotapes of previous years' productions, and talk with the Aboriginal Dance Program dancers, choreographers, and program directors. I've applied to my university for research funds to cover my travel costs, and Cat Cayuga, the assistant program director at The Banff Centre, has arranged a room for me to stay in. I've even received a discounted meal ticket to eat at The Banff Centre dining room. On the plane I read about *Delgamuukw* and try to get a handle on some Canadian land claims history. Then there I am, arrived, ready to research the state of Aboriginal stage dance in Alberta, Canada, circa 1999.

My first day I go over to Aboriginal Arts and meet Nicole Robertson (the publicist), Sarah Williams (the resident adviser), Deborah Ratelle (the project manager), and Cat. All these women are very friendly and helpful but all the same not quite sure what to do with me and so I feel awkward and anxious and keep popping my head in to find Marrie, who is the only one here I've met before. I don't know if I should keep making a nuisance of myself and looking for her, or go off and play or watch the videos they lent me, or what. So I work myself up into a bit of a tizzy about it all, and about the sixth time I check in to see if Marrie is back in her office, Cat says to me, "You know, I think the Sally Borden building is open" (Sally Borden being the gym, pool, and more). I take this to be a hint to go swim or otherwise amuse myself somehow. I am becoming pathetic. And so I do. When I get back from swimming, the phone is ringing as I open the door to my room. It's Marrie, and she says, you made it! You're here! C'mon over! I head over and we talk for half an hour — about how this year the preparation for the Aboriginal Dance Program began with a meeting of an advisory committee to revisit the intention of the program. This began a process to restructure and set future directions.

She hints at the difficulties last year, when they produced four new pieces in five weeks. She explains that this year the program cut back production to two choreographies, rather than four, creating one new work and returning one choreography from repertoire. The program this year, she tells me, has also introduced a two-tiered program to balance the needs of training, creation, and production. The intention, she says, is to use production as a vehicle to build community by adopting cultural methodologies in the process of training, establishing an Aboriginal cultural framework, which includes Aboriginal values and principles in the process of creation and production. This intention, she explains, guides the process and recognizes the need for identifying and affirming Aboriginal systems, and the need for translating these systems to contemporary practices, both Aboriginal and European. "Also part of the process is to identify the effect of colonization on people who come through the program. Colonization shifts you into a way of thinking, which then lives in your body. So, part of what we are doing is deconstructing that way of thinking and reclaiming Indigenous knowledge," she says. One change this two-tiered program has led to is in the dance training that students undertake. "We used to have all our contemporary classes in the morning and our traditional classes in the afternoon. This year, we said, 'Let's not make that separation. Let's begin with the traditional dances,'" she says.

I nod and scribble and ask if she has time when I can interview her more officially and she says yes. Did I know that I have two interviews set up for the next day already? I skip out of her office, flushed and glowing from her warmth and generosity, riding high.

Over the next several days I hope to talk with the choreographers and choreographers' assistants and again with Marrie, and with as many of the dancers as I can, about the work going on at Banff. My requests for interviews, I'm told, need to go through Jacquie Carpenter, the stage manager. I have some officially scheduled and then Jacquie sets things up so I can talk with any dancers who are available backstage in the green room, between sections of rehearsals.

I hang out backstage, waiting for opportunities to interview people. The dancers have all seen me hanging around, but most of them have no idea who I am or what I am doing, and have no reason to trust me. As they plop on the couch or the floor, and look as if they may have a few minutes free before they get called back on stage, I approach them, tell them I am writing about the program here, and ask if I can talk to them and if they mind if I use a tape recorder. I get nervous each time and have to get my nerve up to go up and ask. But everyone I ask says yes and is very helpful and polite, though some seem a bit cool and reserved. Jacquie comes in at one point, when I'm talking to Shalan Joudry, a twenty-year-old Mi'kmaq woman from Nova Scotia.

"You doing okay?" she asks.

"Um, hmm," says Shalan.

"They're being nice?" Jacquie asks me, and we laugh.

Shalan says, "When you're not here we beat her up," and we laugh again and Jacquie leaves and we keep talking.

Many of the interviews I have during my time at the Aboriginal Dance Program start with qualifications. I am cautioned that dance, in an Aboriginal context, can't be separated out from other aspects of Aboriginal life. Marrie explains that even my focus on dance alone doesn't really fit. "Traditionally dance has both a cultural and spiritual significance. Dance, story, song, and drumming are interrelated — they are not exclusive of one another," she says.

Santee Smith, a Mohawk woman who danced in the program for four years and is back this year as the rehearsal master and choreographer's assistant, explains this as well. "Traditionally when we dance, it's a celebration," she says. "It's always been when people gathered. There's always been music, there's always been dancing, there's always the element of almost theatre when somebody's speaking." Because of the way traditional Aboriginal dance is interwoven with story, song, music, and theatre, what is labelled "dance" involves aspects beyond physical movement, and even beyond the focus of these other forms.

Santee contrasts the dance work at Banff with the years of ballet training she's had. "Here it's focused on all three levels. It's not just the physical, it's not just the movement base," she says. "It's traditional, it's cultural, it's spiritual, and people are trying to make that come together in a way that I haven't experienced with any other place."

Other dancers also explain the sense of connection they feel, the sense of dance being more than just isolated physical movement. Penny Couchie, a Mohawk-Ojibway dancer from Toronto, explains how this understanding of dance as something more than physical training translates into the dance work going on at the Aboriginal Dance Program. "Here, there's less of a focus on 'This is the shape that you're making with your body' and more of a focus on 'What shape does your body make when you're saying that?'" she says. "Approaching it from the inside out — but then understanding you don't stay on the inside. You understand your relationship. You understand your relationship to everything around you."

Shalan echoes this focus on dancers' connection to the world around them. "I think that good dancers are very connected not only within themselves, but to everything around them, and they know what they're saying. There is a purpose that transcends their physical movement. And I think you can tell by watching someone if they have that greater connection."

At the base of the discussions we're having is an understanding of connection between what might be called "traditional" Aboriginal dance, done within Aboriginal communities as part of ceremonies and celebrations, and the dance being choreographed and staged here at the Margaret Greenham Theatre for primarily non-Aboriginal audiences.

Santee makes brief mention of the potential controversies in staging some kinds of Aboriginal dance, but recognizing what's appropriate to stage and what isn't is more of a given than an issue she focuses on. "There are controversial things about what we can take to the stage," she says. "There are certain things within everybody's nation that are not meant for public entertainment, stuff that is meant for the community." She adds, "But we haven't had that problem here because everybody's respectful of that." The project's focus instead, she and others suggest, is on the relation between Aboriginal dance practices, as aspects of ceremony and celebration, and how the Aboriginal ways of understanding held in that dancing can be translated to the stage.

I get the feeling that the dancers are tired of suggestions that their lives, including their dance lives, aren't sufficiently "traditional."

"What is traditional?" asks Sid Bobb, a Sto:lo man from Vancouver. "Does that mean three hundred years ago? Does it mean a hundred years ago? Fifty years ago? Or does it mean a thousand years ago? To me, I keep intention, I keep the concepts the same. Dance is a reflection of that." He adds, "It's a reflection of who you are. Your dance is a part of the way you envision things."

An aspect of the interconnection that Aboriginal dance enacts, and that the Aboriginal Dance Program explores and engages, is not only between dancers and the world around. Again and again I hear mention of relation between the dancers dancing here, this week, and other generations. "I envision myself as my ancestors," says Sid. "We're not different. People ask today, well, you live in a city or you do this or you do that. I'm no different than I was a thousand years ago, because I'm the same person, reacting to things around me, making choices within things around me. So there's no difference with the man two thousand years ago." He explains, "The way you do things always changes — throughout your personal life, as well as your cultural life. Your culture has a history and it's still changing, it's going somewhere, same as your personal history is changing and going somewhere."

Santee explains this, too. "We think that — a lot of people think here — that we have ancestral memories in our body, and we are just trying to awaken those. That memory is in our body and in who we are. So when we do our performances, and especially when we're talking about intention, about why we're moving in a certain way, what does that mean to us, as the individual performer, that's when we try to call upon that ancestral stuff or try to awaken that."

Shalan says something along the same line. "My understanding is that as we go from one generation to the next, a part of our spirit and body is passed on to our children, and they pass on a bit of their collected spirit, and so on. Therefore, within me is a piece of all my ancestors, and I have that memory within me somewhere. The challenge is to get in tune to that, to hear and feel it, respond to that kind of memory."

Intergenerational connection is more than a concept the dancers are attuned to: it's also part of the everyday comings and goings of the Aboriginal Dance Program. I see the importance of this connection to children and grandmothers all over the place. Penny's almost-five-year-old daughter, Nimikii, is here, everywhere, playing on the floor, coming over to show us her paper dolls, while I interview choreographer Muriel Miguel and Santee in the cultural room. And Santee is here with her baby daughter, Semiah, and Santee's mother, Leigh, has come along to help take care of Semiah, and Cat's daughter, Zeeta, is running around, and Sadie Buck's son, George, and Cat's mother shows up as well, toward the end. Leigh and I are both on the sidelines here, so we cross paths a dozen times a day, say hello, and chat a bit.

When I ask Don Stein, in The Banff Centre's administration, what effect the Aboriginal Arts Program has had on The Banff Centre for the Arts as a whole, I expect him to talk about awareness of Aboriginal issues or politics or culture. He does, but not in the way I expect him to. "Child care! Child care is better for everybody here now," he answers. "When we started working with the Aboriginal community, they brought their whole families with them. So there were enormous strides forward in terms of [The Banff Centre's] sensitivity and facilities and willingness to support family life. Ten years ago, this was one of the things that people often complained about. And now, ten years later, whenever somebody asks if they can bring their kids, we can say, 'Oh, the child care here is fabulous.'"

Connected with this relation to ancestors and to ancestral memory, the dancers suggest, are understandings of the body, and especially the dancing body, as holding and inhabiting histories and ways of understanding that dancers might not even be fully aware of. As Santee explains, "A lot of the work that we do is with taking ownership of our own bodies. There's a lot of things that, through colonization, we don't even realize [affects] the way that we think or the way that we view our own body and our own humanness. A lot of the work that Karla [Jessen Williamson, the Inuit mask instructor] did was very much of reclaiming our own bodies, feeling comfortable in who we are." She adds, "We talk about this in the beginning — that we're going to be doing things that might spark something in you. We're working with our body and a lot of times issues will come up, because we're holding things in our body that we don't realize."

Inuit dancer Feliks Gower-Kappi implies that in this way of understanding bodies, and connection to others through bodies that are dancing, theories that understand what happens on the stage as merely representational — something acted or portrayed (but what Austin would call null or void in any "real" sense) — don't quite hold. "For these pieces here, you really have to be what you're portraying," Feliks says. "It's not just 'Okay, I'm told to be this, and I'll do it.' You have to learn to really become that. That's what Alejandro [Ronceria, the program director and choreographer Feliks is working with] wanted — us to really feel it, be a part of it, to really be that person or to really be that bird. And to think of it in that way, to have that focus, to exercise yourself to have that focus is really challenging," he says. "Because just playing it is not as genuine. It starts to have a feel of 'Oh, just kind of get it over with.'" But once you're being it, it's something. Because if you become it, and if there's something to stop it, it's in a sense a little part of you dying or something, so therefore you want to survive, you want to go on."

This sense of dancing as enactment, not portrayal, comes up again and again in the stated intentions behind the Aboriginal Dance Program productions over the years. In the video box description for his 1997 piece, *Shaman's Journey,* choreographer Raoul Trujillo writes about how the piece is "about seeing into other worlds besides our own." He describes the act of transformation the Shaman in the piece goes through: "He enters other worlds by learning the languages of his guides and even becomes those animal forms." The shaman's "arrival," says Trujillo, is when he enters the spirit world and communicates with the ancient ones. Likewise, Jerry Longboat describes *Raven's Shadow,* a piece he choreographed after working at Banff, as "a contemporary investigation into the process of expanding oneself to experience the threshold between the living and the ancestral." He adds, "I explore dance and movement as spiritual and ritual expression, sculpting a space of Indigenous culture in the contemporary world."

This understanding of dancing as becoming, rather than playing at, extends not just to the people or birds Feliks refers to in *Light and Shadow.* It also underscores the relationship to land that almost everyone mentions to be part of what the dancing they are doing at Banff not only explores, but also enacts. *Light and Shadow,* one of two pieces on the 1999 program, is a dance for Nunavut that premiered during the 1997 season, before the Nunavut land claim act came into effect. This year it is being restaged as a celebration of the land claim and the inauguration of Nunavut as an Inuit province in April. Pablo Palma, a Nahua dancer from Mexico, tells me he relates to the dance, a piece for Inuit land far from where he has always lived, because he can understand the relationship to land he is embodying in his dance movement in the piece. "This dance for Nunavut is for the return to the land of that people," he says. "We can feel the land, and we can feel the beat, and we can feel the vibration, and that is the connection. So, when I begin to feel that, I begin to believe it is possible to make a movement." Sid Bobb also says the connection to and embodiment of both animals and land is a central part of the two pieces they're staging this season. "In both pieces, there is a huge reference to the land. In Muriel [Miguel]'s piece *[Throw Away Kids],* a lot of the connection and a lot of the characters' core is relationship to the land. And then in Alejandro [Ronceria]'s piece, a lot of it is working with animals, seals," he says. "The seal-people are emulating that animal."

Shalan relates this to what Aboriginal dance, including contemporary stage dance, offers. "For us, dance is deeply associated to the animals and land. That's our whole purpose of dancing," Shalan says. "It's all about how things are interconnected. Those relationships to earth being so important and that we never really disconnect from it. Dance then becomes a part of ceremony and a way of speaking, many things. We still view dance in that way. I think that a lot of contemporary kinds of dancers see their craft as a very distinct art. But then for us it's very connected to ceremony and to celebration."

Santee, like Pablo, explains that this understanding of how dance relates to land — how dancing is part of relationship to land and enacts relationship to land — is what connects the dancers from so many different nations. "Even though we are all Aboriginal, we all come from our own communities, and we all come from a movement base which is different, and yet similar," she says. "So there's powwow style and there's the Iroquois dance we do. Then there's Inuit people who come and teach us masking and drumming. But one common thread that's through everything is, Aboriginal dance is very much connected to the ground and to drum beats that are connected to the earth."

Feliks says the same thing. "We might be different, from different climates, landscapes, but we all believe we come from the land. That's our provider. We have the same similarities and respect for things." This, he says, is what he understands "collective memory" to be, this shared understanding, across Aboriginal communities. "Collective memory is memories of different people, from the different places they are from, coming together. And sharing what we have." Penny agrees. "I think that all these stories that we're doing are very much collective memory, because our experience as Aboriginal people has been so similar. The loss of land and laws and social structures and way of life — our whole structure. It's something we have in common as Aboriginal people, all over the world." She adds, "Dance is part of our families and a celebration of the people, and here it's part of political activism. It's part of us saying, 'We are the people who genocide has been performed upon.' It's our voice."

One thing that interests me in these comments is the way that what enables this "collective memory" to be shared across time and place is not a shared Indigenous "bloodline" or gene. Rather, what connects Aboriginal peoples from the Arctic to South America is a common relationship to and understanding of land, and to the animals that share it. This relationship is passed from generation to generation. Another thing that is interesting to me in these articulations is the focus on *connection* across history and geography, time and place. The relation to ancestors the dancers express is not one of surrogation or nostalgia — where a dancer replaces and stands in for a lost past or ancestor. As Sid says, he envisions himself *as* his ancestors, not *like* them or replacing them. By way of his dancing, they *aren't* lost or gone.

In focusing on a "contemporary Aboriginal dance process" for the Banff program, which includes an emphasis on cultural process throughout each program area, Marrie tells me the process also maintains a connection to the land, the elements, and the natural world that surrounds us. "We always spend at least one day a week on the land," she says. "Being in contact with the earth gives us time to reflect, reminds us of who we are and where we come from, connecting us to the great mystery, ancestral roots, and ancient teachings, to guide us in creating new stories that contribute to defining our relationships." Being in contact with the land is part of the dance training, too. "As we were rehearsing we would take it outside," Shalan says. "I don't think you'd see many ballerinas [going] outside to feel the trees and to be connected to the grass. We would take off our shoes to dance on the grass because that's what it's about. I think that it brings a lot more spirit to dance, something stronger to create a more enriched dance. I'm not saying that Western dancers are simply about physical movement because I understand that many of them must feel strongly about expressing themselves as powerfully as possible, but I think that our philosophies such as rehearsing on the grass bring a different kind of spirit." For the dancers and Aboriginal audience members, she adds, this dancing provides inspiration and connection. "It's getting us back to our traditions and our stories," she says. "It's inspiring us to go and learn those dances and those stories and songs, all of them where there's no separation for us, and to bring it back and to put it into a contemporary context of what we see as dance or theatre."

But always undergirding this connection to the land is a politicized awareness of Aboriginal land claims and land title issues. Marrie tells me that part of the program includes connecting to the Aboriginal peoples whose territories are near, "to hear the stories of this land, of the waters and the sacred springs that are here, stories of these mountains." This year, for example, the company was invited to Mii-stuks-koo-wa (Castle Mountain) to hear Siksika Elder Tom Crane Bear and former Chief Robert Breaker speak about their traditional territories and lands. As a term of the historic peace agreement known as Treaty 7, the Crown in Right of Canada set out in 1891 to survey and confirm twenty-six-and-a-half square miles to be set apart as a reserve of the Siksika Nation. The government informed the Siksika that this land was their reserve and encouraged the Siksika people to harvest timber, and hunt and gather for economic and subsistence purposes. Mii-stuks-koo-wa at Castle Mountain was eventually surveyed and recognized as a reserve by the federal government in 1893, before the creation of Banff National Park. The Crown relinquished the land without consent from, compensation to, and compliance with the

Siksika Nation in 1908. Reserves were set aside for the Peigan and Blood Tribe in 1883 by the same surveyor, Ponton, for the same purposes and subject to the same treaty. The Siksika Nation are proactively pursuing the restoration of their rightful reserve title to the lands at Mii-stuks-koo-wa. "Sovereignty, legal, cultural, and political issues all pertain to the land and are part of our spiritual connection to the earth," Marrie says. She points to a passage where Linda Hogan, in her book *Dwellings: A Spiritual History of the Living World,* writes, "A change is required of us, a healing of the betrayed trust between humans and earth. Caretaking is the utmost spiritual and physical responsibility of our time, and perhaps that stewardship is finally our place in the web of life, our work, the solution to the mystery of what we are. There are already so many holes in the universe that will never again be filled, and each of them forces us to question why we permitted such loss, such tearing away of the fabric of life, and how we will live with our planet in the future." Marrie also quotes from Leonard Peltier's book *Prison Writings: My Life Is My Sun Dance:* "To speak your mind and heart is Indian Way. In Indian Way, the political and the spiritual are one and the same. You can't believe one thing and do another . . . We are all leaders. We are each an army of one, working for the survival of our people and of the Earth, our Mother."

One day in the midst of all this, after I've talked to half a dozen of the dancers over the course of a number of hours, I'm exhausted and the dancers are all on stage and again I feel out of place, in the way. So I slip out and head back to my room, where I am reading Silko's new novel, *Gardens in the Dunes,* parcelling it out to myself so I don't curl away in my room and just read all the time. Being here is so much harder than reading books. The interviewing is stressful, though it's my favourite part of each day. It's harder during the rest of the time, when I'm just hanging around, wondering if I should go to the cultural room and try to make friends, or go into town and play tourist, or just go off hiking, or watch the videos over again, or what. Most of the time I really just want to hide and not struggle to approach people I don't know and who may not really want to talk to me. Sometimes the sense of outsiderness and loneliness is overwhelming. And I am only here for a week, with a meal card to use at my convenience and a fine bed and shower and free access to the pool, and a whole tourist town just a ten-minute walk down the hill, where I can (and do) blend in without a hitch any time I want.

I try to bolster my courage by feeling self-righteous about what I'm doing — because Philip Deloria is right: just reading about Native American history and culture and politics is the contemporary way of "playing Indian," without having to have any meaningful interaction with Indian people.[18] I don't know how particularly meaningful my interaction is, really — a week here hanging out and interviewing people — but it doesn't feel safe and it doesn't ever feel like I am Indian, and I am definitely learning things I would never learn poring over documents at my desk. I'm convinced that talking to people, face to face, is more important than holing up in libraries with documents and other people's descriptions. This seems especially true with the topic of Aboriginal dance, given what I've learned of Aboriginal dance history and its relation to official written discourse — its absence in most dance histories, the letters and laws simultaneously invoking and outlawing it, the court findings refusing it agency. At the core of it all, I believe that what I am doing is important, more important than my own uncertainties.

All week, things Marrie said on our panel in Calgary echo in my mind. She told one story about being invited to a community's ceremonies for the first time: she was unsure of the protocol and was afraid she would make many mistakes. Her Grandmother told her to be respectful, to observe and listen. Then her Grandmother laughed and said, "How are you going to learn if you are afraid to make mistakes?" At another point, a young woman in the audience asked Marrie if she would teach them more about Native cultures or tell them where there were Native people who could teach them. Marrie cautioned them that the quest for this knowledge is a journey. Although it is important that they become educated about Native issues and Native cultures so that they can become knowledgeable allies, it is her belief, she said, that it is not the responsibility of Native people to educate non-Native people about Native cultures. Since Oka,[19] she has made the decision to work on behalf of Aboriginal people, to focus her work on building within Aboriginal communities. She recommended that the students learn about Aboriginal cultures through establishing relationships with Aboriginal students at the university, listening to them to gain awareness and understanding. She recommended that they lobby the university to hire Native instructors who are knowledgeable of Native cultures, and that they lobby the university to establish an Indigenous Studies Program, so that cross-cultural work can begin.

On the third night, I finally get the nerve to sit with the Aboriginal Dance people at dinner. They are talking about racist incidents they've had to deal with. They fill me in: the "baby bun heads" (the young ballet students at the ballet program happening at The Banff Centre at the same time) have been harassing a faculty member's eight-year-old son. Apparently, they've been teasing him and not letting him down the hallway, and making disparaging comments about the Aboriginal Dance Program in general. Someone overheard one of them say something about how it smells in the Aboriginal Arts building and then add, "Yeah, well, there's a bunch of Indians in there," or something like that. And other things that they don't really want to repeat. So there is a meeting scheduled to talk about it with the ballet students, two Aboriginal Arts Program advisers, and one of the ballet students' counsellors.

After the Aboriginal Arts advisers leave for the meeting, the rest of us stay and eat our desserts and chat a bit, and then one of the waiters comes by to offer us more coffee. He says to one of the choreographers, "Oh, is your concert tonight? Cool. I'm going to try and see it. I saw an Aboriginal dance program up at the Banff Springs Hotel last summer and it was cool."

We smile up at him, and one of the program managers says, well, tonight is the dress rehearsal so it's free — you should come — but there are only a few tickets left, so you should get there early. And another asks, where did you say you'd seen Aboriginal dancing?

"At the Banff Springs," he says.

"Where?" she asks.

"It's that big tourist hotel," I say. "Right nearby." I'd just had drinks there the night before.

"Yeah, it was cool," the young waiter says. "There was this guy with all these rings, you know? He had all these rings he was dancing with."

"Oh, the hoop dance," they say. "That's the hoop dance."

And he says, "Well, it was so cool! It was like it was getting all the evil spirits out. You could feel it! All the evil spirits coming out of you. And I was thinking, get back in there, I need you! It was great. So I'm going to try and come tonight."

"Oh," they say. The silence of their refusal to engage further with this young man echoes loud and clear. We watch as the waiter goes bouncing off to pour coffee at some other table, and a sense of exhaustion hangs heavily in the air at having constantly to deal with incidents like these — racist ballet students, waiters oblivious to the ignorance in the images they spout and to their right to spout them. It stays quiet for a while.

Then one of the advisers comes back from the meeting with the ballet students and says it went really well. The Aboriginal Arts people gave the students an earful about teasing an eight-year-old boy — "What has he ever done to you?"

"But it gets tiring," they say to me. After that we mostly talk about dessert (have I mentioned the desserts?) and tease the resident adviser about a guy who seems to be giving her the eye.

I see the performances four times, from different places in the theatre. Wherever I sit I am at ease, comfortable and relaxed, watching from my place as "audience member" in the dark. I know this role well. I have been in theatres much like this one many times before. The first piece, Muriel Miguel's *Throw Away Kids,* tells the story of two women, Cosmos (danced by Penny Couchie) and her daughter, Star Girl (danced by Teme-Augama-Anishnaabe dancer Sandra Laronde), and their struggles with life on a very present-day Earth. It interweaves three narratives: a portion of the Haudenosaunee creation story, *Sky Woman Falling;* contemporary fallout from the legacy of generations of stolen Aboriginal children; and a striving for cultural renewal, celebration, and laughter, in a present-day world in which, in Canada, half the Aboriginal population is under twenty-five. The second piece is the revival of Alejandro Ronceria's *Light and Shadow,* first staged at Banff in 1997. It is "a contemporary work, inspired by the Arctic landscape and its profound role in shaping the life and spirit of the far northern culture," the advance release announces, and is presented this year in celebration of Nunavut.

Each time I see *Throw Away Kids,* I follow different threads through it and see something I didn't see the night before. At first I find it frustrating and confusing and a bit all over the place — too ambitious, trying to do too much, needing more narrative drive. Yet each night, I'm moved and intrigued, and more than once have those "Ah, okay" moments, those glimpses when you connect and feel amazed. Each time I see it, I want to see it again. In a way there is something about it being so raw that fits with the dancers, who are young and passionate, and with the concept of *Throw Away Kids.*

The piece opens each night to the sound of a heartbeat, then a moaning wail from a woman on stage. "It was a long long long long long long time ago," a voice-over says, and then Cosmos dances like Janet Jackson, elbows out, to the heartbeat beat. These threads — a birth, a past that is also present, a dance that is, and isn't, the image that what one might think of as "Native" or "Aboriginal" — run throughout the piece. The music works with these threads in fun and funny ways: the Beatles sing lines from "She's Leaving Home" and Cosmos pleads, "Don't go!" rubbing her belly, leaning forward and back, contracting, giving birth, it seems, to Star Girl all over again. The Supremes sing "Baby love, my baby love," and Cosmos bops and twirls, her arm bent at the elbow and flicking out from her waist as she turns, a kind of Native-inflected hip-hop move. But the story the piece tells is dead serious. After this opening section, the heartbeat starts again and Star Girl comes forward. "I had a three-week-old baby girl," she says. "I want her to be okay. But I do not want her."

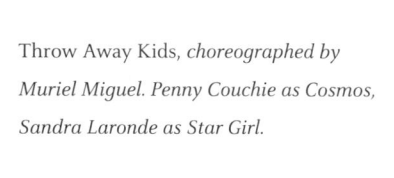

Throw Away Kids, *choreographed by Muriel Miguel. Penny Couchie as Cosmos, Sandra Laronde as Star Girl.*

This is the dark narrative running through *Throw Away Kids:* the cycles of abuse and abandonment that Aboriginal daughters who've been thrown away are caught up in and revisit on their children. This is where the Aboriginal sons enter, also caught up in these cycles. A young man with long, dark hair and a bare torso and a brightly beaded loincloth comes on stage, dancing in a skipping, twirling kind of way, looking beautiful and angry. It is Carlos Rivera, a Mixteco dancer from Mexico. He is called Mean Thing in the program, but in my head I refer to him as "Peter Pan Indian" because the next moment, when he steps behind one of the screens and looms large, still dancing, his silhouette looks like a Disney stereotype.

Throw Away Kids, *choreographed by Muriel Miguel. Carlos Rivera as Mean Thing.*

The image is stark and huge and familiar, and it's jarring to realize it's the same man who was just on the stage. It's like he's stepped into an image he now has to contend with. He emerges again from behind the screen, wearing a yellow tie, and romances Star Girl, enticing her into a nightclub partner dance and then back behind a screen again, where their silhouettes struggle with each other. Their shadows crouch down, and he hits her.

With this image of violence lingering, Cosmos returns and tells us a story. It's about a Miss South Dakota beauty pageant contestant who performed a Native American burial dance ritual for the "talent" part of her competition. "The lights shimmered off her short buckskin dress," Cosmos snarls, spitting each syllable in disdain and disgust.

Star Girl joins Cosmos. "A three-week-old Native baby dies in her sleep," she says.

"These events collide in my mind," Cosmos says. "Enough!"

"Enough!" the two women scream together. "Enough!"

And here the narrative starts to turn, slowly and with struggle, toward renewal. From behind the screen come two young men, Mean Thing and Mean Thing's Shadow (Sid Bobb) who looks just like him, but darker. They stomp out onto the stage together, crouched low, knees bent, stomping their feet to a fast double beat, looking like boys playing "Indian," as they move toward Cosmos. She engages with them in the dance, moving against them, then throwing herself onto them so they have to carry her. When she slides off, they retreat, stomping out the way they came, and Cosmos turns to the audience and smirks, with a little shrug, to have gotten rid of them, and we chuckle with her. But pushing the men away isn't the answer either; Star Girl comes back, and when Lisa Loeb sings "Let's Forget about It," Star Girl says, "I feel a cold in the lining of my heart."

The second man returns as Star Boy. He dances, by himself, off to one side. He dances with his legs apart, moving slowly, rhythmically, in place, his arms bent, his torso curving and twisting, lost in his own rhythm, his own thoughts. "Trying to weave the past with the future," he says. "Trying to connect." The music shifts to a stronger beat and he dances more intensely, though still alone. He is wearing a baseball hat with a feather tied on it.

"Babies came, babies went," says Cosmos. "Some drank, took drugs. Some did not." Cosmos, Star Girl, and Star Boy dance separately, each in front of a screen.

"Some girls are like that," says Star Boy. "Some girls are like that," he repeats. "This is another beginning. This is where it stops and starts," says Cosmos. "And he stayed," says Star Girl. "Was there." Star Boy moves to centre stage and stands behind Star Girl. "I am here," he says.

The theatre fills with a sense that, with Cosmos, Star Girl, and Star Boy standing together, centre stage, the process of healing has begun. "A three-week-old Native baby dies in her sleep," Star Girl tells us again. "Her mother, grandmother, and great grandmother mourn her." "Young mothers and fathers grieve for her," Cosmos says. "It could have been one of theirs." They have a brightly coloured felt blanket wrapped in a bundle and they toss it between them until it unbundles. Star Boy wraps his arms around Star Girl.

"We miss everyone we lose," says Cosmos. Together they face the audience and say, "We are the people who genocide has been performed upon." As the stage darkens, we see projected onto the three giant floor-to-ceiling screens, which have big hands printed on them, slides of dozens of smiling Native faces, young and old, one after the other. A voice-over reads the epigraph from the program: "Sovereignty is that wafting thread securing the component of a society. Sovereignty runs through the vertical strands and secures the entire pattern. That is the fabric of Native society."

One night I write in my notes, "I think in a way the piece is a lot about fathers." Other nights I try to work through what I think the piece is saying about image and screens and the stage. The disjunction is so striking between the silhouette of Mean Thing, whom we see dancing through the screen, and the colourfully, almost gaudily, dressed character of Mean Thing, who really looks very little like the image he projects, even though the dance movement is the same. It might suggest that the image is not "true," that it's "just" a stereotype. And yet even more strongly, I find, it suggests just the opposite. This looming "Indian" image creates a truth that he then has to live in relation to; it has a power beyond itself in creating who and how he is. It is the Hollywood screen, the TV screen, as well as a screen of images and expectations between him and the audience. It registers both the pop image of a "dancing Indian," stomping rhythmically, and the dance as having a function outside of the image it projects.

The last night I see the piece, I think I've finally got it: the piece is really all about the beauty pageant story Cosmos tells. Cosmos describes how the Miss South Dakota beauty contestant performs a Native American bereavement dance. She puts it on as if it's a play, as if it were nothing but an act she can wear, a buckskin miniskirt that looks good in the lighting. The contestant doesn't seem to have any awareness that there may be a political aspect to representing bereavement and mourning practices on a public stage. She not only takes the dance and uses it inappropriately and for her own means, she also disconnects it (or at least thinks of it as disconnected) from its effect on people and the world, its relation to bereavement, the change it effects in dealing with death and loss and thrown-away Native children. She treats it as if it were just a performance. In the process, she suggests that her white, scantily clad body, moving in "Indian" motions in this contest for acclaim according to Western standards of beauty, is a substitute and surrogate for both the Native dead and the surviving Native mourner.

Her representation effaces the bodies of Native American peoples from the living (by embodying the old trope of the "vanishing Indian" and showing Native peoples as always already on the verge of disappearance) and from the stage, replacing them with her own. She seems oblivious to her performance's implication that South Dakota Native Americans are dead and missing, to the complexities of replacing a Native dancing body with hers, and to her relation (as a white woman living on land in South Dakota) to the erasure she represents and reinforces. No wonder Cosmos is beside herself.

The second dance on the program, *Light and Shadow,* also raises questions for me about stage dance in relation to Aboriginal history, culture, and politics. Unlike the Native dance that Miss South Dakota performed without any apparent understanding of its relation to and effect on present-day Native peoples and cultures, the dance of *Light and Shadow* suggests a performative relation between this dance on a stage in Alberta and the life and spirit of Nunavut.

From the start, it's an eerie piece, the mood ponderous and breathtaking, the vocal music and drumming beautiful, rhythmic, and deep. The piece opens with two dancers (Carlos Rivera and Mohawk dancer Cheri Smith) hanging in harnesses, like bats in suspension, floating and curling and turning, and then lowering to the earth. Then Inuit drum dancers move in from the sides, each carrying a big round drum and baton, swaying on bent legs as they drum, together, in slow rhythmic beats. Although the stage remains dark, they are all wearing white, and the light on the white makes them luminous. Behind them, the screen has the glow of a red sky, with one full moon, or sun, surrounded by two half orbs faintly shining. In the middle, a dancer (Feliks Gower-Kappi) perches on a rock and slowly, like a bird being born, struggles to stand.

"Neighbours" from Light and Shadow, *choreographed by Alejandro Ronceria. Cherith Mark, Pablo Palma, Leslie Qammaniq.*

At other points the mood shifts to silly: two dancers (Pablo Palma and Leslie Qammaniq, the other Inuit dancer at the program this summer) with reddish brown fur-trimmed green masks on their faces and hands, and fox heads hanging from their groins, wiggle on stage and cavort with each other, bumping butts and sparring for space on the rocks. The sky is now a luminous blue and purple. A huge silly statue, smiling in a rather subtle, bemused manner, peeks in from the wings. Then it is darker, the light only a faint orange glow, and then that fades, too.

Throughout the piece, the music and sky keep changing. At one point, four dancers appear (Sheri Smith, Shalan Joudry, Carlos Rivera, Sid Bobb), with scrunched-up faces as they bend forward, moving toward the audience, stamping their feet and swaying their heads back and forth like fish. Next come the seal-people. Three dancers (Nakoda Sioux-Stoney Nation dancer Cherith Mark, Sid Bobb, and Feliks Gower-Kappi), wearing masks on the sides of their heads, creep out on their bellies, moving behind and around the rocks, carrying what look like giant claws or clubs. They stretch and walk on stage, knees bent deep, at times turning their heads so their faces, tongues out in grotesque contortions, face us. One scratches himself with his claw club, his back, his leg, his groin, before walking off. Now the sky is crossed with lines of light as if through the mouth of a baleen whale.

"Seal People" from Light and Shadow, *choreographed by Alejandro Ronceria. Feliks Kappi, Cherith Mark, Sid Bobb.*

A physical and political relationship to land — the rocks, the animals, the climate — comes across clearly and compellingly in the dancers' physical involvement with the rocks, the darkness, the sky. The dancers' movements — the swaying drum dancing, the playfulness in darkness, the bodily response to the light that starts to fill the stage toward the piece's end — convey a relationship to specific place. Of course, these are stage sets: the "rocks" are constructed, darkness and sky light are created through stage lighting; the dancers are on a stage in Alberta far from Nunavut land. I do not mean to argue for the dance's immediate ability to mystically conjure Nunavut land on a stage in Alberta, or that certain dance movements caused the Nunavut land claim agreement to come into effect in any sort of "mechanical magic"[20] way. At the same time, I *do* mean to suggest that what the dancers enact, in dancing in celebration of Nunavut, is "real" and has "real" effect on the world. In large part, I think, this effect comes from the context of the piece. It is a production of the Chinook Winds Aboriginal Dance Project, engaged with Aboriginal politics, celebrating Nunavut at a time when Aboriginal dancing, as an element of oral history, has begun to be understood even in Canadian courts in legal (and therefore, again according to the viewpoint of the courts, actual or provable) relation to land and land claims. The context of the dancing thus echoes and strengthens a relationship to "Nunavut" as Inuit land and celebrates governmental recognition of it as such. At the same time, I think that the actual movement of the dancing, and the dancers' skill at embodying a connection to specific land, is itself part of this enactment. As a performance of continuing Inuit movement practices (drum dancing, masking, seal-people) with much much longer histories, the dancing also performs and enacts the relation to Nunavut land that is part of those practices. The celebration of Nunavut through this public dance performance underscores for the audience ways that — though this is a performance, not a parliamentary enactment — dance functions in a way similar to court documents and legal declarations that enact what they name. On the other hand, because the performance occurs outside of what the courts and legislature declare, it shows how new governmental recognition merely reflects what the dance shows to have long been the case.

Two final sections of *Light and Shadow,* called "Nostalgia" and "Inukshuk," demonstrate this a bit more concretely. In "Nostalgia," the dancers move slowly on stage in pairs, some men with women, some women with women, some men with men. They lift one another and slide off, curling together, sex-like, in the dark. The dancers move apart curling and lifting, and then slowly they move together in the centre and lift one dancer horizontally above them, turning her as she curls. In the next section, "Inukshuk," a voice-over tells a story in Inuktitut. The dancers sit on rocks and bring their hands to their faces, like they are washing or eating, and then push the rocks together, their hands over their ears. Moving apart again, they each lift a rock and creep slowly back, carrying the rocks, and piling them up so they make the "Inukshuk" rock formation that signals "Nunavut," with one long rock horizontal from a pillar.

Then the light comes up: daylight. Just at that moment, when after all those shades of darkness, day has come, Leslie Qammaniq reappears, down stage left, dressed in Inuit clothes, looking like a tourist poster of an Inuit woman. She holds a small airplane in her hand and flies it in swoops and swirls across the stage while we hear the sound of an airplane overhead. The tourists are arriving.

The end takes my breath away each evening, that moment when after all that time in darkness, all that sombreness and sex and silliness, that full life happening, the airplanes arrive, propelled by the Inuit image, who is also Leslie in *Light and Shadow,* dancing.

This piece, like *Throw Away Kids,* plays with the audience's relationship to the images of Aboriginal culture we hold, and their relation to what is "real." Like the men in *Throw Away Kids,* whose silhouettes through the screens contrast so startlingly with their presence in front of the screens, Leslie, in her Inuit clothing, plays both herself and an image of herself playing a stereotype. Her startling transition from being one of the white-clad dancers, part of the *Light and Shadow* ensemble, to performing like a tourist image of an Inuit woman underscores her distance from this image, her relation to it, and the image's continuing (tourist and ideological) effect on the Nunavut the dance piece celebrates. At the same time, it refigures a tourist relation to Nunavut by showing ways Leslie controls, or at least propels, that relation. If in one sense the arriving airplane is propelled by what looks like the poster image of an Inuit woman, in another sense Leslie is holding it and directing it herself, swooping it up and down across the stage like a plaything.

This is not the "nostalgia" of lost and mourned and romanticized Inuit culture, a tourist image of an authentic "Inuitness" that's now gone and for which dance performance now provides a surrogate. The "nostalgia" in the title of the penultimate section of the piece refers to not a lost past but young Aboriginal dancers. Leslie, like sixty per cent of the Inuit population of Nunavut, is under twenty-five years old. Her body, lifted horizontally by the other dancers, carries reference to the Inukshuk that signals both official Canadian sign of, and guide and relation to, Inuit land. This dancer at the end is active and present, wearing traditional regalia and propelling an airplane. She is not just an image, a representation. She also has agency and effect. She is not just playing at what she's dancing. She is being it, as well as acting as it, and in so doing enacts herself as an Inuit woman, with connection to Nunavut as Inuit land and to ancestors who had a relationship to the land and have passed that to her. This, in turn, is related to the return of Aboriginal land that the Nunavut Act marks. These understandings of stage dancing as enacting rather than representing enactment, I think, complicate contemporary theories that see what happens with "actors" during stage performances as "hollow or void" and thus distinctly separate from "real-life" "performative" actions.

The first night — the dress rehearsal — I sit next to a fourteen- or fifteen-year-old man. We chat a bit before the show starts, and he tells me he is from Montréal, at Banff this summer to participate in the ballet program. We both sit quietly through the performance, comfortable and at ease in the dark, in our theatre seats, politely watching and applauding at the end. As we are leaving I ask him, so did you like it? Was it what you expected? And he says yes he liked it, but no, it wasn't what he thought it would be. I ask, how so? He says, well, it was a lot more modern. Out in the lobby I eavesdrop on other ballet students, around whom I can hover, unnoticed. The whole group of them has come to see the dress rehearsal. One young woman — a Québecoise with a bouncy brown ponytail, tight pants, and chunky platform shoes — is holding court, the other dancers gathered around her. "They looked so out of place!" she says. "It's like they feel so out of place in our society. Do you think that is how they feel in our society?" I wonder at her comments, the acceptance she presumes "our society" to accord her, a ballet student, on and off the stage, the implication that she and her fellow ballet dancers look and feel "in place" against the "out of place" appearance that "they," the Aboriginal dancers, project. What effect will her reception of these dance pieces have, both her perceptions and her failures to perceive? I wonder to what extent her response matters, or if the Aboriginal Dance Program will do what it does with or without whatever its audience members — mostly non-Native people like this young woman and me — take away.

The next day, after the opening-night performance, there's a reception. We gather for food and drink and thank-you speeches. The ceremony opens with Elder Tom Crane Bear from the Siksika Nation, who welcomes us all to Siksika land and thanks the dancers for their dancing and the program for the work it does, and everyone especially for this year's support of the return of Nunavut. He says it is an inspiration and that, as most of us probably know, they too are fighting for the return, right here, of Siksika land. The dancers and choreographers speak next, thanking the Elder and one another, and lots of other people who've helped with the program. Then we eat and drink and mingle, and there is a video about Nunavut playing off to one side, and a box full of information packets on Nunavut for us all to take home and keep.

Now it is the fall of 1999, and I am long back at my desk in California. I sit in my swivel chair and turn the Nunavut "toonie" I've saved over and over in my hands and riffle through the Government of Canada Nunavut packet, chock-full of official documents printed in English and French (with a few sections in Inuktituk). There are chronologies and informational sheets and "fast facts" on Nunavut history and its economy and the land claim settlement. There are big colour maps and colour prints of the Nunavut coat of arms and glossy "Welcome to Nunavut" brochures. There is a Nunavut "activities" sheet listing fourteen Inuktituk words for snow and suggesting that students draw them. The official documents inscribe "Nunavut" as "real" history, a geo-political fact taught to children in grades 5 and 6. And this governmental recognition is cause for celebration, which is the spirit in which the Nunavut packets were handed out at the Aboriginal Dance reception. Of course, Nunavut has been here all along, recognized by practices, like dance, that legitimate and enact connection to it: it doesn't require a coin or a coat of arms to be official, just to be seen as such. At the same time, it seems important not to discount this documentation or suggest that only oral and performance practices are "authentic" markers of Aboriginal relation to the land; instead, the official documents extend a recognition that Inuit peoples have long asserted and performed.

All the same, these documents call for an attentiveness to the histories of hegemony that have accompanied, and continue to accompany, "official" documents and sanctioned "expert" discourse on Native culture. At issue is the way that, in these documents and discourses, Aboriginal people are often literally and figuratively displaced and discounted. This displacement is blatant when a non-Native like the Miss South Dakota contestant, invoking a "disappeared Indian" trope, performs as an "Indian" mourning her dead, deploying Native culture in a bid to gain the currency of a Miss America title.

But it happens too easily in other arenas as well, including dance studies, when official dance histories and theories, dance conferences and essay collections, ignore Aboriginal dance and Aboriginal peoples' expertise in it. In a sense, the flip side of the "toonie" with the drum dancer on it is a depiction of Aboriginal dance that circulates as commodity to legitimate the Crown. Again, it seems important not to discount the agency that comes with commodification — the way that Leslie, dressed as "Inuit woman," plays with and propels the tourist economy she invokes. But even in this instance, it seems crucial to attend to the question of currency — who produces and profits from "representing" and "documenting" Aboriginal culture? And where are Native peoples and cultures in this document production and what it accrues? In other words, I am struggling, given my position as a university scholar — complicit in systems of institutional racism that have long dismissed Native voices and rewarded outside experts that record, and edit, and themselves tell Native peoples' stories — with the place of this scholarly document I've just produced.

In *Chinook Winds,* Jerry Longboat writes about the role of the choreographers at the Aboriginal Dance Program:

> They recognize the need to train our own choreographers and writers. I think there's real danger in other people appropriating our stories and telling us who we are. We've begun to awaken to the effects of this through the telling of history and we are reclaiming our truth in our own words, in our ceremonies,

> through our stories. Dance is a prolific part of this healing and self determination.[21]

These words on Aboriginal self-determination, like the *Throw Away Kids* voice-over on sovereignty — "that wafting thread securing the component of a society" — need to resonate for dance studies, circa 1999 and beyond. To quote Cosmos, "This is where it stops and starts."

acknowledgement

I would like to thank the dancers, choreographers, and administrators at the Aboriginal Dance Program for their time and effort in helping me with this piece; a very special thanks to Marrie Mumford for her patience and generosity. I am also grateful to the friends and colleagues who read and commented on drafts of this essay, and whose insights have informed my thinking and been with me as I wrote. Thanks especially to Hershini Bhana, Rebecca Monte Kugel, Jerry Longboat, Susan Leigh Foster, Cynthia Franklin, Elyse Vosen, and Deborah Wong.

notes

1 Dara Culhane, *The Pleasure of the Crown: Anthropology, Law, and First Nations* (Burnaby, BC: Talon Books Inc., 1998), 123.

2 Ibid., 257.

3 Ibid., 247.

4 J. L. Austin, *How to Do Things with Words*, Marian Sbisa and J. O. Urmson (eds.) (Cambridge, MA: Harvard University Press, 1975), 22.

5 My information on this ruling comes from the David Suzuki Foundation Series publication *Delgamuukw: The Supreme Court of Canada Decision on Aboriginal Title*, Stan Persky (commentator) (Vancouver: Greystone Books, 1998), 27.

6 Ibid., 29.

7 Ibid., 75.

8 Ibid., 76.

9 Culhane, *The Pleasure of the Crown*, 370.

10 For example, Native American studies and government professor Dale Turner has argued that *Delgamuukw* was lost when Gitxsan and Wet'suwet'en claims for "ownership" were abandoned (conference presentation on "Indigenous Oral Histories, Political Sovereignty, and the Law in Canada and the U.S." on 29 October 1999, at the American Studies Association conference in Montreal, Canada). For a discussion of the change in claims, see Persky, *Delgamuukw*, 26–7.

11 For a brilliant analysis of nineteenth-century anti-potlatch laws in British Columbia, see Christopher Bracken, *The Potlatch Papers: A Colonial Case History* (Chicago: Chicago University Press, 1997).

12 A copy of this letter is included in Heather Elton, Florene Belmore, and Paul Seesequasis (eds.), *Chinook Winds Aboriginal Dance Project* (Banff: Banff Centre Press and 7th Generation Books, 1997), 12. The inclusion of this letter in the Aboriginal Dance Program's inaugural season marks the program's awareness of and explicit relation to this official Canadian declaration of Aboriginal dance as indulgent, injurious, and unrelated to "serious work" or productive usefulness. As such, it presents itself as both ironic performance of bemused, defiant relation, and in official response to this state document. A video documentary on the project invokes the letter as well. The video opens with a single Native dancer moving slowly across the stage while a voice-over reads the text of the 1921 Scott letter. "[U]se your utmost endeavours to dissuade the Indians from excessive indulgence in the practice of dancing," Scott directs. "You should suppress any dances which cause waste of time, interfere with the occupations of the Indians, unsettle them for serious work, injure their health or encourage them in sloth and idleness."

13 Culhane, *The Pleasure of the Crown,* 228.

14 Ibid., 226.

15 In Canada, "Aboriginal" refers to First Nations, status and non-status, Inuit, and Metis.

16 Elton, *Chinook Winds,* 90.

17 For a dazzling exploration of how an Indigenous context can inflect and reform Western philosophic conceptions of mimesis, see Michael Taussig, *Mimesis and Alterity: A Particular History of the Senses* (New York: Routledge, 1993).

18 In his insightful and compelling analysis of how generations of white Americans have negotiated their identity by imagining themselves as Indians, Philip Deloria writes, "During the past thirty years, playing Indian has been as much about reading books as it has been about meeting native people" (*Playing Indian* [New Haven: Yale University Press, 1998], 189).

19 Marrie is referring to July 1990, when "an historic confrontation propelled Native issues in Kanehsatake and the village of Oka, Quebec, into the international spotlight and into the Canadian conscience"(video jacket, *Kanehsatake*). For further reference, see *Kanehsatake: 270 Years of Resistance* (National Film Board of Canada, 1993), a film written and directed by Alanis Obomsawin, an Aboriginal filmmaker. The film provides "insight into the Mohawks' spiritual beliefs and fierce pride in their ancestry that governs the unyielding determination to protect their land." Obomsawin's portrayal of the Mohawk community places the Oka crisis within the larger context of Mohawk land rights, disregarded by white authorities for centuries and destined to culminate in the 1990 standoff. "'The Oka crisis changed the lives of all Aboriginal people in this country,' says Obomsawin. 'We cannot go back.'"

20 See Vine Deloria, "Sacred Lands and Religious Freedom," in *For This Land: Writings on Religion in America* (New York: Routledge, 1999), 210.

21 Elton, *Chinook Winds,* 79.

bibliography

Austin, J. L. *How to Do Things with Words.* Marian Sbisa and J. O. Urmson (eds.). Cambridge, MA: Harvard University Press, 1975.

Bracken, Christopher. *The Potlatch Papers: A Colonial Case History.* Chicago: Chicago University Press, 1997.

Culhane, Dara. *The Pleasure of the Crown: Anthropology, Law, and First Nations.* Burnaby, BC: Talon Books Inc., 1998.

Deloria, Philip. *Playing Indian.* New Haven: Yale University Press, 1998.

Deloria, Vine. "Sacred Lands and Religious Freedom." In *For This Land: Writings on Religion in America.* New York: Routledge, 1999.

Elton, Heather, Florene Belmore and Paul Seesequasis (eds.). *Chinook Winds Aboriginal Dance Project.* Banff: Banff Centre Press and 7th Generation Books, 1997.

Hogan, Linda. *Dwellings: A Spiritual History of the Living World.* New York: Touchstone, 1995.

Peltier, Leonard. *Prison Writings: My Life Is My Sun Dance.* Harvey Arden (ed.). New York: St. Martin's Press, 1999.

Persky, Stan (commentator). *Delgamuukw: The Supreme Court of Canada Decision on Aboriginal Title.* Vancouver: Greystone Books, 1998.

Radul, Judy. "The Specialists: Performing the Heterosexual Couple." In *Private Investigators: Undercover in Public Space.* Banff: Banff Centre Press, 1999.

Taussig, Michael. *Mimesis and Alterity: A Particular History of the Senses.* New York: Routledge, 1993.

retrieving

they were singing and dancing in the mountains

cheryl blood- (rides-at-the-) doore

High along the chain of majestic Rocky Mountains that embrace the clear turquoise sky is an imaginary chiselled line — a border — that separates the United States and Canada. This is the traditional territory and land of the proud Blackfoot Confederacy. Depending on the season, it is a place of rolling golden prairie, a thick emerald green carpet, or snow-white fields. The weather brings both fierce blowing winds and warm chinook breezes and silence so still you can hear the echo of a bird chirping. This is the home of Olivia Tailfeathers, Night Flying Woman (Siipiipotakii), and Orton Eagle Speaker, both Blood Tribe members and teachers of traditional songs, music, and dance.

The mother of four handsome sons, Olivia is a strong role model for her children and students at Tatsikiisaapo'p Middle School, where she teaches music. From this environment, interested students are selected to perform with the Kainai Grassland Singers. Aside from her bright, smiling, beautiful face, Olivia can steal your heart away with her melodious voice and interpretive musical style.

Olivia's music and dance influences began early, when her grandmother and mother, *otsitoi'paamoka,* sang lullabies. Her uncle Emil Wings and grandfather Emil Wings Sr. used to whistle Nistsitapii (Blackfoot) melodies and songs at night, tapping on a wall to keep the melody and rhythm. Olivia and her younger brothers and sisters fell asleep listening to these songs.

In mid-summer, during the Sun Dance, Olivia heard songs sung by the Buffalo Woman Society and the Horn Society and began to internalize these musical influences from Blackfoot culture. Traditional and cultural values permeated her environment. Late into the night, larger-than-life shadows of Elders' movements danced on teepee walls while the song voices carried loud and clear through the camp.

Living in two worlds, Nistsitapii and European, Olivia was also influenced by the Anglican church, where she was encouraged to become a choir member by the Reverend Stan Cuthand, who later became her mentor. He supported her by going to listen when she competed in public school music festivals. Olivia's eyes dance with delight as she remembers these happy memories that instilled strong values, a gift she shares by supporting musical endeavours of our youth.

Because her father was an avid country-and-western music fan, Olivia also listened to Wilf Carter, Hank Williams Sr., Loretta Lynn, and Tammy Wynette. She performed with local bands during the spring, summer, and fall at rodeos and other events.

Olivia has a traditional dance background and as a little girl dreamed of owning a white tanned buckskin dress. In 1980 her dream was finally realized. This buckskin dress, which she was directed to sew by a Blackfeet woman in Browning, Montana, was proudly worn in the Chinook Winds dance performance.[1] According to Olivia, "This dress always seems to be worn by young women who want to dance. It is significant because the five hides have served a valuable purpose for young women to learn about their identity and to have pride in their cultural ways. Most people would be reluctant to share their dress with so many strangers because of the monetary value; however, it seems to have its own purpose because it has been shared with so many artists. There are times I have not recognized my own dress because it takes on its own beauty depending on the individual wearing it."

The first time Olivia was invited to the Aboriginal Arts Program at The Banff Centre, she felt a lot of emotion and synchronicity in the old trails our ancestors travelled. She says, "En route I was moved by the stirring traquillity in the hills and I knew I had to be there. The gift of music was given to me and I felt I had to share my songs and music with the students. In exchange I would learn about the variation and styles of our music whether it be Mohawk, Oneida, Blackfoot, or Inuit."

The sacred circle signified an understanding and a renewal in our unity as First Nations people. As part of the community outreach aspect of the program, some Chinook Winds dancers attended our Sun Dance on the Blood Reserve. This was an opportunity to hear sacred songs and drumming when Horn Society members danced out of the centre lodge.

At The Banff Centre, Olivia shared and taught the dancers her personal compositions, Blackfoot songs, and culture. They heard serenade songs from the Sun Dance and "Sacred Stone," a song given to the family of the late Ben Calf Robe, of the Siksika Nation. Olivia says, "I feel it is very important to teach our children about who they are and where they come from, so they know where they are going. Music and dance are the best ways we can learn about ourselves as Nistsitapii, and I felt very honoured to be there as an instructor because it proved we were all one as the Creator's children. When I saw the performance of Chinook Winds, I cried because I could feel the spirits of our ancestors who have gone on."

The fusion of new and old inspired Olivia and me to return to our past. To research Nistsitapii song and dance, we decided to interview various Elders, a few who still remember when the drum first came to southern Alberta. It is with respect for our Elders that we must confirm with them what we are writing about.

Late one evening, we drove to Lower Standoff, one of the oldest communities on Canada's reserve, to speak with Orton Eagle Speaker. We walked up to his old white house and gently knocked on the door. No one was home. Just as we were leaving, a big truck came speeding into the driveway. Inside was Orton, his wife, grandson, and great-grandson. He got out and quietly said that he had to take his grandson to town, and then he'd rush back because he knew we would be here. He returned and his wife served us tea and banana bread. Orton's blue-eyed great-grandson kept teasing him, and I could see he had Grandpa wrapped around his baby finger. Orton confidently, and with pride, began to tell us stories about his involvement with song and dance.

Orton Eagle Speaker is a rare person. He is a kind, generous, and intelligent man, a father, grandfather, and great-grandfather. He honoured us by sharing with us a lifetime of learning. He told us many stories.

"Historically our songs and drumming came from different societies, and therefore they were ceremonial," he said. "We had many different societies: Black Tail Society, Brave Dog Society, Mosquito Society, Yellow Pigeon Society, Magpie Society, Skinny Horse Society, and others too numerous to mention. Most have died off. We have lost many of our dances from the past and if we could bring back some of our Elders who had the knowledge, we could revive these dances. We had many different dances from our societies before the Mandans (Earth Dwellers) and Kaispai gave us songs and dances."

Orton told us that social drumming and singing originally came from the Omahas when the Kaispai visited Omaha traditional territory and observed them singing and dancing around a fire. He said, "When Blackfeet raiders went to Kaispai territory and came back home, they held a dance. In later years, the Mandans came up to Lethbridge; it was just a small town then in the 1800s. Somewhere around Weasel Fat Flats, near the medicine wheels (it was the first snowstorm in September, a deep, wet snow but not cold), one man got up to get firewood to start a fire and when he sat down to take a rest, he saw some people across the river, on the hills wandering around. He invited them over — I cannot remember if it was two men and one woman, or two women and one man — anyway, they spoke English.

"When they began to talk, the Mandans said, 'We came to give you some war dances, an Owl Dance, Rabbit Dance, Round Dance; these are free. We also have some articles for the dance: whip, drums, eagle bustle, bone whistle, hand drums, woman and man trailing headdress. These items you will have to pay for. Invite all the people and we will demonstrate the dances.' Some riders went around to Old Agency, Standoff, and headed south from there to invite people to the dance, which was to be held in four days. An explanation was also given to the people about payment for the articles."

In four days, numerous people had gathered. "The dance was packed and some of the people couldn't get in," Orton said. "The Mandans told stories about how and why each dance came to be. War dances were done before people go on a raid and, when successful, another dance is done. Kaispai and Mandans were dancing years before us.

"In the past, before the time of powwow, women sat on one side of the room and men on the other. In the Round Dance, or women's dance — *Aki Paskan* — people go to honour people and they would dance in doubles. There were a few people who didn't know how to dance so they danced by themselves and that is how the Round Dance started. Owl Dance is always a woman's choice, and when the man sits down, he would go and pay the woman who asked him to dance because she demonstrated honour and out of respect he would return these values with material exchange. It's a custom you don't see anymore these days."

Orton remembers that the Mandans also brought with them the first large powwow-style drum. "Mandans brought over the big drum, Omahkisttokimaa, designed with eagle claws on one side and painted yellow and red on the other side, representing day and night," he said. "Over a hundred horses were given in payment for the articles they brought with them. The Mandans brought them to Lethbridge and sold them to pay for their train tickets back to North Dakota. We, the Bloods, paid for our dances and that is how we got them. I do not know how the Stoneys, Sarcees, and Crees got their dances."

Orton Eagle Speaker is a traditional songwriter who has composed hundreds of songs. We asked him about his creation process and about ownership protocol. He said, "Some songs come in dreams or visions, or you can fast. My uncle George Shields — Naatoisaopoi Natoisaopoi (Sacred Plume Bonnet) — would fast sometimes four to eight days without food and water. His sacred war bonnet had every animal represented. I hear stories about five, ten, twenty people going to fast in the mountains together and I have to laugh because in the past you would go and fast at Chief Mountain by yourself.

"Traditionally, songs come from dreams, visions, and ceremony. The holy songs and powwow songs were passed through lineage. Honour songs were passed down through various societies.

"While most songs are passed on through lineage, a person may be honoured by the owner and thereby given a song directly. Great-grandfathers to grandfathers, fathers to sons and, yes, some songs are women songs, too. Some of the songs I made I keep — especially Honour songs. My daughter asked me for an Honour song for her son, my grandson, and I gave him a song and gave it to her on a tape to keep it for him so that when he gets older he can learn it and use it. My uncle made a song and I keep it and no one else can use it.

"My friend from the United States visited me one summer and told me, 'I will give and teach you some appraisal songs.' Appraisal songs evaluate the worth or significant accomplishments of an individual. They set status or value of an individual. He said, 'I will teach you five now, and when you come and visit me I will teach you eight more, and that will be thirteen songs in total.' Well, he taught me the five songs that summer, but he died before I made it to see him again. I don't know if anyone else knew those songs, but he died with the eight more he was going to teach me. Cree, Blood, Blackfoot, and Blackfeet, you have to go through ceremony to sing appraisal songs."

We asked Orton if he remembered when words first started to be used in songs. He said, "Our ceremonial songs were the only ones I remember having words in the beginning. In the past, just straight songs were used and then the Kaispai began to tape songs with words and that's how we started to use Blackfoot words in songs. Different tribes, the Bloods, for example, use Blackfoot and English words — 'When the dance is over I will take you home, honey, on my grey mare, hiya aiya' — and the Cree do that, too."

Orton thinks that some songwriters today no longer approach the material with the same cultural values. "I used to sing a lot. I would make songs. Nowadays, we have copycats who don't make their own songs. I wonder, do they know what they're singing about? When I make songs I usually put together four or five songs and once I get a song to be a good song, then I put it to a drum. I use the rhythm. A lot of singers don't have the rhythm, you can tell when you get up to dance. The main singer, or start singer, is the rhythm, and if a group doesn't have the rhythm they are no good.

"This young man once came to me and told me he was a good-time singer. I thought to myself, then he should know all the different society songs, because that's what a good-time singer is. Anyway, I went to Heart Butte, Montana, for a powwow, and this man, George Old Person, he is deceased now, he came to me while I was sitting in the bleachers and he said, 'Come and sing with our drum.' I was happy to sing with them. I sang with the Star School Drummers at this ceremony. George Old Person went to this group of Levern singers and asked them to sing a Fast Race Horse Society song and none of the drummers knew it. I knew it and I offered to sing for them. When the singing was over he threw me sixty dollars on the drum and said, 'Split it with your singers.' I never got one cent for singing for them even to this day. When you call yourself a good-time singer and are requested to sing, you should know all the society songs."

Listening to the stories of this humble man, we knew that his memory is precious and extends far into the past. "The first Rabbit Dance song was brought from the South Dakotas around Pine Ridge area," Orton said. To prove his point he sang us the first Rabbit Dance song and it was so beautiful. Honoured, humbled, I ached deep inside and felt emotion stirring, then rising, until I choked back the tears of sorrow, joy, and loneliness for the people gone to the other world and, finally, peace. At this moment, no other singer could compare. Orton's song was the language that reached and spoke to our souls. We were left breathless in awe. This is a sacred power of song and dance. It has the ability to heal one's being and soul in this world and the other world.

This article was first published in Heather Elton, Florene Belmore and Paul Seesequasis (eds.), *Chinook Winds: Aboriginal Dance Project.* (Banff, Alberta: Banff Centre Press and 7th Generation Books, 1997). Reprinted here with permission of the author.

notes

1 Chinook Winds: Aboriginal Dance Project, 1996, at The Banff Centre for the Arts, Banff, Alberta, Canada.

ballet in black:

louis johnson and african american vernacular humour in ballet

thomas f. defrantz

> African-American humour . . . emanates from the social and political predicament of the group; for African Americans, their predicament has been based on their status as outsiders.[1]

During the first two-thirds of the twentieth century, African American dancers interested in ballet approached the form "sideways," supplementing their mastery of other forms of dance rather than becoming accomplished classical performers. Strict segregation precluded sustained ballet study by black children before the 1960s, causing the few African American classical dancers of that era to begin their ballet training as adults. While the African American presence in classical ballet crystallized with the founding of the Dance Theatre of Harlem in 1969, wider African American interest in the form grew more slowly alongside waxing American interest in theatrical stage dancing.

This essay explores the history of African American participation in classical ballet before the abatement of segregation and focuses on the work of Louis Johnson, a master choreographer whose ballets employ sparkling fragments of African American vernacular humour. Although an African American presence in ballet has been circumscribed by ambiguous race relations in the United States, Africanist compositional strategies have had a dynamic impact on contemporary ballet choreography.

overview

Ballet captured the interest of a broad American public only after tours by Diaghilev's Ballets Russes provided entertaining "high art" in the early part of the twentieth century.[2] Diaghilev's repertory included a fantastical coordination of settings, costumes, music, and choreography that propelled modern ballet into American cultural landscapes. But assumptions that the European outlook, history, and technical theory fundamental to ballet were alien to the black dancer's culture, temperament, and anatomy discouraged African American interest in the form for generations. Dance aesthetes wrote about the unsuitability of the Negro dancer's "tight joints, a natural turn-in rather than the desired ballet turn-out, and hyper-extension of the knee [and] weak feet."[3] Most black dancers, barred from all-white ballet schools, turned to performing careers in modern and jazz dance. Ballet training, however, remained the basis of many theatrical dance techniques, ensuring that African American dancers studied ballet when and wherever they could.

Although general American interest in ballet broadened, few performing opportunities were available to classically trained African American dancers.[4] From the 1930s to the 1960s, racial division led to the formation of several short-lived "all-black" ballet companies. While these companies provided much-needed artistic outlets for dancers and, in fewer cases, choreographers, they also promoted a voyeuristic exoticism of black bodies that placed the dancers outside the emergent mainstream of American classicism. These early companies withstood a dual-pronged challenge to prove that black bodies could master classical technique while simultaneously entertaining their mostly white audiences and critics within familiar, stereotyped performance contexts. Not surprisingly, the repertory of each all-black company employed and expanded upon prevailing stereotypes.

Eugene Von Grona's American Negro Ballet debuted at Harlem's Lafayette Theater on 21 November 1937.[5] Von Grona had been a modern dancer and was trained by the German choreographer Mary Wigman before moving to the United States in 1925. He formed his own company of African American dancers to address what he termed "the deeper and more intellectual resources of the Negro race."[6] Although the company's original program included a version of Stravinsky's *Firebird* choreographed by Von Grona, its more popular works were set to jazz music by Duke Ellington and W. C. Handy. In an apparent attempt to attract a larger audience, Von Grona reformed the company as Von Grona's American Swing Ballet in 1939, when it appeared in producer Lew Leslie's musical spectacular *Blackbirds* and at the Apollo Theater.

Other lesser-known companies mimicked the racially inspired use of African American musical forms to accompany ballets made for African American dancers. Joseph Rickhard, a German émigré and former dancer with the Ballets Russes, founded the First Negro Classic Ballet in 1948. Rickhard taught ballet to African American students in Los Angeles, where his company first performed in 1949. Its concert material included *Variations Classiques,* a suite of dances set to Bach, as well as a reworking of *Cinderella* with African American materials. Although the company achieved critical success and toured the West Coast for seven seasons, almost no documentation of its repertory has survived.[7] In 1956, Rickhard and several of his dancers moved to New York, and the company merged with the New York Negro Ballet.

The most important company before the Dance Theatre of Harlem was Edward Flemyng's New York Negro Ballet, founded as Les Ballets Négres in 1955. This group began as a loose collection of dancers who took daily technique classes with Maria Nevelska, a former member of the Bolshoi Ballet. Flemyng, a charismatic African American dancer born in Detroit, Michigan, organized private sponsorship of the company, which led to the landmark 1957 tour of Great Britain, with stops in England, Scotland, and Wales.[8] The company's tour repertory included a purely

New York Negro Ballet. Edward Flemyng, Cleo Quitman, Theodore Duncan, and Barbara Wright in Ernest Parham's Mardi Gras, *1957.*

classical pas de deux from *Sleeping Beauty* danced by Delores Brown and Bernard Johnson, as well as *Waltze,* an abstract classical work for twelve dancers by Louis Johnson. Other pieces in the repertory mined more recognizably "Negro" themes. Ernest Parham's carnival ballet *Mardi Gras,* set to music by Les Baxter, ended with a group possessed by a mysterious primitive ritual.

Raisin' Cane, by Graham Johnson, with music by Claudius Wilson, told a comic story of a country boy who becomes lost in the big city and is seduced by a barroom siren. Joseph Rickhard's *Harlot's House,* also with music by Wilson, depicted a young girl's strange attraction to a brothel she passes while strolling with her boyfriend.

Even with repertory that traded on the time-worn stereotype of black bodies as sexually available primitives bewitched by "low" jazz music, none of these companies survived their contemporary marketplaces. Over time, singular efforts by African Americans to use classical technique resulted in similarly abbreviated programming with blatantly sensationalist overtones.[9] Even as African Americans were recognized for their achievements in modern dance and jazz dance, there was widespread ambivalence toward the idea that black dancers could master classical technique or that African-derived performance practice could influence American ballet.

The beginnings of an integrated classical dance in the United States began after World War II, when individual dancers became briefly associated with larger organizations. At New York's Ballet Society, Talley Beatty appeared in Lew Christiansen's 1947 *Blackface* and Arthur Bell danced in Frederick Ashton's 1950 production of *Illuminations.* Janet Collins, the most famous African American classical dancer from this era, achieved the stature of prima ballerina at the Metropolitan Opera from 1951 to 1954, where she danced in *Aida, La Giocanda,* and *Samson and Delilah.* In 1952, Louis Johnson, a student of the School of American Ballet, created a role in Jerome Robbins' *Ballade* for the New York City Ballet.[10]

The affiliation of African American dancers with mostly white companies accelerated throughout the 1960s. The Harkness Ballet of New York ran an aggressive recruitment program in consultation with Thelma Hill, an alumna of the New York Negro Ballet, which by 1968 had successfully placed five black members in that company. Choreographer Alvin

Ailey, who created *Feast of Ashes* for the Joffrey Ballet in 1962, also made *Ariadne* (1965), *El Amor Brujo* (1966), and *Macumba* (1966) for the Harkness Ballet. Ultimately, the founding of the Dance Theatre of Harlem (DTH) in 1969 conclusively ended speculation about the appropriateness of African American interest in ballet. Arthur Mitchell's company and its affiliated school provided performing opportunities and training for black dancers and choreographers from all parts of the world.

As DTH performances set a standard for black classicism, African American influences on ballet began to be recognized and documented. Choreographer George Balanchine, who served on the original DTH board of directors, successfully articulated a neo-classical style of ballet that emphasized thrust hips and rhythmic syncopations commonly found in African American social dance styles. Prominent in his works *The Four Temperaments* (1946) and the "Rubies" section of *Jewels* (1967) are references to the Charleston, the cakewalk, the lindy-hop, and tap dancing.[11]

The critical success of DTH hinged on its dancers' abilities to embody these social movement styles within classical technique. The company excelled in resilient performances of the Balanchine repertory and also in works that explored affinities between ballet and ritual dance, including Geoffrey Holder's *Dougla* (1974), a stylized wedding ceremony combining African and Hindu motifs, and Billy Wilson's *Ginastera* (1991), a combination of Spanish postures and pointe dancing.

black classicism

The consummate versatility achieved by DTH is, of course, directly related to the articulation of "black classicism." Because African American dancers were denied access to sustained study of dance technique, they excelled in choreography that embraced a continuum of idioms as a compositional strategy, in work that explored the spaces between modern dance, social dance, and ballet technique. I want to suggest that dancing well "in between" idioms became a hallmark of African American achievement in ballet and a recognizable standard of black classicism.

The artistic achievement of DTH, the presence of innumerable individual African American artists in companies around the world, and George Balanchine's neo-classic fusion of classical technique and African American dance styles have led to a contemporary ballet repertory that is indisputably bound up with Africanist aesthetic principles. These principles have been vividly realized in works by the European American choreographers Gerald Arpino, William Forsythe, Jerome Robbins, and Twyla Tharp. Ironically, vernacular African American dance styles, which value subversive invention, participatory interaction, and an overwhelming sense of bodily presence, diverge from ballet's conception of strictly codified body line, a silenced and motionless audience, and movement as metaphoric abstraction.

But what are the principles of African diaspora performance? In 1966, art historian Robert Farris Thompson proposed a series of aesthetic commonalities in dance and music-making based on his extensive travels through sub-Saharan Africa. This "aesthetic of the cool" described four shared traits of West African music and dance: the dominance of a percussive concept of performance, multiple meter, apart playing and dancing, and call-and-response. In addition, he chronicled a large category of performance that he termed "the songs and dances of derision."[12] Thompson's work held profound implications for the study of expressive culture in the African diaspora including concert dance.

Thirty years later, dance theorist Brenda Dixon Gottschild elaborated on Thompson's principles by naming five intertextual traits that work together to produce aesthetic balance in an Africanist aesthetic. These traits are a precept of contrariety, in which "difference, discord and irregularity are encompassed, rather than erased or necessarily resolved"; polycentrism and polyrhythm, in which "movement may emanate from any part of the body, and two or more centres may operate simultaneously"; high-affect juxtaposition, in which "breaks that omit the transitions and connective links valued in the European academic aesthetic" are explored; ephebism, the principle that "encompasses attributes such as power, vitality, flexibility, drive, and attack"; and the aesthetic of the cool, the attitude that "combines composure with vitality."[13]

These theoretical hallmarks of Africanist dance are typically discussed in relationship to social dance and modern dance performance.

I'm interested in how they emerged in ballet choreography, especially as African American artists began creating works for classically trained dancers. A close look at two ballets created by Louis Johnson will shed light on how these principles are realized as compositional strategies. I acknowledge that a single choreographer cannot produce a narrative of cultural coherency. But Johnson's work does embody an obvious engagement with Africanist dance practice, especially in his unexpected use of humour to produce a recognizable "ballet in black."

louis johnson

Although Johnson was among the first African American choreographers to work consistently in the ballet idiom, his life and career have been poorly documented. A brief biographical note outlining his early career is in order.

Born in 1932 in Statesville, North Carolina, Johnson developed an interest in dance after his family moved to Washington, DC. Acrobatic play at the local YMCA led to dance study as a teen at the Doris Jones-Clara Haywood School of Dance, an important studio that trained many accomplished African American and Latino dancers. Johnson's potential in ballet was confirmed during a single year of study there and, with classmate Chita Rivera, he auditioned and was accepted as a student at the School of American Ballet in 1949. After high school, he moved to New York in 1950 to study at the School of American Ballet, as well as the Metropolitan Ballet and the Katherine Dunham Dance School. After only two more years of study, Johnson created a role in Jerome Robbins' ballet *Ballade,* alongside dancers Nora Kaye, Janet Reed, Tanaquil Le Clercq, Todd Bollinger, and Robert Barnett. His participation at New York City Ballet was short-lived, however, and he was not offered a permanent position with the company.

Johnson danced on Broadway in several productions during the early 1950s, including *Four Saints in Three Acts, My Darlin' Aida, House of Flowers,* and both the stage and screen versions of Bob Fosse's *Damn Yankees.* He began his significant choreographic career in 1953 with *Lament,* a lyrical ballet set to music by Villa-Lobos and first presented with an integrated cast at the Third New York Ballet Club Annual Choreographers' Night. After this successful showing he continued making small-group dances, including the character studies *Kindergarten* and *Harlequin,* as well as early explorations of African American experience titled *Spiritual Suite* and *How Many Miles?* He also made abstract dance suites during this period, including a decidedly neo-classical trio titled *Variations.*[14]

Louis Johnson and Barbara Wright in Variations. *Choreography by Louis Johnson.*

For the New York Negro Ballet's tour to Great Britain in 1957, he created two works: the classically styled *Waltze* and *Folk Impressions,* a suite of dances set to Morton Gould's orchestral arrangements of folk songs and spirituals. But after the New York Negro Ballet company folded in 1959, Johnson found few outlets for his classical choreography.

In other spheres, however, Johnson's reputation grew and he settled into a career making dances for television, film, the Broadway stage, and nightclub appearances.[15] His experience in show business deeply influenced his choreographic method. When he resumed making ballets for classically trained dancers, his choreography began to freely mix movement idioms, setting social dance next to classical ballet technique, Dunham-inspired modern dance forms, spiritual dancing, and acrobatics. His mature work is consistently concerned with style juxtaposition, as was evident in his large group ballets, especially *Forces of Rhythm,* created for the Dance Theatre of Harlem in 1972, and *Fontessa and Friends,* premiered by the Alvin Ailey American Dance Theater in 1981.

Forces of Rhythm, subtitled "A Fusion of Classic Ballet, Ethnic, and Modern Dance Styles," is ostensibly an abstract suite of dance variations, and it offers fine examples of Johnson's choreographic method. The dance is structured as an agon between four groups of dancers all costumed in black and white: a quartet of ballerinas on pointe, a quartet of male ballet danseurs, a quartet of female "Katherine Dunham" dancers clad in white ceremonial dresses, and a quartet of social-dancing men who wear very little. The dance exploits the tension between these four groups and their "appropriate" movement ideas, then mixes up any notion of choreographic propriety as the groups perform in one another's idioms.

The ballet begins with three of the identifiable groups of dancers on stage. The ballerinas, danseurs, and Dunham dancers approach the audience performing movements that satisfy the charges of their costumes. They demonstrate a working vocabulary for the piece as the ballerinas scoot through petite allegro passages, the danseurs execute expansive jumping phrases, and the Dunham dancers charge passionately through a series of turns and contractions. Without warning, the four "social dance" men leap onto the stage and cavort through the space with patently invented "neo-African" steps. Their gestures are at definite odds with those of the other groups, their very presence undermining the propriety established in the opening sequence of the dance.

Throughout *Forces of Rhythm,* these "social dance" male dancers interrupt the flow of other dance episodes. Their appearance often prompts an abrupt shift in the pre-recorded musical score, from a classical orchestral selection to a rhythm-and-blues song.[16] The juxtaposition of musical selections mirrors the flagrantly contrary quality of their actions in relationship to that of the other dancers. In one variation, four ballerinas "trap" one of the clowning social dance men within a series of precise geometric formations. In the dance's central pas de deux, a ballerina and danseur are joined by a comic figure who teases his way into the dance, counterposing his fluid, low-to-the-ground neo-African movements with their formal, lengthened classical partnering. The members of this trio interact with a poignant curiosity, the social dance man partnering the ballerina in a series of lifts, while the danseur tests his way through sinuous motions with a released torso and articulated hip and shoulder isolations. It is as if the dancers are "learning" one another's appropriate modes of expression.

In the final section of the ballet, set to Rufus Wright's song "Do the Breakdown," all the dancers achieve the neo-African movements proposed by the social dance quartet.[17] First, each of the four groups offers a brief summation of its basic dance idiom. Here, the four comic men strut, tap dance, and perform the cakewalk, an African American social dance of derision that was popular at the turn of the twentieth century. As the vocals in the musical score call the dancers to "do the breakdown, children!" the dancers carefully promenade toward the audience in unison, then pulse in a neo-African gesture of supplication, their torsos pushing toward the ground as their feet stamp from side to side. The dancers find a common language in this gesture and seem to dance with and for one another, rather than simply at the same time. Each group exits the stage in character, the last being the four social dance men. They leave dancing the breakdown, an African American social dance popular in the early 1970s.

Obviously, *Forces of Rhythm* comments on the variety of dance impulses available to African American dancers — in this case, the classically trained dancers of the Dance Theatre of Harlem. While the choreography draws lines between four "types" of dancers, the audience is challenged to remember that all sixteen dancers on stage are members of a classical ballet company. The choreographer clearly takes delight in feeding non-balletic movement to some of these dancers, as he simultaneously tests his audience's ability to comprehend connections between several dance idioms. In some sections of the piece, individual dancers test and master movements borrowed from other idioms until the differences between these groups of dancers are ultimately laid bare.

Most interesting to me are the social dance men. Their idiom in the dance as a whole is never clearly defined. They are, of course, trickster figures. In several passages they perform neo-African movements borrowed from the Dunham technique and a host of African American social dances, while humorously mimicking the classical ballet postures of the danseurs.

Overall, they are the outrageous comic glue that ties the piece together. The choreographer invests them with the ability to inhabit other idioms represented in the dance. They are agents of vernacular inversion, equalizers who target the pride and pretension of other dance idioms with a wink and a smile.

DTH "Tricksters": William Scott, Homer Bryant, Samuel Smalls, and Roman Brooks in Louis Johnson's Forces of Rhythm.

The social dance men embody the ability of the African American vernacular to absorb influences from Europe and the Caribbean and derisively expand on the implications of those influences. This ability is one of Thompson's aesthetic commonalities. Throughout *Forces of Rhythm,* aspects of Africanist composition emerge in the phrasing of percussive movement, complex metrical subdivisions, passages of physicalized call-and-response dancing, and sections that require the dancers to work apart from one another as pieces of a larger, unified whole. Also apparent in the choreography are vestiges of Gottschild's intertextual traits of Africanist performance. These are evident in the blatantly contrary structure of the work and the juxtaposition of dance idioms and musical selections within a classical ballet setting.

Clowns: Members of the Alvin Ailey American Dance Theatre in Fontessa and Friends *by Louis Johnson.*

In his later work, *Fontessa and Friends,* Johnson revisited the depiction of tricksters who derisively tease the conventions of ballet. In this dance, the tricksters appear as clowns and are led by a tattered character recognizably drawn from minstrel shows. His name is Ragtime. The ballet tells the story of an evening in the life of Fontessa, described by the choreographer as "a crazy lady."[18] Fontessa is a lonely countess who hosts an imaginary party. Ragtime and his clowns number among her guests, along with a young couple of balletic lovers and a golden slave character borrowed from *Scheherazade.*

The ballet follows a complicated scenario full of outrageous juxtapositions and abrupt shifts in mood. At its opening, Fontessa commands the stage with a searing portrayal of melancholy as she carefully prepares for the imaginary party. Her "guests" first arrive only in pantomime, and then in the flesh when Ragtime, his clowns, and the young lovers suddenly emerge from the wings. Ragtime repeatedly invades the mood of the other party-goers by breaking in on the young lovers' idylls. He presents Fontessa with a wardrobe trunk that contains her very own golden slave. The broadly drawn humour in this piece ranges from the male clowns' mimicking of traditionally female corps de ballet movements, to Fontessa's pratfalls as she chases after the preening golden slave. The flirtation is consummated when the couple disappears inside the wardrobe trunk.

Fontessa and Friends includes a phantasmagoric sequence in which Fontessa, wearing a sequinned G-string, struts across the stage to the strains of a disco version of "If They Could See Me Now." During this sequence, the clowns accompany her post-coital outburst with singing-group backup movements. The dance draws toward its close as the young lovers flit across the stage to lead a series of humorously stereotypical ballet endings full of multiple turns, impossibly fast leaps, and unattainable lifts and balances that involve all of the cast members. In a short coda, Fontessa finds herself alone again, bejewelled but singular as she recalls the imaginary party to the plaintive strains of the tune "Fontessa," played by the Modern Jazz Quartet.[19]

What I find most striking about this dance is the flamboyant indulgence that Johnson employs to tell Fontessa's story. Huge juxtapositions of musical style force seemingly contrary idioms into a compressed expressive space, as the assembled score careens from modern jazz to disco music to symphonic selections. The ballet is permeated with a feeling of queer excess, not only in the mannered, mincing gestures of the male clowns, or the even more obvious use of disco music and Las Vegas showgirl kick-line routines, but in its abundance of technical demands. Johnson's choreography here is laced with difficult feats, all to be performed with a patent theatricality and sense of coolness. *Fontessa and Friends* is a rare achievement; a ballet that frames classical technique within vernacular comedy.

Forces of Rhythm and *Fontessa and Friends* each questions the "suitability" of classical ballet for African American dancers, placing ballet in direct dialogue with movement styles and strategies of humour traditionally practised by African Americans. Through their strategic uses of humour, these dances tease fundamental assumptions surrounding the black body in ballet. Ultimately, Johnson's choreography proposes a belief in the power of classical ballet technique to provide an effective metaphorical rendering of human conditions — so long as that technique is slyly framed within recognizable black vernacular humour.

Johnson came of age in the 1950s, when the mood of the New York dance world was remarkably optimistic, well before the variety of impulses we now call Africanist had been documented. His tenure at the School of American Ballet (SAB) was marked by his status as a pioneer. In a 1976 interview for *The New York Times,* dance critic Jennifer Dunning described Johnson as the first "black black" at the school, dancing at a time when "blacks were rarely hired."[20] In that interview, the choreographer expresses an affinity for classical ballet borne of his training at SAB: "'It's so funny,' Johnson sighed, 'When I was into classical ballet all those years, I couldn't get hired or fired. There were just no outlets for blacks. And now, all of a sudden, here I am doing *Dance of the Hours.*'"[21]

By the time of the 1976 interview, Johnson was staging *La Gioconda* as resident choreographer for the Metropolitan Opera. It is a striking irony that the *Dance of the Hours* had been performed at the Met in the early 1950s by light-complexioned African American ballerina Janet Collins — during the same period that Johnson was at SAB.

Johnson's training in acrobatics combined with his dance studies at the Dunham school and at SAB surely contributed to his vision of aggressive style juxtaposition in his ballet choreography. To be performed well, his dances require consummate mastery of several movement idioms. As if to draw on the experiences of his African American predecessors who were interested in ballet, but denied opportunities for sustained study and performance, Johnson makes work that investigates the space *between* movement idioms. His dances suggest classicism with a difference — a powerful, hybrid black classicism that draws on African diaspora aesthetic principles within ballet technique. For Johnson, vernacular humour serves as a salve to the longstanding predicament of African Americans as outsiders to ballet.

Portions of this essay appeared in the subject entry "Ballet," Encyclopedia of African-American Culture and History *(MacMillan Press, 1995).*

notes

1 Eugene Nesmith, "Langston Hughes' *Simply Heavenly* and African American Humour," in Pamela Faith Jackson and Karimah (eds.), *Black Comedy: Nine Plays* (New York: Applause Books, 1997), 458.

2 Lynn Garafola discusses this issue in depth in *Diaghilev's Ballets Russes* (New York: Oxford University Press, 1989). See also Lynn Garagola (ed.), *Diaghilev and His World* (New Haven: Yale University Press, 1999).

3 Don McDonagh, "Negroes in Ballet," *New Republic,* 2 November 1968, 44.

4 The "Classic Black" panel, developed by Dawn Lille Horwitz and Jonnie Green at the New York Public Library, 12 February 1996, explored issues of African American dancers seeking training and performing opportunities in segregated ballet schools and companies of the 1940s and 1950s. Participants included Delores Browne, Louis Johnson, Betty Nichols, Walter Nicks, Cleo Quitman, Carmencita Romero, and Marion Spencer.

5 Joan Ross Acocella, "Van Grona and His First American Negro Ballet," *Dance Magazine,* March 1982, 22–4, 30–2.

6 Ibid., 24.

7 Zita Allen, "Blacks and Ballet," *Dance Magazine,* July 1976, 65–70.

8 For more information about the tour and repertory, see Dawn Lille Horwitz, "The New York Negro Ballet in Great Britain," in Thomas DeFrantz (ed.), *Dancing Many Drums: Excavations in African American Dance* (Madison: University of Wisconsin Press, 2001).

9 For example, Helena Justa De Arms performed toe dances in vaudeville in the 1910s, Mary Richards danced on toe in the 1923 Broadway production of *Struttin' Along,* and Josephine Baker performed on toe for at least one number in her appearances at the Paris Opera.

10 Collins began her career in vaudeville and was a member of the original Katherine Dunham troupe. John Martin, the influential dance critic for *The New York Times,* wrote a column praising Collins' debut in 1949. See John Martin, "The Dance: Newcomer," *The New York Times,* 27 February 1949, II, 9.

11 Several scholars have documented African American influences on Balanchine's neo-classical style, most notably Brenda Dixon Gottschild and Sally Banes. Balanchine was fond of telling his dancers to "dance jazz" in certain neo-classical works.

12 Robert Farris Thompson, "Dance and Culture: An Aesthetic of the Cool: West African Dance," *African Forum* 2, 2; Fall 1966: 88. The concept of apart playing and dancing refers to the tendency in African forms to allow each artist a unique contribution to the whole. Strict unison is seldom desired; rather, dancers and musicians "unite music and dance, but play apart" (Ibid., 93).

13 Brenda Dixon Gottschild, *Digging the Africanist Presence in American Performance: Dance and Other Contexts* (Westport, CT: Greenwood Press, 1996), 13–6.

14 Although the actual premiere dates for these ballets are not clear, they were all created between 1953 and 1957.

15 In 1970, Johnson received an Antoinette Perry (Tony) nomination for his choreography of the Broadway musical *Purlie!* Since then he has continued to alternate musical staging with

concert choreography, film, and opera choreography. He is also a noted teacher, and in 2000 continues to serve as the coordinator of the Dance Program at the Henry Street Settlement in New York City.

16 The score for *Forces of Rhythm* juxtaposes classical music by Tchaikovsky to pop music by Rufus Thomas ("Do the Breakdown"), Donny Hathaway ("He Ain't Heavy, He's My Brother"), and others.

17 Two sections of *Forces of Rhythm* are included on the videotape *Dance Theatre of Harlem,* telecast on *Dance in America* by WNET Channel 13, New York, 23 March 1977.

18 Johnson describes Fontessa briefly before the screening of the ballet on the videotape *Dance Black America,* produced by the State University of New York and Pennebaker Associates, Telecast on Great Performances, PBS Channel 13, New York, 27 January 1985.

19 The score for *Fontessa and Friends* includes music by John Lewis and the Modern Jazz Quartet, James P. Johnson, Scott Joplin, Aram Khachaturian, Dorothy Fields, Cy Coleman, Giuseppe Verdi, and Linda Clifford. Louis Johnson designed the costumes for the ballet.

20 Jennifer Dunning, "Louis Johnson: 'I Love Dance — Any Kind of Dance,'" *The New York Times,* 28 September 1975, II, 6.

21 Ibid.

bibliography

Acocella, Joan Ross. "Van Grona and his First American Negro Ballet." *Dance Magazine,* March 1982, 22–4, 30–2.

Allen, Zita. "Blacks and Ballet." *Dance Magazine,* July 1976, 65–70.

Banes, Sally. "Balanchine and Black Dance." In *Choreography and Dance,* 3, part 3. Reading, UK: Harwood Academic Publishers, 1993: 59–77.

Barnes, Clive. "Barnes on . . . The Position of the Black Classic Dancer in American Ballet." *Ballet News,* 3, 9, 1982: 46.

Dunning, Jennifer. "Louis Johnson: 'I Love Dance — Any Kind of Dance.'" *The New York Times,* 28 September 1975, II, 6.

Emery, Lynne Fauley. *Black Dance in the United States from 1619 to 1970.* Palo Alto: National Press Books, 1972.

Goodman, Saul. "Brief Biographies: Louis Johnson." *Dance Magazine,* August 1956, 38–9.

"Harlem Under Control, Negro Ballet Gives 'Fire Bird' and Park Ave. Approves." *Newsweek,* 29 November 1937, 28.

Hering, Doris. "The New York Ballet Club Third Annual Choreographers' Night." *Dance Magazine,* June 1953, 10.

—. "Reviews: Geoffrey Holder and Louis Johnson, 22 November 1955, 92nd Street 'Y.'" *Dance Magazine,* January 1956, 76–8.

Horst, Louis. "Reviews of the Month." *Dance Observer,* January 1956, 10–2.

Horwitz, Dawn Lille. "The New York Negro Ballet in Great Britain." In Thomas DeFrantz (ed.),

Dancing Many Drums: Excavations in African American Dance. Forthcoming from University of Wisconsin Press, 2001.

Jackson, Harriet. "American Dancer, Negro." *Dance Magazine,* September 1966, 35–42.

Kisselgoff, Anna. "Limning the Role of the Black Dancer in America." *The New York Times,* 16 May 1982, 10–32.

Latham, Jacqueline Quinn. "Louis Johnson: Outstanding Choreographer." In "A Biographical Study of the Lives and Contributions of Two Selected Contemporary Black Male Dance Artists — Arthur Mitchell and Alvin Ailey." Diss. Texas Women's University, 1973, UMI xerox, 159–65.

Long, Richard. *The Black Tradition in American Dance.* New York: Rizzoli International Publications Inc., 1989.

Manchester, Phyllis Winifred. "Geoffrey Holder and Louis Johnson and Companies." *Dance News,* January 1956, 7.

—. "Third Choreographers' Night." *Dance News,* May 1953, 8.

Martin, John. "The Dance: A Negro Art Group." *The New York Times,* 14 February 1932, VIII, 11.

—. "The Dance: Newcomer." *The New York Times,* 27 February 1949, II, 9.

McDonagh, Don. "Negroes in Ballet." *New Republic,* 2 November 1968, 41–4.

"Negroes in Ballet." *Dance and Dancers,* October 1957, 9.

"Newest Ballet Star." *Ebony,* November 1954, 36–40.

Schulman, Jennie. "New York Ballet Club." *Dance Observer,* August-September 1953, 119.

Stahl, Norma Gengal. "Janet Collins: The First Lady of the Metropolitan Opera Ballet." *Dance Magazine,* February 1954, 27–9.

Terry, Walter. "To the Negro Dance." *New York Herald Tribune,* 22 January 1940.

Thompson, Robert Farris. "Dance and Culture: an Aesthetic of the Cool: West African Dance." *African Forum* 2, 2; Fall 1966: 85–102.

Vaughan, David. "Transatlantic View 4: Breaking Down the Barriers." *Dance and Dancers,* September 1956, 20.

Williams, Wilson. "Prelude to a Negro Ballet." *Dance Magazine (American Dancer),* March 1940, 14, 39.

Young, Stark. "Slightly Ghosts." *New Republic,* 8 December 1937, 131.

melville herskovits, katherine dunham, and the politics of african diasporic dance anthropology

kate ramsey

In this essay, I want to pose the study of African diasporic dance as a problem in the history of North American cultural anthropology, focusing specifically on its status in the field of "New World Africanism" pioneered by and most closely associated with Melville J. Herskovits. Such a topic might seem initially unpromising, given the discouraging statements that Herskovits published on this subject throughout his career — writing perhaps most decisively in his *The Myth of the Negro Past* that "no method has as yet been evolved to permit objective study of the dance."[1] Indeed, almost every time Herskovits turned to the question of dance anthropology in his writings, it was to cite the methodological problems and descriptive challenges that were inherent to, and inhibiting of, the development of this field. Yet reading such pronouncements against their apparent grain, I would like to propose that the development of an anthropology of African diasporic dance — or as he termed it, of "New World Negro dancing" — was a career-long disciplinary preoccupation and project for Herskovits, and one that is particularly illuminated by his professional relationship with the choreographer and anthropologist Katherine Dunham, whose fieldwork he advised in 1935–6, when he travelled to the Caribbean to study dance cultures in Jamaica, Martinique, Trinidad, and, particularly, Haiti.

In examining Herskovits' investment in the development of an anthropology of African diasporic dance, and Dunham's intervention in that project through her fieldwork in Haiti and, later, her ethnographic memoir *Island Possessed,* I want to think in broader terms about methodological and representational conventions that have historically worked to marginalize dance as an anthropological object. Such disciplinary prescriptions, particularly turning, as Herskovits suggests above, on questions of "objectivity" have been subject to intense critique and revision over the past thirty years, both within and outside the field.[2] More

Melville J. Herskovits

specifically, I am interested in the particular narrative of "New World" African cultural continuity that this earlier moment in the history of North American anthropology inaugurated, and the way that African diasporic dance was figured in its highly influential and controversial project. Drawing on recent cross-disciplinary work in African diaspora studies, I want to question a conception of continuity that fixates on origins and authenticity at the expense of comprehending how African diasporic cultures emerge from and speak to particular black Atlantic histories and contemporary political situations. I see the ethnographic work of Katherine Dunham as being exemplary in this regard. Thus, as much as this essay looks historically at her intervention in Herskovits' project, I also want to situate her work in the context of contemporary epistemological and political debates, and consider ways in which her research of, and writing on, dance ritual in Haiti represents openings for new ethnographic practices and poetics.

Melville Herskovits' case for the survival of Africanisms across the Americas, which he first publicly formulated in the early 1930s,

Katherine Dunham (far right) with friends in Haiti, 1936.

countered both scientific racism's long-standing denial of meaningful existence to African histories and cultures, and the assimilationist thesis, advanced by many mid twentieth-century liberal social scientists, that African cultures had been destroyed under American slave regimes. Herskovits himself had subscribed to this latter position during and just following his studies under anthropologist Franz Boas at Columbia University in the early 1920s. In Howard University philosopher and cultural critic Alain Locke's seminal 1925 anthology, *The New Negro,*[3] Herskovits argues, against the claims of segregationists, that black Americans were not culturally distinct from any other American group, but were rather, of "[t]he same pattern, only a different shade!"[4] The underlying premise of this assertion was subtly contested by other contributors to the volume, including W. E. B. Du Bois, Langston Hughes, Countee Cullen, and folklorist Arthur Huff Fauset, whose writings, in different ways, connected contemporary African diasporic cultural expression and political identity to a refigured African present and past. In his article in the anthology, "The Negro Digs Up His Past," Harlem bibliophile and essayist Arthur A. Schomburg calls for further scientific study of African cultures as a means of building greater self-respect and pride among black Americans, concluding: "The Negro has been a man without a history because he has been considered a man without a worthy culture."[5]

That within a decade Herskovits would himself be closely identified with this position is testimony, as historian Walter Jackson has argued, to the impact that the Harlem Renaissance and diverse forms of cultural nationalism among African American artists, writers, intellectuals, and activists during the mid- to late 1920s had on the development of the central problematic of Herskovits' subsequent research. Jackson notes that Herskovits' ongoing exchange with black scholars and theorists such as Locke "coincided with the emergence of theoretical problems in [his] research that undermined certain of his initial assumptions."[6] Notably, it was Herskovits' discernment of similarities in African and African American dance styles that seems to have first propelled him to ponder seriously the possibility of widespread African cultural "retention" in the Americas. In a 1927 letter to German ethnomusicologist Erich von Hornbostel, Herskovits wondered if "this element of motor behavior might not be a cultural remnant brought to America by the African slaves, which their descendants retained even after the songs themselves were fundamentally changed according to the European pattern?"[7] Disagreeing with von Hornbostel's suggestion that perceptible affinities between African and African American movement styles stemmed from a common "racial" endowment, Herskovits theorized that such similarities were more likely "carried over as a behavior pattern handed down thru [*sic*] imitation and example from the original African slaves who were brought here."[8]

I will return to the problematic place of dance in Herskovits' evolving theory of "New World Africanism," but for the moment I want to flag that his earliest musings on African cultural continuity in the United States and elsewhere frequently focused on what he termed "motor behavior" among black Americans. It was not until three years after these private communications with Hornbostel that Herskovits publicly reversed his earlier assimilationist views regarding the virtual if not total obliteration of African "culture patterns" under slavery, and laid out a methodology for studying African cultural "survivals" in the United States and across the Americas. In the meantime, he had begun teaching in the sociology department at Northwestern University and had undertaken two summer research trips to Surinam (then a Dutch colony) with his wife and collaborator, Frances. There they were strongly struck by the resemblance of certain

Saramaccan cultural forms to West African counterparts. In his landmark article, "The Negro in the New World: The Statement of a Problem," written soon after the second trip to Surinam and published in *American Anthropologist* in 1930, Herskovits proposes that relative degrees of African cultural retention across the New World could be quantified, measured, and plotted on a "scale of intensity of Africanisms," with West and Central Africa anchoring one end of the continuum and the United States the other.[9]

The dependence of this chart, and thus Herskovits' project, on the construction of fixed, stable, and determinate African cultural origins from which extended a diasporic continuum of measurable degrees of Africanism has been frequently and deservedly problematized in recent years for its essentialism and ahistoricism.[10] "Aboriginal purity" was the implicit presupposition of a methodological apparatus designed to chart the relative proximity of "New World Negro" cultures to Africa. On the far end of the continuum lay the United States, which Herskovits figured as the place where the "departure from African modes of life was greatest, and where such Africanisms as persisted were carried through in generalized form, almost never directly referable to a specific tribe or a definite area."[11] The Caribbean, a primary locus of Herskovits' own "New World" ethnographic research, occupied a critical space in this scheme as the middle linking term between the two poles, making attenuated retentions in the United States recognizable and connecting them, metonymically, to a verifiable African cultural origin. Echoing Arthur Schomburg's argument in *The New Negro*, Herskovits contended that research of such continuities would both instill greater self-esteem and pride among peoples of African descent by culturally validating their connection to an ancestral past and, at the same time, dispel the racist myths about that past that served, in his view, as "one of the principal supports of race prejudice" in contemporary American society.[12]

Herskovits' scale of Africanism worked on two interconnected levels — on the one hand, comparatively charting degrees of retention among New World cultures taken monolithically, and on the other, breaking each cultural "whole" down into constitutive units, or cultural "traits," which, he argued, could be plotted according to the extent to which they manifested or departed from "aboriginal patterns." Here, the historical record shed light on why Africanisms were retained to such differing degrees in, as he put it, "the several parts into which any human culture can be divided."[13] Herskovits argued that while the conditions of plantation slavery militated against the survival of "African forms of technology, economic life and political organization," there had been greater possibilities for retention in religion, magic, and "the non-material aspects of aesthetic life," such as storytelling, music, and dance.[14]

I want to turn, in this context, to the highly prominent and thoroughly paradoxical status of dance and movement in Herskovits' charting of New World Africanism. Despite his oft-repeated caveat against cross-cultural generalization, he states in *The Myth of the Negro Past* that dance "has in characteristic form carried over into the New World to a greater degree than almost any other trait of African culture."[15] He accounts for this resilience ethno-historically, with reference to the centrality of dance in West and Central African religious practices and expressive cultures, as well as its ambivalent status under slave regimes — perceived by planters to be alternately a locus of resistance or a harmless entertainment, even encouraged by them as a "safety valve."[16] If dance formations were, according to Herskovits, arguably the greatest of diasporic cultural retentions, they did not manifest the same degree of Africanism in every cultural setting, but rather followed the general scale or continuum that mapped African "aboriginal purity" and widespread "acculturation" in the United States, through the intermediary forms of the Caribbean and parts of South America. Herskovits singled out dance in rural Surinam and Haiti — the sites of his own early New World field research with Frances — as particularly exemplary of Africanisms, proposing in the case of coastal Surinam that "these descendants of Africa are but repeating motor habits current in the homeland of their ancestors," a continuity that is total, becoming repetition.[17]

What Herskovits characterized as the prominence, pervasiveness, and "high visibility" of New World Negro dance added another dimension to its stature in his project. One of the potentials of anthropology's "modern scientific method," as he termed it, was to authoritatively counter racist images of African and diasporic cultures that often fixated on dance and ritual forms. Herskovits had undertaken fieldwork in Haiti during the summer of 1934, just as the nineteen-year occupation of that country by US marines was coming to an end. In the ethnography that came of this research, *Life in a Haitian Valley,* he attacked the sensationalized representations of the Voudou religion that proliferated in American imperial literatures over the course of the occupation, commenting dryly that Voudou's ritual dances had "been more frequently observed and reported on than any other rites of the cult."[18] At best, he wrote elsewhere, "available data on the dance" was limited to "scattered literary descriptions of various occasions on which persons, usually untrained in the study of dance, witnessed ceremonies of one kind or another"; yet, he continued, "no method has as yet been evolved to permit objective study of the dance."[19]

I would like to suggest that this marks the site of a great disciplinary impasse in Herskovits' work. Figured as possibly the greatest African diasporic cultural retention, with social and political stakes resting on its scientific study,[20] "New World Negro dance" was not accessible to scientific research or ethnographic representation. Herskovits contrasted the predicament of dance anthropology with the "objective nature" of data collection in the field of music studies, contending that notation systems and the recording phonograph had permitted extensive documentary transcription of African and diasporic rhythms and songs, making comparative analysis possible and degrees of retention and continuity "measurable." The absence of such methodological tools for the anthropological study of dance thwarted not only the imperative of empirical quantification, but also, notably, the possibility of textual representation: "To attempt descriptions of dance types," he writes, "requires a technique as yet scarcely developed; since analysis must also await the utilization of motion pictures as an aid to the study of these special aspects of motor behavior, we can here but record the fact of its prominence in the culture, and its pervasiveness in the life of the people."[21]

Throughout his corpus, Herskovits returned to this paradox — the importance of dance to his studies of diasporic Africanism and the insufficiency of his methodologies to study it. And throughout his professional correspondence, like a counterpoint to those published statements, Herskovits recorded what I am suggesting was a ongoing career-long preoccupation with the development of a dance anthropology. Interestingly, his papers (collected at Northwestern University) make clear that he never imagined or intended that he would build the field himself, but rather insisted that its pioneers should themselves be dancers. In 1953 he wrote to a dean at Northwestern: "It is a much neglected [field], and one that I feel can only be [established] by someone thoroughly trained in the dance who would then get enough anthropological training to work out methods and conceptual approaches for this cross-cultural study."[22] Thus his correspondence with and support of Franziska Boas (daughter of anthropologist Franz Boas), who was a dancer herself and an advocate for dance anthropology during these years, and his communications with Maya Deren, dancer-turned-filmmaker and author of *Divine Horsemen: The Living Gods of Haiti* (1953).

One of Herskovits' strongest statements regarding the urgency of developing a dance anthropology occurs in a 1946 letter to the Guggenheim Foundation, in which he asks to be put in touch with choreographer Martha Graham (an ex-fellow of the foundation), whom he had just seen dance, was much impressed by, and who, it had struck him, might know "someone who could start doing a job in the field of the dance *that I think needs doing as much as any other single job in . . . anthropology*" (emphasis added). He elaborates: "The fact is that so little work on the comparative study of the dance has been done, that we don't even have a vocabulary for it. Yet it is an extremely important manifestation of culture everywhere, and I have long felt that if someone could be found who was competent in the dance field and interested in getting anthropological training, that person could make a first-rate contribution."[23]

But by far the most important testimony to Herskovits' investment in the development of a cross-cultural anthropology of African diasporic dance was his support of Katherine Dunham. She became his student at Northwestern University in early 1935, several months before her departure for the Caribbean on a Julius Rosenwald Fellowship to make a comparative study of dance on the islands of Jamaica, Martinique, Trinidad, and Haiti. Dunham, of course, went on to become one of the great pioneers and innovators of dance modernism, developing a concert dance idiom based on African American and Caribbean forms that has influenced generations of choreographers and performers since the 1940s. Dunham appears in Herskovits' discussion of the predicament and possibilities of the comparative study of "New World Negro dancing" in *The Myth of the Negro Past*, published in 1941. By this point, she had completed her master's degree in anthropology at the University of Chicago working under Robert Redfield and had starred in the musical *Cabin in the Sky* on Broadway. She would go on to establish an international reputation as a choreographer and performer during the forties, touring with her company in such productions as *Tropical Revue* and *Carib Song*. Herskovits cites Dunham's fieldwork in the Caribbean in 1935–6 as marking an important beginning for the development of comparative studies of "New World Negro dance": "To the present time," he writes, "the most important result of Miss Dunham's field investigations has been in her own creative dancing." Noting approvingly the "popular success achieved by her reproductions of the dances she studied," he proposed that this choreography, based on Caribbean forms, was familiarizing North American audiences with the African elements of their own indigenous dance traditions, in the same way that, on his scale of Africanism, the West Indies performed a kind of cultural mediation between Africa and North America. "Such reactions," he writes, "despite their impressionistic nature, are not without significance in terms of the search for African survivals, pointing to the rich returns to be gained from systematic scientific analysis, on the basis of comparative studies, of the tenacity of African dance styles and the effect of acculturation on New World Negro dancing."[24]

A growing body of critical and biographical work focuses on Dunham's choreographic career and, as VèVè Clark has generatively analyzed it, her "research-to-performance method."[25] Here, I want to focus more strictly on Dunham's ethnographic work, looking at how she intervened in and moved beyond the impasse that made the development of an anthropology of African diasporic dance an ongoing preoccupation and priority for Herskovits, but also an irresolvable problem within the positivist terms of his science.[26] I want to look briefly at the ethnographic approach that Dunham evolved toward the study of ritual dance during the course of her fieldwork throughout the Caribbean, and particularly in Haiti, where she departed most significantly from the program of research and documentation that Herskovits had laid out for her, as well as from the objectifying practices of fieldwork that he more generally considered requisite.

Herskovits' support of Dunham's fieldwork in the Caribbean from June 1935 through late April 1936 can be read as reflecting both his extremely high estimation of her abilities and the seriousness of his commitment to the development of this anthropological sub-field, which he clearly believed she would pioneer.[27] Their correspondence was unbroken throughout her travels, with letters crossing between them at least twice and sometimes three times a month. In the early stages of Dunham's research, these exchanges were usually structured around her mailings of reels of film that she was taking as she went, recording dances (some staged for her) on each island with a motion picture camera on loan from the Rosenwald Fund.[28] In recently discussing her early research in the Caribbean, Dunham noted that she had been "very conscientious about trying to do all the filming that I could. And, you know that's a great deal of work when you're by yourself."[29] Their correspondence over this footage, with Dunham expressing concern about her techniques of filmmaking, and Herskovits offering reassurance and coaching after viewing each instalment (for, of course, he was seeing the entire series before she did), reveals the extent to which her early research in Jamaica, Martinique, and Trinidad was oriented around, even dominated by, the demands of filmic documentation.[30] This was at Herskovits' direction, for he was convinced that the development of dance anthropology could proceed only through the ethnographic utilization of the motion picture camera.

It was a position that he repeated throughout his published statements on the subject and particularly in *The Myth of the Negro Past,* where he cites, as a salutary beginning, a study done by the French anthropologist Marcel Griaule in what was then the French Sudan in the mid-1930s, in which dance sequences were filmed and then broken down into a series of outline drawings taken off single frames of footage.[31] The drawings were then miniaturized and placed above a musical staff on which were figured the transcribed drum rhythms to which the movements had been performed. Herskovits writes of this technique: "The movements of the dancers are thus presented in their bare essentials, which makes it simpler than any other means yet devised to compare these figures with others similarly treated, or for those interested in dancing to reproduce the dance figures."[32]

I want to think more about the methodological implications of Herskovits' investment in filming, in the context of shifts that took place in Dunham's field research after her arrival in Haiti in late 1935. On her way there from Trinidad she wrote in one of her letters to Herskovits: "If all goes well in Haiti, I shall have a little controversy with you, I think. I shall try to be initiated, which means that I will probably have to do away with [the] . . . picture machine for a while . . . Unless I'm dealing with purely social affairs, must go easy on the equipment. I've seen the difference between something staged and something real, and besides people don't like it. That is, if they are doing something serious."[33] That conclusion was no doubt some time in coming, but stemmed most immediately, as she writes in her memoir *Island Possessed,* from an upsetting experience in Trinidad, when she was caught filming a Shango ceremony that was being held in secrecy.[34] It was during Dunham's stay in Trinidad that Herskovits cautioned her that she was "taking a bit too much scenery" in her footage. "[J]ust remember," he wrote with regard to the latest batch of film she had sent back to Northwestern, "that twenty-five feet of films of nothing but scenery is an awful lot, and ten feet gives you about everything you need."[35] Yet this tendency seems to have become yet stronger once she got to Haiti, where, Dunham admits in *Island Possessed,* she shot "hundreds of feet of limpid ocean beach, palm trees, cane fields" but otherwise had "little use" for filming. "During most of my stay in Haiti," she writes, "the movie camera would have been strikingly out of place."[36]

Clearly, as Dunham herself indicates, a shift had taken place in her project by the time she arrived in Haiti, of which the setting aside of her camera was only one, albeit highly symbolic, marker. Her decision not to film the sacred dances she was studying there represented a break with the methodological program of study Herskovits had laid out for her — one that she made explicit in her letters to him, as above. Herskovits was invested in film technology as the best hope for the "objective study" of dance, by which he meant an analysis in which dance forms could be broken down into constitutive units, fixed perhaps, as in the study cited above, on single frames of film, and comparatively and positivistically examined in relation to a West or Central African standard. The camera, in some sense, then, served as an instrument of measurement. Yet, interestingly, it also guaranteed another constitutive dimension of Herskovits' methodology from which Dunham was breaking.

Following her first announcement that she planned to forsake her camera to become initiated, Dunham wrote to Herskovits from Haiti: "Dancing a lot and feeling rotten . . . I shall start initiations when I feel better and hope that before leaving Haiti I can reach the second stage . . . They are amazed at my dancing. All of which will facilitate initiation."[37] Herskovits wrote back immediately: "Once again, I am disturbed at the amount you are trying to do, this time principally because of your health . . . I am a little disturbed also at the prospect of your going through the *canzo* ceremony and I am wondering if it would not be possible for you to attend merely as a witness . . . However you know best in such matters."[38] A few weeks later, after hearing from Dunham that she had been counselled against seeking the second stage of initiation by a priest of Voudou, Herskovits replied: "I am glad that he advised you not to go through with the *kanzo,* for as I wrote you, I was a little afraid of it . . . I take it that in any event you will be able to see a *kanzo* ceremony, and careful notes on it are the most important thing to have."[39]

Herskovits was *not* an advocate of anthropological participant-observation, a position that he emphasized at the end of his ethnography *Life in a Haitian Valley,* which, I want to emphasize, he was preparing for publication during the very months Dunham was studying in Haiti in 1935–6.[40] Their correspondence reveals, in fact, that he had her do some last-minute research and fact-checking for the book.[41] In an unusually forceful statement, he writes in his final chapter, "Some Comments on Method": "Much nonsense has been written about the need for the student of the customs of a people to become a 'participant observer' of those customs, by doing what, in common parlance, is termed 'going native.' This may be feasible among some folk — in the South Seas, perhaps — but let it be stated emphatically that this is neither possible nor of benefit among West African Negroes and their New World Negro descendants."[42]

Having made that encompassing pronouncement, Herskovits immediately qualifies the prescription along lines of race and gender: "The ethnographer, again, especially if he be a white man, has what has been called a high degree of social visibility." And a few lines later: "In Negro cultures the white student must be content to remain what he actually is, an observer."[43] In other words, the border that Herskovits so strenuously marks off between the white ethnographic analyst and the African diasporic "object" of anthropological study seems not to necessarily or strictly apply to the researcher of colour. Given the extent of Herskovits' correspondence with Dunham in Haiti as he was readying this manuscript for publication, and the shifts that she was reporting in her own research at the time, I would argue that *her* participation was a strong factor in this qualification, first compelling his interrogation of the assumed whiteness and maleness of the ethnographer, and then motivating, in effect, an exception to his rule.

Yet the politics of such an attribution of exceptionality raise important questions, insofar as African American ethnographers such as Dunham and Zora Neale Hurston (who travelled to the Caribbean to undertake research in Jamaica and Haiti in April 1936, just as Dunham was returning to Chicago) were often perceived, on racial grounds, to have "greater access" in their studies of African diasporic cultures than white researchers. Swiss ethnologist Alfred Métraux, for example, in writing an appreciation of Dunham in the early 1960s, attributed the success of her fieldwork in Haiti to her "racial origin," along with her scientific background, and her talent as a dancer. It is important to stress that Dunham herself believed her racial identity to be a factor of crucial importance in her research, for as she describes in her monograph *The Dances of Haiti,* the "negative aspects of being a woman field worker," and American in post-occupation Haiti, "were often counterbalanced by the positive elements of racial affinity."[44] The external perception and attribution of such access, however, was potentially double-edged, opening up questions of "objectivity" and "critical distance" that could, and in certain cases did, result in the anthropological marginalization of her work.[45] For example, in the October 1970 issue of *American Anthropologist,* Erika Bourguignon (a cultural anthropologist who had been a graduate student under Herskovits and had also done her dissertation field research in Haiti during the late 1940s) wrote a negative review of Dunham's *Island Possessed* in which she contended: "This book is of interest not as an ethnography, nor for what it may tell us about Haiti, but as a personal document of an American Negro woman, an artist seeking identity and roots . . . while uprootedly traveling about the world in the exercise of her art."[46]

Such critiques responded to the challenge Dunham's work posed to disciplinary conventions by categorizing it as autobiography: a genre from which anthropology proper could feel safely insulated. In closing, I want to argue that Dunham's memoir of her early work in Haiti is of interest *precisely* as an ethnography — both as a document of her research and as a textual representation of that experience, strongly focused on the *writing* of ritual performance. As Faye Harrison and Ira Harrison have noted, Dunham's reflexivity and blurring of genre in this work anticipate recent experiments in ethnographic writing that have accompanied anthropology's postmodernist turn and contemporary critiques of ethnographic "objectivity" and authority.[47] Published in 1969, more than thirty years after Dunham's first return from Haiti, *Island Possessed* is self-consciously filtered through the prisms of history, memory, and sometimes nostalgia, and drawn with a plenitude of detail that is a hallmark of all of her later writings.[48] I want to focus briefly here, in particular, on the way Dunham figured her own ritual participation and, indeed, initiation in this work, making the crossing of ethnographic boundaries a central issue, theme, and problem in her narration and description of those experiences.

Island Possessed is structured by two ritual events: Dunham's *lave-tête* initiation into Voudou and simultaneous "marriage" to the Voudou *lwa* Danbala in late 1935, and, secondly, her "promissory" ceremony to this god just before returning to Chicago in April 1936. Dunham's descriptions of the space of ritual are not simply catalogues of visual data — in fact, the visual has no primacy in her text (one might well remember here the laying aside of her camera). Rather, they are multi-sensory evocations of her experience of these ceremonies, insinuated, for example, with the smells (sweat, bad breath, damp earth, burnt kerosene oil, cheap perfume) that contemporary ethnographic theorists Mary Louise Pratt and James Clifford have rightly commented on as being absent from the pages of most ethnographies.[49]

The experiential quality of Dunham's writing of ritual is best captured, though, in her descriptions of the dances performed during these ceremonies, which took place on the outskirts of Port-au-Prince, in the area known as La Plaine. In these passages she is concerned with representing not only their "choreography," but also their affective "sense" in the context of a community of worshippers: "All of us who could crowd into the *peristyle* . . . shuffled in the warm earth, effacing vévés, raising dust, rocking from side to side as we progressed, knees relaxed, turning now and then with the concentrated shuffling, shoulders moving like pistons of a high-powered locomotive. The joy of dancing overwhelmed me . . . It was so good in every sense of the word to dance to the drums of the gods that Sunday in Cul-de-Sac, and this feeling of the rightness of these cult dances has never left me."[50]

Yet, if these ceremonies were the locus of joy, they were also occasions of confusion and crisis, accounts of which are built into, rather than written out of, Dunham's ethnography. Indeed, ritual becomes the space in *Island Possessed* where Dunham interrogates most rigorously, and often painfully, the feeling, as she describes it during one such meditation, "of being outsider within, or vice versa, as the occasion dictates," and of standing on "a fringe border of belief and nonbelief."[51] She appeals at one point: "Could Herskovits tell me . . . could Téoline or Dégrasse [two of her Voudou advisors in Haiti] tell me what part of me lived on the floor of the houngfor, felt awareness seeping from the earth and people and things around me, and what part stood to one side taking notes?"[52]

Repeatedly in the course of her narrations of these experiences — the banality, profundity, and tedium of her initiation; the anxiety, fear, trauma, and relief of her ritual promise — Dunham brings her reader's attention back to this border, which she chooses to inhabit and theorize in *Island Possessed,* rather than seek the security that might be constructed, however illusorily, on either of its sides. This is a position of honesty as well as risk, and it points to one of the most generative and exemplary dimensions of Dunham's work for contemporary ethnographic practices. In continually returning to this borderplace, which is so marked for her, as for Herskovits, by the question of participation, Dunham rejects the claims of both an objectifying ethnographic authority on the one hand, and a mystifying experiential authenticity on the other. *Island Possessed* neither suppresses the fact of Dunham's initiation, nor makes it the grounds for a new authority, opposed but analogous to that conferred by science.

Rather, her account of participation becomes a site in which the ethnographic balancing act between subjectivity and objectivity is continually explored, but never stabilized. As she puts it at one point: "I am there to believe or not believe, but willing to understand and to believe in the sincerity of other people in their beliefs, willing to be shown, to participate, and where the participant begins and the scientist ends, I surely could not say."[53]

acknowledgement

I am grateful to Katherine Dunham for sharing memories of her early research in Haiti with me. I would also like to thank Elizabeth Chin, Yvonne Daniel, Anne Flynn, Susan Leigh Foster, Susan Manning, Jacqueline Shea Murphy, Halifu Osumare, Tim Watson, Joe Wood and the participants in the January 1999 conference at the University of Calgary for their helpful questions and comments on earlier versions of this article. My thanks go as well to the staff of the Melville J. Herskovits Library of African Studies at Northwestern University, and the staff of Special Collections/Morris Library, Southern Illinois University at Carbondale, where the Katherine Dunham Papers are held.

notes

1 Melville J. Herskovits, *The Myth of the Negro Past,* 1941 (Reprint, Boston: Beacon Press, 1958), 269.

2 See, in particular, James Clifford and George E. Marcus (eds.), *Writing Culture: The Poetics and Politics of Ethnography* (Berkeley: University of California Press, 1986).

3 This anthology of fiction, poetry, drama, and essays began as a special March 1925 "Harlem" issue for *Survey Graphic* magazine on the topic, entitled "Harlem: Mecca of the New Negro." Locke's reservations about the radical *dis*continuity that Herskovits ascribed between African and African American cultural "patterns" might be surmised by the "editorial note" published alongside the article, in which Locke suggests that "external" perceptions of "Negro life" might not tell the entire story (Alain Locke, editorial note to Herskovits, "The Dilemma of Social Pattern," *Survey Graphic* 6, March 1925, 676).

4 Melville J. Herskovits, "The Negro's Americanism," in Alain Locke (ed.), *The New Negro,* 1925 (Reprint, New York: Atheneum, 1968), 353.

5 Arthur A. Schomburg, "The Negro Digs Up His Past," in *The New Negro,* 237.

6 Walter Jackson, "Melville Herskovits and the Search for Afro-American Culture," in George W. Stocking Jr. (ed.), *Malinowski, Rivers, Benedict and Others: Essays on Culture and Personality* (Madison: University of Wisconsin Press, 1986), 105.

7 Letter from Herskovits to Erich von Hornbostel, 10 June 1927. Quoted in Walter Jackson, "Melville Herskovits and the Search for Afro-American Culture," 107.

8 Ibid.

9 Herskovits writes: "It is quite possible on the basis of our present knowledge to make a kind of chart indicating the extent to which the descendants of Africans brought to the New World have retained Africanisms in their cultural behavior" (Melville J. Herskovits, "The Negro in the New World: The Statement of a Problem," *American Anthropologist* 32, 1930: 149).

10 See, for example, the excellent articles by David Scott, "That Event, This Memory: Notes on the Anthropology of African Diasporas in the New World," and Andrew Apter, "Herskovits Heritage: Rethinking Syncretism in the African Diaspora," *Diaspora* 1, 3, 1991.

11 Herskovits, *The Myth of the Negro Past,* 122.

12 Ibid., 1.

13 Ibid., 111.

14 Ibid., 136–7.

15 Ibid., 76.

16 Anticipating the recent work of Roger D. Abrahams, Herskovits writes that this was especially true during so-called slave holidays, when African based dances "were enjoyed by the masters who watched them as much as by the slave dancers and singers" (Herskovits, *The Myth of the Negro Past,* 138). See also Roger D. Abrahams, *Singing the Master: The Emergence of African American Culture in the Plantation South* (New York: Pantheon Books, 1992).

17 Herskovits, *The Myth of the Negro Past,* 219.

18 Melville J. Herskovits, *Life in a Haitian Valley,* 1937 (Reprint, Garden City: Doubleday and Co., 1971), 178.

19 Herskovits, *The Myth of the Negro Past,* 269.

20 He writes in *The Myth of the Negro Past:* "The recognition by the majority of the [United States] population of certain values in Negro song and Negro dance has already heightened Negro self-pride and has affected white attitudes toward the Negro" (299).

21 Ibid., 76.

22 Melville J. Herskovits to Dean Prior, Northwestern University, 14 December 1953 (Melville J. Herskovits Papers, Africana Manuscripts, Northwestern University Library, Evanston, Illinois).

23 Melville J. Herskovits to Henry Allen Moe, Guggenheim Foundation, 20 March 1946 (Herskovits Papers). Moe replied in a 10 July 1946 letter: "This is a belated response to your letter of March 20, but I did, as soon as it arrived, write to your fellow Fellow, Miss Martha Graham in the sense you suggested. Miss Graham may have been in touch with you: I hope so. But I have had no response." There is no record of a reply from Graham in the Herskovits Papers.

24 Herskovits, *The Myth of the Negro Past,* 270.

25 See VèVè A. Clark, "Performing the Memory of Difference in Afro-Caribbean Dance: Katherine Dunham's Choreography, 1938-87," in Geneviève Fabre and Robert O'Meally (eds.), *History and Memory in African-American Culture* (New York: Oxford University Press, 1994), 193.

26 In focusing the essay in this way, I am indebted to the work of Joyce Aschenbrenner, VèVè A. Clark, and Faye V. Harrison. See Joyce Aschenbrenner, *Katherine Dunham: Reflections on the Social and Political Contexts of Afro-American Dance* (New York: Congress on Research

in Dance, 1981) and "Katherine Dunham: Anthropologist, Artist, Humanist," in Ira E. Harrison and Faye V. Harrison (eds.), *African-American Pioneers in Anthropology* (Urbana: University of Illinois Press, 1999), 137–53. See VèVè A. Clark, as detailed in note 25. See Faye V. Harrison, "'Three Women, One Struggle': Anthropology, Performance, and Pedagogy," in *Transforming Anthropology* 1, 1990: n.1, 1–9. My thanks go to Gina Ulysse for alerting me to Harrison's article.

27 As a condition of this funding, Dunham spent the semester before her departure for the Caribbean working with Herskovits at Northwestern. In early May, he reported to Edwin Embree of the Rosenwald Fund that "her work with me has been excellent, not only from the point of view of class work and scholarship, but more importantly for the purposes of her fellowship, as regards the manner of her approach to her problem and the way in which she has grown into it" (Melville J. Herskovits to Edwin Embree, 2 May 1935, Herskovits Papers).

28 Herskovits acknowledges Dunham's Caribbean filming in *The Myth of the Negro Past:* "An attempt to begin the comparative study of dancing among Negro folk of the New World was made during 1936 by Miss Katharine [*sic*] Dunham in applying her training and experience as a dancer to the comparative study of Negro dancing in Jamaica, Martinique, Trinidad, and Haiti. Motion pictures of various dances were taken by her, to make possible comparisons between these and the motion pictures of dances obtained in Dahomey, the Gold Coast, Nigeria, Guiana and Haiti during the field work on which has been based much of the approach to the comparative study of Negro cultures and survival of Africanisms in the New World discussed in these pages" (270).

29 Interview with author, Habitation Leclerc, Haiti, 9 April 1997.

30 For example, Herskovits wrote to Dunham upon receipt of reels of film from her stay in Martinique: "I certainly do not feel that you need be afraid that your Martinique trip was wasted for the dances you filmed are magnificent and came out beautifully . . . All in all you are becoming very adept with your camera and you should have the makings of a very extremely interesting film. There is only one suggestion that occurs to me at the moment and that is that in filming the dances, you pay a little more attention to the drumming. Closeups showing the way in which the drummers use their hands would be especially valuable" (Melville J. Herskovits to Katherine Dunham, 25 October 1935, Herskovits Papers).

31 See Marcel Griaule, *Masques Dogons* (Paris: Institut d'Ethnologie, 1938). Griaule's ethnography is a fascinating early anthropological attempt to cope with the challenges that dance and performance raised for objectifying ethnographic methodologies. As Griaule explains and exemplifies in this text, Dogon dances had been filmed, and then rendered as individual sketches, frame by frame: "In the case of very rapid dances," he writes, "all the images are reproduced; in the inverse case, one single image is retained of two or three" (716; all quotes are my translation). Griaule proposed that this notation system was not only valuable for anthropological analysis, but might also enable the reconstruction of dances that "have disappeared [but] that some older informants still know" (716, n.1). It is important to emphasize that Griaule's advocacy of ethnographic filming assumed, in keeping with the French anthropological tradition at this time, the participation of a *team* of specialized researchers, a fact that makes Dunham's comment quoted above, on the difficulties of filming on her own, yet more well taken.

32 Herskovits, *The Myth of the Negro Past,* 269.

33 Katherine Dunham to Melville J. Herskovits, 15 November 1935, Herskovits Papers.

34 Dunham, Katherine, *Island Possessed,* 1969 (Reprint, Chicago: University of Chicago Press, 1994), 218.

35 Melville J. Herskovits to Katherine Dunham, 25 October 1935, Herskovits Papers.

36 Dunham, *Island Possessed,* 218.

37 Katherine Dunham to Melville J. Herskovits, 28 December 1935, Herskovits Papers.

38 Melville J. Herskovits to Katherine Dunham, 29 January 1936, Herskovits Papers. See also VèVè Clark's discussion of this exchange in "Performing the Memory of Difference in Afro-Caribbean Dance: Katherine Dunham's Choreography, 1938-87," in *History and Memory in African-American Culture,* 192–93.

39 Melville J. Herskovits to Katherine Dunham, 29 January 1936, Herskovits Papers. Note that Haitian Creole orthography was not officially standardized at this time. Today, "kanzo" would be the correct spelling of this initiation ritual, as Herskovits writes here.

40 He described his own methodological approach to his and Frances' research in Haiti thus: "In the field, the procedure followed in earlier investigations was continued; a house was found in the village where it was possible to settle down and quietly observe life as it drifted past the door" (Herskovits, *Life in a Haitian Valley,* 325.)

41 For example, in his letter to Dunham of 13 December 1935, Herskovits wrote: "If you go up to Mirebalais, give everyone my best regards. And if you go there, I wonder if you would do something for me? In the center of the place in front of the tribunal that is between the national palm trees is a tomb of the Duc de Mirebalais. I wonder if you would copy the inscription and send it to me? I don't know whether I told you or not, but I have changed my plans for this winter, since I was invited to prepare my Haitian manuscript for publication . . . I shall want to use this inscription, and would therefore greatly appreciate having it." (Herskovits Papers).

42 Herskovits, *Life in a Haitian Valley,* 326. The reference here is to the research of Bronislaw Malinowski in the Trobriand Islands of the Southwestern Pacific. Malinowski is closely identified with the development of "participant-observation" as an anthropological fieldwork methodology.

43 Herskovits, *Life in a Haitian Valley,* 327.

44 Katherine Dunham, *Dances of Haiti* (Los Angeles: University of California, Center for Afro-American Studies, 1983), 15.

45 This seems particularly significant in terms of reports of Herskovits' own alleged reluctance to support research by African Americans in Africa because he doubted their ability to be "objective" in studying African societies. Such allegations are particularly troubling given Herskovits' role as a "gatekeeper" for research funding in Africa and the African diaspora during the 1940s and 1950s. Faye Harrison and Ira Harrison note that "[b]y the 1960s Herskovits' attitude had clearly changed. Johnnetta Cole was able to conduct her dissertation research in Liberia. At this later juncture, the Ford Foundation helped provide institutionalized incentives and support for a black American presence among Africanists" (Harrison and Harrison, *African-American Pioneers in Anthropology,* 28, n.16). See also in that volume, Gwendolyn Mikell, "Feminism and Black Culture in the Ethnography of Zora Neale Hurston," 51–6, and Cheryl Mwaria, "The Continuing Dialogue: The Life and Work of Elliot Skinner as Exemplar of the African-American/African Dialectic," 274–92.

46 Erika Bourguignon, "Review of *Island Possessed*," *American Anthropologist* 72, 5, October 1970: 1132–3.

47 See Harrison and Harrison, *African-American Pioneers in Anthropology*, 19.

48 See, in particular, Dunham's memoir of her childhood, *A Touch of Innocence*, 1959 (Reprint, Chicago: University of Chicago Press, 1994).

49 See James Clifford, "Introduction: Partial Truths," in Clifford and Marcus (eds.), *Writing Culture: The Poetics and Politics of Ethnography*, 11.

50 Dunham, *Island Possessed*, 131.

51 Ibid., 105–6

52 Ibid., 228.

53 Ibid., 106.

dance and intertextuality:

theoretical reflections

naomi m. jackson

In 1985 dancer and anthropologist Cynthia Novack created a solo entitled *Artifacts (The Empire after Colonialism)*. In this work there were two sections. Part I, "Diorama," consisted of Novack conveying certain images taken from Agnes de Mille's *The Book of the Dance*, a pictorial history of dance from 1963 that attempted to cover Western and some "world" dance. In this section, Novack slowly shifted into and out of positions depicting such figures as a dancer on an Etruscan tomb, a European folk dancer, the image of the sculptured god Shiva, a lindy-hop dancer, Uday Shankar, Carlotta Grisi, and Nijinsky. In Part II, "Possession," Novack exploded into movement, improvising on each image based on the qualities suggested to her by the photographs.

Her activity accelerated until she ended by stopping and facing the audience in an open and challenging way. The piece, according to Novack, as discussed in the 1992 issue of *Women and Performance* devoted to feminist ethnography and performance, was intended as an implicit critique of de Mille's work. Novack argues that *The Book of the Dance* is an ethnocentric representation of non-Western dance that wrongly assumes that non-Western dance is a form of primitive dance occurring earlier on the evolutionary scale than European forms. By alluding to images from de Mille's book in *Artifacts* but mixing up the chronology and classification of the pictures, Novack hoped the implied hierarchy presented in the book would be subverted. She also believed that by conveying the images in an altered form she would present the ambiguity of her feelings about them —"their simultaneous evocations and reductions of dancing" from different times and places.[1]

Novack's work is characteristic of a trend in *some* postmodern choreography to consciously allude to other dancers, dances, and styles as a means of providing a commentary or critique on the nature of dance and how we experience it. The trend may be traced to choreographers of the

Judson Dance Theater in the 1960s. They challenged the supremacy of modern dance and ballet, usually by juxtaposing symbols of these traditional forms with awkward, mundane actions. A dancer wearing a tutu changed a car tire, for instance, or struck a balletic fifth position, said "Oh no!" and then fell slowly to the side.

More recently, choreographers such as Mark Morris, Stephen Petronio, and Twyla Tharp frequently make references in their works to such icons as Isadora Duncan, Martha Graham, and Nijinsky. This may be in order to parody older dance conventions, or to pay homage to them. Other times their work is seen as a way of self-consciously presenting the kind of multiple bodily references that postmodern dancers are said to carry within themselves, having been trained in a wide range of styles and taught to regard dance history as a storehouse of movement possibilities on which to draw.[2]

In our current high-tech "information" society, where cutting and pasting words, images, and behaviours is a large part of our daily experience, it seems inevitable that quotation and allusion should be so prominent in contemporary dance. The increased visibility of so-called intertextuality in art, however, is also closely connected to recent developments in literary criticism that have focused on, theorized, and popularized this aspect of making and looking at art. The claim by many authors is that while scholars have always been interested in tracing influences among artists through quotations and allusions, it was not until the term "intertextuality" was coined in the mid-sixties that people began to perceive the power of this concept not only for literature but for other art forms and popular culture.[3] This essay advocates its relevance for dance.

So, what *is* the meaning of "intertextuality"? At its most straightforward, the term refers to the quality of literary texts to quote or allude to another literary text, thereby setting up a relationship between the two works. Within the context of poststructuralist theory, the term focuses on the idea that no text is an untouched, unified whole, but the result of many "grafts" of other texts. These grafts need to be analyzed for where they lie comfortably together, or where their intersections create points of juncture and stress. Annette Levitt, in her introduction to *The Intertextuality of Joyce Cary's* The Horse's Mouth, describes well the way the term includes all the implicit as well as explicit references in a particular literary work; the social as well as artistic "texts" to which it alludes and with which it is intimately interconnected. She writes:

> Intertextual analysis is a critical approach which looks closely at a text . . . in the context of its worlds . . . suggested by allusion and direct reference in the text itself — worlds of art, music, politics, even other literary texts, which intersect with the work one is reading so that knowledge of the various texts in this interaction sheds light on all of them . . . In looking closely at a literary work, intertextual analysis notes the origins of its references, both literary and non-literary, words and events as well, and provides a map of these "intertexts," it reveals the interplay of issues enacted in these texts and the primary text, the dialogue between the primary text and its intertexts.[4]

Although intertextual studies have gained in popularity in literary criticism, they are also on the rise in other artistic fields. With the advent of Barthes and other French theorists, the notion of "text" has been applied to any semiological system, not only literature. There are now books that discuss intertextuality as it relates to art and architecture. A work edited by Janet Adshead-Lansdale has recently been published on intertextuality and dance (to which I contributed the chapter that is the precursor to these reflections). As Adshead notes, the appropriateness of a method of analysis based on intertextuality "can be seen in the way it opens up the discourse of 'art' to cultural practices more widely without encouraging simplistic cause-effect propositions."[5]

Most of the authors of these intertextual studies seem to pursue a dual purpose. On the one hand, they examine how and why a particular writer, artist, or choreographer uses certain references in his or her work. This is important because methods of allusion run the gamut, from the most explicit form of direct quotation to the least conscious referencing of a particular artwork or social practice. The reasons for allusion also vary considerably, from those who quote others as a way of validating their own ideas and providing an "authenticating authority," and those who quote in order to debate with, or satirically subvert, their opponent's opinion.

People also unconsciously, or consciously, splice together various traditions in the process of establishing their own identities.

The other purpose of intertextual studies is to discuss the implications of such an analysis for an interpretation of the meaning of the primary text. Here there exists a debate between diehard poststructuralists who would see intertextual analysis more as disrupting a work's unity and undermining meaning located in the text, and those who see the process as articulating a complex web of relations that actually enrich understanding and "emphasize the significance of these relations for the meaning of the individual text."[6] For instance, in the case of Cynthia Novack's *Artifacts*, described above, one person might argue that tracing the various images to *The Book of the Dance* leads to a better grasp of the dance's meaning, while another would argue that an ambiguous relation between the poses makes a cohesive interpretation impossible.

I tend toward the belief that intertextual analysis can provide a valuable means of seeing dances as webs of interrelations that may sometimes be at odds with one another, but nonetheless can be mapped out from the perspective of specific individuals living in particular communities, at particular time periods, themselves defined by multiple influences.[7] Given this assumption, I will briefly consider some of the more obvious ways in which dances might be looked at as intertextual "events," culminating in a more detailed look at the implicit nature of intertextuality in Sophie Maslow's *The Village I Knew* and what it suggests regarding the usefulness of such an approach in the field of choreographic analysis.

Beginning with what may be considered the most obvious form of intertextuality, quotation, it is interesting to note that unlike writers including phrases from other writers, choreographers rarely include whole phrases of movement from other choreographers' works in their dances as part of a broader choreographic "argument." Perhaps it is due to the emphasis in dance-making on the originality, uniqueness, and individuality of dance, especially in the modern dance tradition, or maybe because of a belief that such quotation would constitute stealing, but it hardly ever occurs in an explicit fashion.

Sally Banes recalls that Trisha Brown quoted an improvisation by Steve Paxton that she learned from video in one of her dances, but this seems to be a rather singular occurrence.[8] The only place where extensive quotation does occur is in the constantly reworked versions of the Romantic and Classical ballets, where steps from previous choreographers are noted only by knowledgeable viewers. In countless Sleeping Beauties and Swan Lakes one can often trace sequences of more authentic material spliced together with choreography by the current production's artistic director/choreographer. In this instance, an intertextual reading would be fascinating in examining how the various sections were indeed stuck together, and what this signifies for a particular interpretation of a work.

Much more prevalent, especially in contemporary American dance, are fleeting allusions to famous people's behaviour or to other dancers, which are often referenced, as stated earlier, as part of the choreographer's larger plan to critique or parody the past. In Petronio's solo #3 he splices together the gestures common to about seventeen people who are recognized cultural idols, such as Frank Sinatra, Judy Garland, and Ronald Reagan. His interest is in multi-layering images of these people in his body and playing them off each other in a seemingly critical commentary, as is suggested by the twisted, bodily distortions that result. Such dances as Morris' playful *Ten Suggestions,* in which Morris romps like an early modern dancer performing music visualizations, or Twyla Tharp's *Pergolesi,* where Baryshnikov makes rapid allusions to familiar ballet characters, are examples of the more humorous side of this practice. More extended parodies based on allusion can be seen in the performances of Les Ballets Trockaderos, where entire versions of familiar dances are enacted with a humorous twist, or in pieces like Morris' *Hard Nut,* which reconceives the nineteenth-century *Nutcracker* as a 1970s, disco, comic strip fantasy.

This latter case, in which the older musical score is maintained, but with new choreography and adjusted narrative, points to another form of intertextuality demonstrated in other attempts to reconceive nineteenth-century ballets. I am thinking here of Matthew Bourne's *Swan Lake,* or Mats Ek's *Giselle,* both of which make reference to prior dance texts not as a means of parody so much as to engage in a reflective manner with the earlier versions and suggest new interpretations of their subject matter. Critics are already examining what this multiple referencing means within today's society, but an extended intertextual analysis could enrich their efforts.

Another kind of intertextuality prevalent in dance might be termed "interdisciplinary intertextuality." This involves the inclusion of references to other art forms and popular culture within a piece. It may happen in dance when the performers actually enact a famous painting or text, for instance, da Vinci's *Last Supper,* or Martin Luther's "I Have a Dream" speech — both of which occur in Bill T. Jones' *Last Supper at Uncle Tom's Cabin/The Promised Land.* Or the *original* painting or reading of a text might be included through the incorporation of slides, film, video, or audio recordings.[9] Sometimes the resulting form is more like a montage, in which the references blend together to create a particular atmosphere, as in a Pina Bausch work.

John Henry in Singing Myself a Lullaby

Or they may be linked as part of an unfolding personal narrative, as in Ellen Bromberg's *Singing Myself a Lullaby,* based on the life of dancer/choreographer John Henry. In this piece, video by collaborator Douglas Rosenberg was used to allude to significant influences on Henry, such as actress Lauren Bacall, who represented the kind of glamorous performer he wanted to be. What was interesting in this piece is that the work was constructed especially around Henry's dying of AIDS. As his health faded, more and more video projection from prior performances was used to compensate for his inability to move, the intertextual references thereby becoming more pronounced and central as the environment became increasingly mediated. The result was an unsettling yet moving reversal of normal practice — the large, projected images of Henry gained a powerful presence in the theatre, while his own live body lost its resonance.

Since the 1980s, a fascination with blending cultural and stylistic influences in dance has led to another form of intertextuality based on fusing different sets of movement conventions and beliefs. Choreographers now blend ballet and Butoh, Cunningham technique with Bharata Natyam, and hip hop with modern dance. Fred Darsow, for instance, is a choreographer based in New York who, since the late 1980s, has experimented with fusing postmodern dance and flamenco. Or there is the American Ralph Lemon, who has recently explored combining African and postmodern dance. While Darsow tends to approach his work from a more formalist perspective that is interested in playing with movement vocabulary, choreographic structures, music, and costuming, Lemon has framed his intercultural research in a highly charged atmosphere marked by concerns regarding cultural appropriation, gender, and race.[10]

The recent boom in fusion work is often seen by the dance world as a means of embracing the "other," whether it be the lower class other (for example, combining street or social dancing with ballet or modern dance), or the cultural other (combining a non-Western form with a familiar dance style). Work in this vein is regarded as an attack on the so-called traditional Eurocentric (white, upper class, male) tradition in art. As part of its mission, fusion dance has also highlighted the intertextual nature of dance. Audiences are now encouraged to see that a performance combines different styles and cultural influences as part of a broader multicultural agenda that seeks to embrace and uphold difference.

What is misleading about contemporary trends in postmodern dance is that promoters and enthusiasts would make it seem as if it is only recently that dances have had this characteristic of intertextuality. What is important to realize is that this is far from being the case. It is possible to see the synthetic nature of all dance, not only that within the so-called postmodern idiom. Any dance or dance style, when considered closely, can be seen to be a complex network of references and associations.

If the above examples, then, are of more obvious ways that dances may be regarded as intertextual, I will now focus on the usefulness of regarding *all* dances as being open to intertextual analysis, especially those that seem to be seamless wholes, complete within themselves, and with no clear quotations. My example will come from American modern dance, because this style is frequently juxtaposed with postmodern dance as an example of a purist style, untouched by the kinds of stylistic and cultural fusions and associations of more recent years. Seeing it as marked by various intersecting influences suggests a revision of our perception of this style and reveals a strong continuity with contemporary trends that was not thought to exist before.

For the purposes of this paper, looking at Maslow's *The Village I Knew* from the perspective of intertextuality clarifies particular American Jewish and modern dance "texts" of the 1940s and 1950s and explores how they interacted with one another to create a new American Jewish identity and broaden the dominant modern dance narrative of the time.[11] *The Village I Knew* was premiered on 18 August 1950 at the Palmer Auditorium, Connecticut, New London, as part of the American Dance Festival (ADF). The piece was an expanded version of a dance titled *Festival,* which had been presented by the company at ADF the previous summer.[12] *The Village I Knew* was based on the stories of Sholom Aleichem, the paintings of Marc Chagall, and events of significance in Jewish lives drawn from ritual and oppression.[13]

Within the history of dance, *The Village I Knew* has often been treated as a charmingly competent work in the modern style. From its original performances in the early 1950s, through several revivals, critics have frequently interpreted the dance as a warm and tender depiction of Jewish life in Tsarist Russia, offering straightforward evaluations of what they consider a relatively simple piece. The work is enjoyed but considered lightweight beside the designated masterpieces of a choreographer such as Graham. The power of an intertextual reading of dance, in contrast, reveals the complexity of the work and the sometimes complementary and sometimes conflicting Jewish and modern dance texts in *The Village I Knew.*

After World War II, second- and third-generation American Jews were beginning, on a visible scale, to rediscover their Jewish "heritage" and to re-imagine and recreate their Jewish identity. *The Village I Knew* shows that this process was marked by two somewhat conflicting strands. First, there was a move to locate Jewishness in traditional Judaism and the religious community. In the dance, women cover their eyes and circle their arms as they perform the blessing over the candles in "Sabbath," while five men *daven* (a praying motion involving rocking back and forth) upstage. In another section, students appear engaged in study (this is mimed) of the great books of Judaism (the Torah and Talmud), during which they assume expressions of meditation, questioning, and insight.

At the same time, for Jews like Maslow, there was an interest in remaining true to contemporary American society and its support of individual expression and secular humanism. In the dance, this is marked by the presence of modern dance practices that simplified, stylized, and abstracted the material. The housewife character, for instance, moves barefoot in a stiff, doll-like way, performing some technical *développés* and turns, and gesturing with her hands in a simple, exaggerated way. In the dance, Maslow adhered to the theories of modern dance, which validate individuality, creativity, and universalism of communication, all of which were part of her training and exposure to people like John Martin and Martha Graham. The result was quintessential images of Jewishness that were uplifting, timeless, and spiritual, yet largely purified of any negative associations of the old world, immigrant life, or actual Orthodoxy.

An intertextual reading of *The Village I Knew* helps clarify the presence of these conflicting texts present in the dance. On one hand is a narrative of Jewishness tied to traditional beliefs and practices as defined by the religious community. On the other lie conventions of "contemporary American woman" and "dance as art" that move constructions of Jewish subjectivity toward individual freedom and away from ancient tenets. For the progressive Jewish viewer of the 1950s, the texts lay together relatively well, embodying a new form of Jewishness shaped by individuality, artistry, and female consciousness. For the more observant, traditional Jew, however, the texts were glaringly exposed as opposing entities unacceptable in their implications regarding the nature of Jewish identity, as can be seen by the negative response of various rabbis to the piece in the early 1950s.

An intertextual reading also sheds light on the way the coming together of Jewish and non-Jewish "texts" deeply affected the evolution of modern dance. During the 1940s and 1950s, modern dance in America fully matured and crystallized as a form distinct from ballet and social or revue dancing. Internally, however, debates lingered between the more art-for-art's-sake and activist dimensions of the form. Many involved in the promotion of modern dance followed John Martin in defining it as a largely apolitical, pure art characterized by universally expressive movement, best exemplified through the works of Graham and Humphrey.

At the same time, the progressive orientation of Jews like Maslow led to a continuing challenge to modern dance to recognize and embrace racial, gender, and ethnic diversity. Within this debate, Jewish forces in New York (in particular) played a central role in trying to re-frame modern dance as an expression of social and political consciousness and as a hybrid style with disparate ethnic and religious influences. This reorientation was attempted through patronage of African American, Hispanic, and Jewish artists at institutions such as the 92nd Street Young Men and Young Women's Hebrew Association (YM-YWHA) and through choreographic experiments that focused on minority experiences.

The challenge to the purist notion of modern dance is represented in *The Village I Knew* in numerous ways, including where it was premiered in New York, namely at the 92nd Street Y, and the casting choices. The dance included two African Americans, Ronne Aul and Donald McKayle. Aul played the "fiddler" and McKayle danced a variety of roles, including a student. McKayle later recalled his enjoyment and appreciation of working with Maslow as a beginning modern dancer. He also remembered an incident that underscored the way African American dancers, in particular, were faced with a mixed message elsewhere in the modern dance world. According to McKayle, John Martin had "said he didn't understand why there was a black boy in a Russian Jewish Village." McKayle continued:

> I wrote to him . . . and said well if he really was interested in why there was a black boy in a Russian Jewish village he should ask the

> question why there wasn't a Russian Jew in that whole Russian Jewish village because there wasn't one on stage . . . because that didn't seem to bother him only that there was one that was black.[14]

Martin responded, much to McKayle's disgust, that with McKayle present on stage, the work lacked "verisimilitude." Clearly, blacks were not allowed to represent others, despite the openness otherwise espoused by Martin.

Intertextuality conceives of dance as inherently and necessarily a cultural discourse that is inseparable from society. Individual dances are seen as specific textual arrangements that can be analyzed only in relation to the general cultural fabric of which they are part and which, in turn, is part of them. By tracing the intertangled textual strands in a choreographic work, a dance historian or critic can juxtapose methods and master narratives, showing how they shape subjectivity and either challenge or support culturally dominant views about gender, race, ethnicity, and the arts. Implicit in this approach is a critique of any notions of dance as "authentic" or "true" in a universal sense. Instead, what appears "natural" is shown to be a cultural construct of a particular group of people at a particular time and place in history. At the same time, the richness and complexity of the human condition is recognized and validated in a manner that can provide greater sensitivity to choreographic efforts.

notes

1 Cynthia Novack, "Artifacts (The Empire after Colonialism)," *Women and Performance: Feminist Ethnography and Performance,* 5, 2, 1992: 86.

2 Such a perspective is presented in Sally Banes' text for the film *Retracing Steps,* directed by Michael Blackwood.

3 Mikhail Bakhtin, Julia Kristeva, and Roland Barthes are often seen as the main theorists of the concept of intertextuality.

4 Annette Shandler Levitt, *The Intertextuality of Joyce Cary's* The Horse's Mouth (Lewiston: Edwin Mellen Press, 1993), 2.

5 J. Adshead-Lansdale, "The Concept of Intertextuality and Its Application in Dance Research," Society of Dance History Scholars (U.S.). Conference (22nd: 1999, Albuquerque, New Mexico). *Proceedings*, 111.

6 Udo J. Hebel, *Intertextuality, Allusion, and Quotation* (New York: Greenwood Press, 1989), 12.

7 The role of the viewer here is important and requires further elaboration outside the scope of this paper.

8 Communicated to author in phone discussion, December 1998.

9 It should be noted that each of these mediums has its own unique conventions, along with histories, which add to the complexity of any intertextual analysis.

10 See my paper "Intercultural Fusion in American Choreography with Specific Reference to the Work of Ralph Lemon and Fred Darsow," forthcoming in *Proceedings, Voice of the Artist: Synthesis in Contemporary Choreography*, Volgograd, Russia, 1999.

11 For a more in-depth look at this piece in relation to intertextuality, see my contribution "Jewishness and Modern Dance in Sophie Maslow's *The Village I Knew*," in J. Adshead-Lansdale (ed.), *Dancing Texts: Intertextuality in Interpretation* (London: Dance Books, 1999).

12 *Festival* was loosely based on Sholom Aleichem's story "The Merrymakers," about three men (Alek the Mechanic, Kopel the Brain, and Mendel the Tinman) who sing and dance through the village on *Simchas Torah*.

13 The seven sections were, briefly: "Sabbath," celebrating the coming of the Jewish Sabbath; "It's Good to Be an Orphan," showing an older woman giving some boots to a young girl; "A Point of Doctrine," about a verbose housewife who presents the details of her domestic difficulties so vividly that a rabbi faints; "Festival," a collective dance of celebration; "The Fiddler," showing a girl who is in love with a poor fiddler against her mother's wishes; "Why Is It Thus?" concerning three studious young men; and "Exodus," portraying Jewish villagers fleeing persecution. The version described here is based on a film of a performance of the piece at the Riverside Church, New York City, May 1977. Dance Collection, New York Public Library.

14 *Speaking of Dance: Donald McKayle, Conversations with Contemporary Masters of American Modern Dance*. Produced by American Dance Festival (ADF) Video, 1993. Producer/director: Douglas Rosenberg. Note that other members of the initial cast, as listed on the program for the January 1951, 92nd Street Y recital, included: Jane Dudley, William Bales, Alvin Beam, Rena Gluck, Billie Kirpich, Donald McKayle, Muriel Manings, Anneliese Widman, and David Wood.

bibliography

Adshead-Lansdale, J. "The Concept of Intertextuality and Its Application in Dance Research." Society of Dance History Scholars (U.S.) Conference (22nd: 1999, Albuquerque, New Mexico). *Proceedings*, 109–15.

— (ed.). *Dancing Texts: Intertextuality in Interpretation*. London: Dance Books, 1999.

Cancalon, Elaine D., and Antoine Spacagna (eds.). *Intertextuality in Literature and Film*. Gainesville: University of Florida Press, 1988.

Hebel, Udo J. *Intertextuality, Allusion, and Quotation.* New York: Greenwood Press, 1989.

Levitt, Annette Shandler. *The Intertextuality of Joyce Cary's* The Horse's Mouth. Lewiston: Edwin Mellen Press, 1993.

Novack, Cynthia. "Artifacts (The Empire after Colonialism)." *Women and Performance: Feminist Ethnography and Performance,* 5, 2, 1992: 82–9.

Plett, Heinrich F. (ed.). *Intertextuality.* New York: Walter de Gruyter, 1991.

dancing in the canadian wasteland:

a post-colonial reading of regionalism in the 1960s and 1970s

lisa doolittle and anne flynn

Dancers of the Young Canadians were required to stand in front of mirrors at home and practise their smiles. Their director, Randy Avery, wanted the dancers and singers to have "natural smiles," and one achieved that by practising. During the grandstand performances, there were "monitors" placed at the foot of the stage to check on the dancers' smiles. Anyone not smiling properly was encouraged to "turn on."

Why practise natural smiling? Because you want to show the world you are having a good time at the Greatest Outdoor Show on Earth, the Calgary Stampede, and to ask the international tourist crowd to join your fun, to invest in your down-home and upbeat vision.

Betty Poulsen, who was a dancer and then teacher/choreographer with the Young Canadians from 1970–8, remembers a proliferation of "Western" dances in the grandstand shows. The dancers had gun-handling classes just as they had ballet, jazz, and acrobatics. They learned combinations of twirl, catch, double-twirl, and reverse, and they had to practise until they were all in perfect unison. According to Betty, the dancers were fined if they dropped a gun or missed a holster. Precision was a marker of high quality.

Why guns? Because this is the Wild West and these are not registered guns, and we can control their every move.

• • •

Contemporary dancers at the University of Calgary were discouraged from smiling; theirs was a serious, solemn, very clean kind of dancing. Their director, Yoné Kvietys-Young, had to educate the reporter who shot this staged photograph: "The three non-smiling people on the cover are dancers. But they aren't about to break into a soft-shoe routine. They are contemporary dancers (and smiling is a no-no in contemporary dance)."[1]

Why refuse to smile? Because you are engaged in higher learning at the University of Calgary, where Plexiglas polygons and immobile lips proclaim your modernity, your depth of erudition, and you want your local audiences to climb with you to new heights of aesthetic elevation.

• • •

Yoné created a children's show at the University of Calgary Theatre. One work the company performers choreographed was *Junk Dances,* a suite of movement studies using tin cans, coat hangers, cardboard boxes, and rags. The procedure for choreographing was to use movement to transform these objects in funny and ingenious ways. It was an absurd, goofy, and super high-energy show, kind of like a *Waiting for Godot* for children.

Why junk? Because this is the wild and wacky West, the frontier where anything goes, where you can make something out of nothing, and we can show you how.

"What I really learned was how to stay in line, how to do spacing, how to be a very, very disciplined dancer for somebody. In other words, how to respond quickly, how to be a vehicle. I learned how to try to do what I was told to create a vision that was being asked for outside of itself." Betty Poulsen[2]

Why a vehicle, why outside itself? A vehicle so you can go somewhere else. Outside itself so you can strive for the best.

"Yoné introduced me to creating work of one's own and 'going out on a limb' to perform it, however personal, raw, or sometimes literally naked it was. She gave us the freedom and latitude to make work freely — instilling a kind of creative confidence that has remained with me since. I credit those years with . . . having the confidence to 'speak with my own voice.'"
Norma Wood[3]

Why raw, why your own voice? Raw so you can be true. Your own voice so you can say whatever you want.

Writing history is a way of recording lived events and a way of describing or reflecting back to ourselves, the lives we live, and how the way things were then appear to us now. In Alberta, some of the region's early history is still told by people who participated in its making, and this is especially true in the dance community. This paper is about two women artists who worked in radically different styles of performance dancing and who knew about each other but never met, working as they did in very separate spheres. They both still live in Calgary today. Margot McDermott choreographs and teaches young dancers and singers, and Yoné Kvietys-Young has been a visual artist for twenty-five years. In this essay, we dig around in their pasts to make a broader socio-political analysis of their choreography, teaching, and institutional affiliations.

The story of their parallel worlds, and how they came to live and work in Calgary, is the starting point for a more general discussion about two related themes. We will examine the multi-layered connotations of "regionalism," and how seemingly "natural" ideas about the artistic desolation of Canada's West affect dance artists in regions that are isolated from the mainstream of North American concert dance. Further, we intend to use the women's stories as a case study to reveal the broader cultural process of colonization. Post-colonial writers suggest that the body is always a site of resistance. "As well as being the site of knowledge-power, the body is thus a site of resistance, for it exerts a recalcitrance, and always entails the possibility of a counter-strategic reinscription, for it is capable of being self-marked, self-represented in alternative ways."[4] We wish to trace evidence of both colonization and resistance in two sets of dancing bodies that coexisted in Calgary during the 1960s and early 1970s.[5]

Yoné's high art and creative dance and Margot's popular/populist cowboy and spectacular dance were "neither the passive reflection nor the active initiator of cultural values, but rather they participated as one of an ensemble of practices that danced out the social and political choreography of (their) time."[6] Juxtaposing the two contrasting dance styles, choreographic approaches, and biographical moments helps clarify processes that may otherwise be obscured by the individual stories.

The bodies who are creating this text are Canadian dancing bodies who see the consequences of the choreographies that have gone before. We see dancing here and now that is either intensely "regional" or "global," those two categories remaining mutually exclusive and unequally rewarded. The dancing is mostly white and is deeply divided along class lines as high or low art, popular or serious. The dance world is gendered and the vast majority of women's lives in dance are limited by structures that define appropriate age, reproduction habits, and access to power. Dancing is rarely noticed in the story that is told about the region we live in and the lives we lead, despite its power to reveal and inform cultural values. How might those vanished dancing bodies illuminate new pathways for choreographing the future? And how might those dancing bodies enrich our understanding of the past?

To better understand the artistic and social climate in western Canada in the late 1960s and early 1970s that set the stage for the dance artists we will analyze, let us first take you to the early twentieth-century wasteland of Canada's North-West Territories.[7]

• • •

the wasteland — the breadbasket

Conventional historical and cultural considerations of Canada contain a recurring metaphor that casts the prairies of Canada, the "Northwest," as a wasteland. This is a particularly tenacious image that embraced social, political, and cultural spheres. Starting in the 1800s, this image, despite its inconsistency with humans' ability to adapt to varied geographical conditions, has continued to shape concepts and policies in Canada's West to this day. Paradoxically, the image of plenty — of resources ready for plundering — coexists comfortably in the urban colonial imagination with the image of emptiness.[8] The combination of the contradictory myth of the empty wasteland and the untouched Eden provided a necessary ideological framework for the spread of colonial agendas. Common to settler colonial societies, such as Australia, New Zealand, and Canada, the invaders/settlers took scant notice of indigenous inhabitants and had no compunction about appropriating all available resources for themselves. The eastern colonizers could exploit the wealth of the west without feeling any guilt, because, hey, it was actually empty in the first place!

This double-sided wasteland/breadbasket metaphor, which is so prominent in the discourse about this region, is unsurprisingly also the central metaphor used in descriptions of the cultural landscape of this region of Canada. The metaphor gets expressed, in the arts and culture discourse, in its horticultural form, apparently a form common to post-colonial societies,[9] who view their social and cultural practices as seminal rather than cooperative, additive, or transformational. For example, here is Max Wyman, dance critic, in his 1989 book *Dance Canada:*

> Across western Canada, the story of the development of modern dance is the story of a handful of visionaries, mostly women, who

> struggled against great odds to scratch into inhospitable ground enough of a space to give the seed of modernism a chance to grow.[10]

And here is Maxwell Bates, prominent Alberta painter in a 1948 article:

> The three Prairie Provinces have proved themselves even less sympathetic to the original artist than the rest of the country. Talent appears here as elsewhere; *but an unsympathetic environment* [emphasis added] acts as an emetic force on those who do not conform to its philistinism, or do not care to put up with its indifference. Calgary and Edmonton were unable to attract much outside talent. Nor did they seem very open to it. Faced with the task of reinventing the wheel on their own, they struggled, and got off to a slow start after the war. But the seeds that were scattered during those years germinated, and a few took root, and from them has grown the active artistic community that we know today.[11]

Simplistically equating cultural phenomena with geography is a rhetorical practice common to colonized capitalistic ideologies, a fiction that obscures individual or collective embodied agency. We will try to pinpoint its effects on the artistic endeavours of our subjects as they inevitably internalized the messages of the wasteland/breadbasket metaphor to cultivate, produce, and export dancers. With this metaphor, the so-called regional artist's relative insignificance can be blamed on the inhospitability of the land, which is not changeable, rather than on some socio-cultural cause, which might be effectively combatted and changed. With this metaphor we create an excuse for heroic martyrs to the cause of art rather than build a healthy environment for local artistic activity.

the colony — regions as colonies of the colony

Contemporary Canada faces the effects of colonization on two fronts. As a former colony of Britain, it carries the baggage of British political and cultural domination. Canada's geographic proximity to the much larger, and more globally powerful United States means that the threat of

American political and cultural colonization is both a historic and a daily reality. Further, both economically and culturally, Alberta was, and is still, seen by many to be in a colonized relationship with the rest of Canada.[12] The mid-century Canadian arts and culture environment mirrored this layered, post-colonial situation.

The persistent and constitutive myth of the wasteland/breadbasket landscape heroically and maternally cultivated by colonizers was internalized by its inhabitants, including artists. A post-colonial obsession with the creation of the "mother" culture (Britain) was evident in the establishment of richly endowed "national" performing arts entities like the Stratford Festival, which featured imported British artistic directors producing British plays, and the National Ballet, which featured imported British artistic directors producing European ballets.[13] The real threat to Canadian identity, however, was American, not British imperialism. An array of cultural fortifications (nationalism, regionalism, multiculturalism, and bilingualism) were created in the late 1960s and 1970s by the government of Prime Minister Pierre Elliot Trudeau to protect Canadian-ness in the face of our overbearing, if friendly, American neighbour.[14] "Regionalism" held promise for the development of unique artistic cultures across Canada, but it was conceived in a colonial mindset. In the end, the second-class status and perceptual isolation of Alberta as a region was reinforced.

Federally mandated regionalism tended to create what dramatist John Gray calls a "branch-plant mentality," merely duplicating big centres in the form of little centres.[15] Diversity in regional identity was contained within a notion of national unity. And as theatre historians have pointed out, the idea of nationalism was in fact a cipher for "that which reinforces and perpetuates the power of those whose status within the society is predicated on a particular sense of the political entity called the nation."[16] In other words, although creating regional identity through artistic endeavours was important, the most important of all, the "highest quality," were the "national" artistic endeavours that "coincidentally" were the most heavily funded through federal arts grants, and all took place in Toronto and Montréal. In 1970–1, the Canada Council dance section budget was just over $1 million. Ninety per cent of it was given to three ballet companies (Toronto, Montréal, and Winnipeg) and a whopping $900 was spent west of Winnipeg.[17] Nation/region binaries matched high/low or elite/ popular culture binaries and formed the unspoken premise in policies that shaped arts production. Thus, artistic work produced in the "national" centres tended to be seen as high and elite and therefore fundable, while artistic work produced in the "regions" tended to be seen as low or popular and therefore unworthy of federal support.

whiteness — WASP values

Current theories about "whiteness" give us tools for seeing the foreground that our case study occupies, and for noticing omissions, absences, and erasures that mark the development of dance in Canada's regions. Canada's special position as a settler colony meant that whiteness and white values were unproblematically integrated into the post-colonial psyche — unlike, say, South Africa or India, where the dynamics of post-colonialism or decolonization are quite different. The fact that it is more difficult for us to perceive the oppressiveness of these values does not diminish their force as an oppressive system. Whiteness and its associated WASP values were prime motors for colonizing activity in the west and included the Protestant settler values about hard work, creating something from nothing, and persisting, chin up, in the face of enormous odds.

WASP values also included the ideologies of "essentialist universalism," a knowledge frame that comprehends difference only within "totalizing schemas."[18] This is the frame of mind that, for instance, leads to the invisibility or attempted erasure of the First Peoples and their cultural practices. Such a position explains the unproblematic way that we accepted for so long the absence of funding for "ethnic" and Aboriginal dance. When we begin to deconstruct the privileged position of "whiteness," how it forms the basis for the apparently homogenous story of political and cultural development in the west, we can begin to see more plural realities. Our loss of a sense of absoluteness is more than compensated for by our gain of a sense of multiple possibilities. Such a plural perspective is important to our aim of constructing a healthy and inclusive dance community.

dance

Post-colonial theoretical frameworks help to begin to unravel some of the dynamics at work in the situation of Canadian dance in general, and Albertan dance in particular. Where Max Wyman sees two benign "streams of influence" or dual "threads that bind"[19] Canadian culture (an appropriately restraining metaphor), the post-colonial models reveal a more malignant dynamic. A privileging norm, European/American ballet and modern dance, becomes "a template for denial of the value of the peripheral, the marginal, the uncanonized."[20]

Wyman provides two blatant examples. In 1965, critic John Percival of the British publication *Dance and Dancers,* wrote about the Royal Winnipeg Ballet: "It is obvious that the company is to some extent confined by the need to cater to Canadian tastes, which on this showing, were not on the whole notably sophisticated or subtle." And worse, in the early sixties, the Canada Council, the federal arts-funding body, invited advice from a panel of American and British "experts," who suggested Canada should fund only one ballet company as the chosen instrument for dance.[21] (At that time, three major Canadian ballet companies toured internationally and regional companies were rapidly forming.) The council ultimately did not take their advice, but the legacy of imposing external standards of excellence continued to have broad and negative repercussions, at least in terms of the development of a distinct Canadian identity in dance.

Fifteen years later, the same nationalist mentality reared its head in a report from 1982, commissioned by the Department of Communications and CAPDO (Canadian Association of Professional Dance Organizations).[22] This study is a long apology for the centralization of resources for dance in large central Canadian cities. One of its main tenets is that all true dance artists are nurtured in urban environments, thus naturalizing the development of dance in these cities. This report appears to be a reaction against the dispersal of previously centralized money for the arts that was triggered during the Trudeau years.[23]

New federal support for regionalism in the performing arts did not, however, permit funding of popular art forms such as jazz or musical theatre dancing. One rationale offered was that these companies had large regional audiences, and even made money, which was not part of the high art colonizing agenda. Federal funding did not include non-balletic, contemporary dances made by regionals, partly because the central dance entities "needed" all the money to maintain "national" standards. It also did not include non-white art forms such as "ethnic" or Aboriginal dancing.

For dance in the Canadian regions to establish an independent voice, it would have to escape from, or radically rework, the assumptions that adhered to received languages such as ballet and modern dance, assumptions about "aesthetic and social values, the formal and historically limited constraints of genre, and the oppressive political and cultural assertion of metropolitan dominance, of centre over margin."[24] For dance in the Canadian regions to flourish, it would have to create ways for its diverse and pluralistic communities to converge. We will now map out features of regionalism as it was staged here thirty years ago, a co-production of geography and history, and introduce you to our two protagonists, who danced out their destinies, with and against the grain of their place and time.

yoné

Like the early settlers, Yoné Kvietys-Young came from the old country and ended up settling in the west. Born in Lithuania, she trained in European-style contemporary dance in the 1940s, eventually graduating from Rudolf von Laban's Hamburg school. Yoné toured Germany briefly as a soloist, dancing while the bombs fell. An ardent anti-Soviet and one of thousands of East Europeans sheltered in American refugee camps in post-war Germany, she entered Canada in 1948 with a wave of immigrants from Eastern Europe and the Baltic States. Yoné was a political and cultural refugee, what was known in the early fifties as a DP (displaced person). After a short stay in Toronto, where she danced with Boris Volkoff's ballet company, she moved to Montréal, where she founded a company and began a career as a modern dance teacher, performer, and choreographer. She moved back to Toronto, founded another company, and remained for around ten years. In regular trips from Montréal and Toronto to New

York, she was delighted to discover American modern dance and studied with Schurr, Erdman, Graham, Cunningham, Weidman, Limon, and others. Her dancing history thus combines two strands of the particularly Canadian experience of colonialism — Old World European culture and American contemporary culture. Yoné's life story, especially her experiences as a refugee from wartime Europe and from heated and politicized post-war artistic environments in Toronto, mean that she always wants to start from zero and not "build on the past." This impulse is basically the same as the modernist arts premise of rejecting all art "that came before" to create something "totally new." Turning one's back on the past was an aesthetic premise that defined the mid-century evolution of modern dance; it was also a feature of Yoné's life, where a succession of new environments led to the invention of new personas.

Canada's colonialist cultural policies in the 1950s favoured the development of ballet, rather than contemporary work. Yoné was essentially left to her own devices to find ways to support her artistic work, which she did by teaching in her own studios and in a wide variety of university, college, and arts academy settings. The nineteen years she spent performing, forming two companies, choreographing, and teaching, all without a scrap of government support, she describes as "tearing myself to pieces."[25] As long as Yoné stayed in central Canada, she was part of the action; some of her accomplishments in eastern Canada have been officially recorded.[26]

When Yoné married and moved to Calgary in 1966, she began to disappear. Ironically, that year the Canada Council awarded its first-ever subsidy to a modern dance troupe (Montréal's Le Groupe de la Place Royale). In that same year, Brian Macdonald's landmark first full-length all-Canadian ballet, *Rose Latulippe* (a French Canadian girl dances with the devil), premiered at the prestigious Stratford Festival in Ontario, to mixed reviews.[27] It was not until the inception of the Dance in Canada Association in the early 1970s that dancers and choreographers in Canada began to form any clear idea of what was happening in their art form in other parts of the country.[28] So when Yoné moved to Calgary, she knew she would be cut off. She was pragmatic about it and says she had no intention of maintaining a career in dance.

When Yoné arrived, Calgary had a budding downtown performing arts community — the first professional theatre company was Theatre Calgary, founded in 1968. At the University of Calgary's Department of Drama, the young faculty (a largely American and British corps, with a Canadian department head) had experimental ideas and was enjoying a new theatre building, establishing new ways of teaching drama, and keeping up with new trends in the field. Their 1969 Greek tragedy, *The House of Atreus,* used Grotowski vocal techniques and the chorus was clothed in cement. Victor Mitchell, head of the department, invited Yoné to teach movement there. The department's strong connection to ideas emerging in Eastern Europe seems, in retrospect, a perfect fit with Yoné's ethnic and artistic background.

What did Yoné do in this new setting? She "settled" it, artistically speaking — she taught, choreographed, and created companies. She imported her American mentors and their ideas to cultivate her new students. For instance, she brought Charles Weidman from New York to the University of Calgary for a week-long residency and performances. She read to her students about the latest American dance trends — they knew about Twyla Tharp, Steve Paxton, and Anna Halprin. University of Calgary calendar records show that she began to set up credit courses in contemporary dance and creative dance for children, and that by the time she left the university in the early 1970s, the skeleton of a dance program was in place. In the process of colonizing this virgin academic territory, something else happened. Let's take a closer look at how she adapted her imported ideas about the dancing body and its meaning to this region, and at how the forces of regionalism acted on and through her work and the bodies that danced for her.

To this end, let us recreate for you her approach to training bodies for dance. Warm-ups were extremely disciplined and movement had to be scrupulously honest: no macaroni, not artificial, not like ballet. Former student Margaret Dragu remembers, "No narrative. Very clean. Solemn. Rarely even a cupped hand — usually hand/fingers glued together, shooting out of the arm like well-made arrows. Bare flexed feet, rarely a point. Square shoulders and hips, almost heavy."[29] Yet Norma Wood remembers, "Because I didn't fixate on technique, I was able to 'move from within' in a way unfamiliar to me . . . the work was very organic, and connected to the natural body — much of the work came from natural rhythms."[30] Yoné's dancing students experienced weightedness, solemnity, clean lines. The bodies also experienced internal energy, natural rhythms, breathing, and freedom. They were embodying the classic concepts of European modern dance of the 1940s and 1950s, where becoming a "transcendent" dance artist meant first subjugating oneself to a kind of modern dance calisthenics, which would make one free to express one's inner feelings. They were also embodying a pervasive and paradoxical 1970s ethos, where the Space Age faced off against Flower Power. Feats of technological mastery, coming out of rigorous discipline and scientific exploration, coexisted with strong impulses toward natural self-expression, achieved through freedom from inhibitions and obsolete social structures.

In Calgary, Yoné's teaching fluctuated between an insistence on precision and disciplined dance technique and an increasing emphasis on choreographic inspiration and creativity. Over time, the technique part of class shrunk until students spent most of their time doing explorations and improvisations or studies. For whatever combination of reasons (the improvisation-based legacy of Laban, the university environment, which at that time precluded commitment to professional dance training, Yoné's personal journey away from the dance profession), Yoné's work went beyond cultural colonization. A colonizer does not improvise. As instigator, editor, and mentor, Yoné's finest work was to create creators. "The dancers must see themselves not only as instruments, but as people who are able to create . . . In the process of solving problems, students learn to think and to work creatively."[31]

Of course, when we move out of the studio and onto the stage to look at the choreography she and her students danced, the colonial sources for her work are obvious. Her dances carry the stamp of American modern dance trends: Nikolais-like dances of stretchy shapes made by dancers in a bag, Hanya Holm/Nikolais-like concern with space, and a parodic approach to American consumerist pop culture, with Weidman-like wry humour and mime-like skits. German expressionist dance motifs make their appearance in splayed hands, flexed feet, and dramatically dark evocations of death and illness. Sometimes all of these influences appeared in a single production. But when her students danced these dances, created by themselves, they believed they were making something completely new. As they rejected ballet, symmetrical formations, and macaroni, they thought they were striking out on their own. Reviewers described the work thus: "One has the impression . . . that Miss [*sic*] Kvietys-Young inspires her students rather than directs them. Their dances are not a discipline imposed on their bodies, but rather spontaneous fun that springs from inside them."[32] Critics were perhaps surprised to find stimulating and intellectually up-to-date content in, technically, rather amateur dancers: The interest lay in "dances themselves, the ideas behind them."[33] They called them "unusual and worthwhile."[34]

During 1970 and 1971, Yoné's company, composed of university students and a trio of high school students, created two full-length adult productions and a children's production and performed in numerous off-campus community venues. It is important to note that while unnoticed nationally, this sudden quantity of high-art dance activity was well attended. The university's 550-seat theatre, where Yoné's group performed, attracted a cultivated local audience, the intellectual and artistic elite of Calgary. As Alberta historian Howard Palmer remarks, "In the 1970s (because of foreign energy-oil-investment) Alberta had one of the best educated and most affluent populations in the country."[35] There were big, appreciative, educated audiences for this experimental dance work — right in the middle of the wasteland.

Outside the university structure, but using many of the dancers she trained there, Yoné led three years of creative dance summer projects, employing up to ten dancers and musicians for four-month periods. This level of "community outreach" and employment for local student dancers was unprecedented, and employment opportunities of this scope and independence for young local dancers to this day remain a rarity. Over three summers, Yoné received federal Opportunities for Youth (OFY) grants. OFY grants were awarded according to the inventiveness of the projects and the financial need of the individuals involved. These funds, then, were free of the peer-jurying system of the Canada Council that awarded arts grants ostensibly on the basis of "artistic merit," a system that tended to support existing central Canadian work, because it was largely judged by a central Canadian peer group. The summer projects, directed and run by the dancers, gave participants confidence and a degree of professional responsibility, as well as training in self-management. It led directly to the formation of a local experimental dance collective, Co-Motion (1977–81), and was the foundation for many independent careers.

Yoné was a catalyst. Her focus on individualistic expression and the search for the new may derive from the heritage of iconoclasm in modern dance, but she transcended imitation to reread and rewrite her inherited dance aesthetic. Her students did not perpetuate a style, but dispersed to influence both artistic margins and mainstream in Canada and elsewhere. One student from Toronto, David Earle, went on to found part of the modern dance "establishment" — the Toronto Dance Theatre. A Calgary student, Karen Greenhough, became a successful choreographer and teacher at the Laban Centre and later at The Place in London, England. Another, Margaret Dragu, is one of Canada's more eclectic and notorious performance artists. Yoné gave them confidence in their individuality and they took it and ran.

Yoné never spoke openly about her personal history and gave no coherent tracing of her professional experiences. She has become a successful visual artist and declares minimal interest in her own "glorious past."[36] She insists on being remembered as a dual-career person. Her lack of interest in the past is startling in a field where personal martyrdom to the grand cause of Dance is prized. The myth of blazing forth as individual shining beacons can take its toll. It can also get in the way of the development of strong communities.

Yoné's most enduring legacy is the continuing presence of modern dance in the Faculty of Fine Arts at the University of Calgary, but one completely disconnected from its past. When she left the university, the Department of Drama, on her advice, hired a young British immigrant who studied at The Place, Britain's "branch plant" of the Graham school in New York. A new colonizing agenda was begun. I found no record of Yoné's work in the University of Calgary Fine Arts archives, and no mention anywhere of her work after leaving the eastern "centre" for the western "margin" of Canadian cultural life. As recently as 1989, some twenty years after her arrival, a local modern dance group, Dancers' Studio West (immigrants from London, England, via Toronto), was described yet again as breaking new ground for modern dance in Calgary's dance desert. Anne Georg commented, "In 1979 the dance community was still in its infancy with a few independents working in whatever space they could find."[37] The metaphor still holds. The "unusual and worthwhile" dance had disappeared.

margot

An entirely different picture existed outside of the university in a dance community that is characterized by continuity and connections, family and tradition. This is a community where mothers teach daughters, aunts teach nieces, and sisters operate studios together. There are no professional companies, but the choreography and training strives to achieve professional standards, of which the community is keenly aware. This dance community lives in a Calgary whose economic climate is characterized by cycles of boom and bust and whose inhabitants ride these cycles out with a spirit of urban boosterism. Historian Alan Artibise wrote, "To prairie townsmen, not to be a booster — not to be part of the team — showed both a lack of community spirit and a lack of business sense."[38] In 1965, Calgary was home to 965 head offices of mostly American companies involved in the petroleum and natural gas industry, which brought enormous wealth to the city as well as a dramatic increase in population. Calgary, much like the American West, has always represented itself as a place of limitless opportunity for anyone with the drive to create something. Such a representation partners well with a white, WASP ideology that values growth and individual initiative.

Margot Gooder was born in Calgary in 1943 and began studying ballet and Highland dance at age seven with Jean Murdoch Simpson, the sister of Alice Murdoch Adams, who opened one of Calgary's first dance studios in 1927. Margot completed her Royal Academy of Dancing ballet exams with Sybil Rogers, who had been recruited from England to teach at Jean's studio. Given Canada's position as a colony of England, it is not surprising that if a studio was going to offer "serious" ballet training, an examiner from England was essential. Like other dedicated ballet students of her generation, Margot spent her summers studying at The Banff School of Fine Arts (founded in the 1930s), the prestigious Canadian institution located in Banff National Park.[39]

In 1946, Margot won a scholarship to study at the Royal Winnipeg Ballet School and at age thirteen she moved to Winnipeg on her own. She returned to Calgary to finish grade 12, by which time she had decided that her future in dance would be as a teacher and choreographer. After high school, Margot spent a year studying ballet in England, and by age nineteen was back in Calgary to direct the Calgary Ballet Corps, which was affiliated with the Calgary Allied Arts Centre. A 1963 news article reported that her goal was to stay in Calgary and "help get the city on its feet in ballet."[40] Margot spent many summers studying either in New York or England, a tradition she adopted from her first dance teacher and her teacher's teacher. These periods of professional development would last for months. From the 1920s, local dancers had been travelling to larger centres to stay current and bring back the newest styles to the region; Margot had learned this lesson well, and it seemed like the most natural and obvious thing for a dedicated dance teacher to do.

During the 1960s, Margot operated a studio, choreographed for ballet recitals, and steadily became more involved in musical theatre and jazz. While she identifies most strongly with ballet and will tell you that ballet is really her first love, her studies in jazz with Luigi and Matt Maddox in New York, and with Eva von Gencsy at the Banff School, meant that she was also in great demand in the burgeoning musical theatre community. In addition to her work in musical theatre, she choreographed weekly "numbers" for a local television jazz show for about a year. As well, she worked with dancers from her studio to create dances that were performed at a local "underground" jazz music club. She would set some movement material for the group based on the score she received from the musicians, and then each dancer would improvise a solo to mirror the musicians.

Then, in 1965, Margot's career changed significantly when she became involved in the creation of what became a totally unique performing group in the country, the Young Canadians of the Calgary Stampede.

She worked as a choreographer with the newly hired producer/director of the grandstand show, Randy Avery, who was from a Chicago family of vaudeville performers. The Young Canadians would become a Calgary institution. Gone were the Calgary Ballet Corps and the television shows. Gone were the underground jazz club improvisations, and gone was her own business. She went from independent artist and businesswoman to employee of a large organization run almost exclusively by men. Not just men, but prairie businessmen who could spot a good deal when they saw one, and Margot McDermott was not just a good deal, she was a great deal.

The Young Canadians is an amateur performing group whose prime function is to perform at the annual grandstand show of the Calgary Exhibition and Stampede, the largest outdoor rodeo in the world, which dates back to 1912. The decision to create the Young Canadians represented a significant shift in thinking by the Stampede board of directors. Rather than hiring performers from elsewhere, the board was going to invest in developing local dancers and singers. Even more noteworthy was the decision to hire a local person to undertake this training. Although such a move might have been driven by entirely pragmatic rather than ideological considerations, it was an act of resistance to the assumption that Calgary was not capable of producing performers who could hold their own on an enormous stage in front of a large international audience. There were already very skilled young dancers and singers around town, so Margot would provide them with even more training and send them out into the footlights. They would do their best and strive for a high standard of achievement because they had already internalized the message that says if you do well locally, you may get noticed and be able to leave for larger centres, where the "real" work is going on. Although significant external influences continued to shape the choreography of the grandstand show itself and the Young Canadians group as a whole, the creation of an infrastructure for the long-range training of dancers by local teachers was a bold move that transcended the colonial status of Alberta. Especially noteworthy is the fact that the group chose the name Young *Canadians,* not Young Calgarians, which is who they were. The name claimed national status for the group, alongside the National Ballet of Canada and Les Grands Ballets Canadians, which was perhaps their boldest move.

According to Margot, the Young Canadians was originally modelled after the American group Up with People. It's easy to see why the Stampede board, with its mandate to promote Calgary to the world, would be attracted to a model that included young, fresh-faced men and women representing wholesome values. Calgary had lots of fresh-faced young people, and surely someone could teach twenty-four of them how to dance? The group would have a relatively uniform look, with girls maintaining weight limits and wearing their hair long. In addition to the annual grandstand show, the group would also tour and be expected to serve as ambassadors for Calgary. Betty Poulsen recalls that they had very strict rules to follow during road trips and lived with the threat of being sent home if they were caught breaking rules.

Ten years into its development, the Young Canadians group was well known. The plan was working. In a review by *Calgary Herald* critic Jamie Portman, he defended his criticism of a Young Canadian production with this introduction:

> If you're looking for sacred cows, you need look no further than the Young Canadians of the Calgary Stampede. Utter even the mildest criticism of this group and you incur the wrath of a fanatically loyal mob of admirers. They will tell you that you are disloyal and unpatriotic to Calgary, and that you deserve to be reported to the Society for the Prevention of Cruelty to Children. They will remind you that the Young Canadians are an institution and that their reputation both nationally and internationally has given new lustre to Calgary — all of which is meant to suggest that it is a vile act of anarchy to knock an institution.[41]

The WASP value of creating something out of nothing through hard work and dedication is obvious in the spirit of the group. Acceptance into the group was and continues to be by audition, which gives its members a sense of accomplishment before they even start in the program. Once accepted, the Young Canadians receive all their training for free. Considering that many of its members participate for a number of years, this represents a significant financial investment on the part of the Stampede board to produce artistic workers. Parents also get a huge financial break when their dance-passionate children are accepted into the Young Canadians. In other words, this group was guaranteed to be successful because it had something for everyone. Dancers got excellent training and could perform, the Stampede board was investing in a long-term project rather than paying short-term salaries to people who would spend their money elsewhere, parents saved money, and Calgary's citizens could share in the civic pride that came when international audiences were dazzled by such a high quality of production and performers.

Talking about her initial reaction to the invitation by the Stampede board to become the choreographer and director of dance training, Margot said in a 1971 news article, "I wasn't really too keen about the idea at first because I was going to New York to study modern dancing and jazz. But when the Stampede board offered money, I had second thoughts. I'd never been paid for my work before!"[42] Before this, Margot had produced most of her choreography for free. The ballets, the jazz pieces, the musical theatre productions, free. Totally free labour in an endeavour that is exceptionally labour intensive. No wonder she took the job.

Margot accepted the task of preparing these dancers for the requirements of the choreography they would be performing. The study of ballet was the foundation of the program and was supplemented by classes such as jazz, acrobatics, ethnic, and, yes, gun handling. The high art of ballet was juxtaposed with the popular entertainment of jazz and acrobatics, all at once alive and interacting within the bodies of these dancers. They knew how to shape their bodies and attitudes in a ballet class, and they knew how to shape themselves for cancans. Choreographically, the Young Canadians dancers experienced a wide range of dance styles. Betty remembers a belly dance, an acrobatic novelty dance with canes, a Charleston to "Ma, They're Making Eyes at Me," and a cancan kick-line, to name a few. They also performed soft-shoe pieces, tap dances, and lyrical dances. The grandstand show was structured like a variety show, with the singers, dancers, and headliners weaving in and out. Betty says that the singers were really the top bill and the dancers were used more as "fillers." As she says, "kick line and leave." Margot fought for the dancers to have more autonomy, and over the years the show included larger dance sections. Betty says that the time they spent training was totally disproportionate to the amount of actual performing they did, but what Betty didn't know as a young dancer was that Margot was providing her with an intensive program of study in professional theatre dance. They were also embodying the beginnings of the globalization of consumer culture — bodies for hire that could work anywhere in the world.

Despite Randy's disapproval, Margot made certain the dancers took their British Royal Academy of Dancing exams, which introduced them to the idea of working toward an outside standard. Deferring to the wisdom of the motherland is part of the colony's expected behaviour and, in the case of ballet, the deferral seems particularly "natural." Ballet is associated with respectability and high culture and Margot made certain that no matter how many cancans or Charlestons Randy threw at her to choreograph, the dancers would respect themselves and be respected by others because they could do ballet, too.

Her students remember her as being very strict and instilling in them a sense of continually striving to attain greater skill and refinement. Betty says that the dancers all wanted to please Margot and they did that by being "good little girls." She also says they simultaneously loved and feared her. Her former dancers all said that discipline is what they really learned from Margot. She required them to stay poised in class, in rehearsals, and in performances, and expected them to work to a professional standard. These were dancers you could take anywhere.

In addition to the annual grandstand show, the dancers also performed in musical theatre productions. The Young Canadians Dinner Theatre produced shows such as *Hello Dolly, The Music Man, Damn Yankees,* and a show written by Randy about the history of the Stampede called *Big Guy.* According to Betty, Randy invited producers from New York to come and see it. As well, Margot produced an annual spring show that was just for the dancers. No singers, no Randy, no outdoor stage, no one eating dinner, just undiluted dance. Margot invited guest choreographers, she choreographed, and the dancers choreographed. The show took place at the Kinsmen Centre. Margot says that this show was the most satisfying artistically. It was where she felt able to experiment as a choreographer, rather than having to create dances that were small sections of someone else's vision, which she did for the other shows.

Arguments over artistic choices were common between Randy and Margot. Betty says that Margot was always sticking up for the dancers.

Margot remembers storming out of the studio on occasion. The arguing was perhaps inevitable. Randy had one job to fulfill in producing an enormous outdoor entertainment spectacle year after year for international audiences attending the rodeo. Margot's job, as she chose to shape it, was to maintain the same training and aesthetic standards she had applied in her own studio and not to be completely engulfed by the annual product of the grandstand show.

The Young Canadians helped create many careers in dance, and the investment on the part of the Stampede board has been paying off for a long time. Many former Young Canadians work in the commercial world of musical theatre and music video, and Margot speaks with great pride about their accomplishments. These dancers generally move away from Calgary for greater work opportunities, but there are a number of former Young Canadians who have made significant contributions to Calgary's current dance community. Vicki Adams Willis, co founder of a very successful Calgary jazz dance company called Decidedly Jazz Danceworks, is the daughter of Alice Murdoch Adams and the niece of Jean Murdoch Simpson, Margot's first ballet teacher. Vicki was a member of the Young Canadians and later a teacher in the program.

A short diversion into Vicki's story helps us see the continuity in evidence in this community, and the way that indigenous dance, as it has been made indigenous by the settlers, is viewed nationally. Founded in 1983, Decidedly Jazz Danceworks performs in concert settings and is dedicated to preserving the jazz dance tradition. Although the company receives enormous support locally and throughout the Canadian northwest, it has less national recognition. The Canada Council would not consider its application until 1993 because its policy had been to fund only ballet and experimental dance, and it took another six years of applying to the Council before the company actually received funding. The group has only been invited to perform on less prestigious outdoor stages at the biennial showcase for Canadian dance talent, the Canada Dance Festival in Ottawa. It appears that what is mainstream in the region is marginal by national standards.

Let's step back now from these close-ups on two lives. We have selected bits and pieces of these life stories, rather than attempting a cohesive narrative. Our point here is not to add the story of these two lives to the shelf full of trophy tales of Canada's dance heroes. Canada's dance history is a barely sketched-out story at this point, and much of it is told through passionate and valuable biographies of important dance artists. But we want to offer these two pieces of the puzzle together, as connected evidence of the history of arts development in Canada, the history of the Canadian West, and the history of women's, and women artists', lives.

The story of Yoné's disappearance from the historical record of dance in Canada as she moves west illuminates a documentation process where erasure or forgetting characterizes the regional in contrast to inscription and remembrance that characterizes the central. Margot's story shows how work that is marked "regional" or "popular" is easily ignored by the national arts establishment, which orients itself toward urban colonial ideals of high art.

Clearly, both Margot and Yoné fully accepted the notion that the standard of excellence resided in large metropolitan centres, and they sought to do their best within that context. Both enjoyed living in Calgary and making dances there. They didn't feel oppressively colonized at all. Here is Yoné: "I didn't expect to find anything in Calgary. Nothing was going on. Oh yes, there were a couple of old ballet teachers doing some miserable things. But if I expected New York, it would be ridiculous."[43] Still, the colonial framework profoundly affected their work and lives. For example, the above remark demonstrates a debilitating lack of communication between, and mutual support for, local dance communities, brought on by close identification to sources outside the community. Just as colonizing peoples maintain a fiction of being the first to discover new territory, and thus ignore or erase existing populations and ways of living, so too the fiction that immigrating dance pioneers are "groundbreakers" renders their forerunners, and even local colleagues, invisible and illegitimate. The colonial template limits perceptions, too. Images of the work of these two Calgary choreographers still make us giggle at its naïveté or cringe at its derivativeness. The sincerity of the undertaking is disproportionate to the potential for achievement. But we submit that despite being "derivative" or "charming," this regional work must be taken more seriously by dance historians. To dismiss it is wrong for many reasons, ranging from the scholarly to the ethical. Even in this brief study, we have detected cross-national parallels in regional dance history that deserve further comparative investigation. Cross-genre or cross-cultural studies could produce new understanding that may reduce isolation and expose paths we could follow for a healthier dance community.

Study of this kind of work could offer insights into the broader picture of social history in Canada. The above juxtaposition of matching fragments from Yoné's and Margot's disparate lives reveals some surprising consistencies and similarities that signal convergences of private lives around prevailing social/cultural beliefs. For instance, each of our narratives ends with images of students venturing off on their own, an inspired bevy of dance entrepreneurs. Like maverick regional businesspeople, they downsize and invent new paths to success that confound centrist old-money dogma. Calgary — what an unlikely spot for a burgeoning new university dance degree program! And how can it be that an American-inflected, global groove jazz dance ensemble remains such an anomalously successful and deeply loved feature in the Calgary cultural landscape? Surely this tells us about possible forms of resistance to, or at least appropriation of, federal regionalization agendas.

As we look for more correspondences, we find that the privilege of whiteness contributes to success in both stories, reflecting ongoing inequities of race and class in the arts, as in other areas of social endeavour. From Margot's Young Canadians to Decidedly Jazz Danceworks, and from Yoné's creative dance companies to the University of Calgary dance program, participation remains largely white and upper middle class, inaccessible to many, despite earnest but still ineffective attempts at racial and class inclusiveness. Although it seems we could hardly have chosen two more different personalities than Margot and Yoné, some similarities in the trajectory of their personal lives (which we have chosen not to discuss here) are startling.[44] These two remarkable women, with all their accomplishments, remain part of a cultural choreography that limits women who attempt both careers and families, perhaps even more so in the body-bound field of dance.

Above all, we need to remember that the myths that become structures that choreograph our activities — such as "regionalism," high versus low culture, the privilege of whiteness, and the inequities of how society structures gender roles — need constant re-examination, and that we can and must work to choreograph history as we wish to dance it.

postscript: anne flynn

We bring our own agenda to all our tasks. I write about someone else's work thinking that I am preserving it, but I am just making room for myself and my own memories, my own history. My father taught me how to tap dance in the kitchen of our Brooklyn house, where his family had lived since 1921. I stood in lines that wrapped around entire city streets, wearing wool and leather leggings waiting to get in to see the 11 A.M. performance of the Rockettes Christmas show at Radio City Music Hall. I saw the film *West Side Story* there when I was six. Miss Renee's Dance Studio was less than twenty-five metres from my childhood home, and we idolized her son Mark, who was a Broadway gypsy. I danced on my father's shoes every Sunday night to the music of Lawrence Welk, and I co-produced afternoon-long song and dance productions in our backyard. We hung a curtain from fence to fence, we had seating, we had a slate stage area, we served refreshments, and we charged admission. I clearly remember our version of *Around the World in Eighty Days* and our Beatles medley lip sync.

Then, in college, I discovered modern dance and I erased these earlier experiences from public versions of my dance history. In 1977, I performed with Richard Bull's company in the Larry Richardson studio on East 14th Street in Manhattan. My family would finally get to see me dance. I wasn't in several of the pieces on the program, so I could watch my family watching the dances. My dad and brothers sat with their programs covering their faces because they were laughing so hard and my heart sank that I would have to admit a connection to these obviously uneducated dance viewers. Didn't they see the great art unfolding before them? What I could never bear to even think until now was that their hearts sank too because after four years in a university dance program, this was what I had learned. Hell, there was no music, or only some saxophonist doing circular breathing improvisations. There were no lines, no kicks, no tapping, no rhythm, and no pretty costumes. There was no dancing really, just a bunch of us moving around.

Now my father has died and so has Richard Bull. Maybe they're having a great talk about dance improvisation, or maybe Richard's got a pot on his head learning the soft-shoe we used to call the "Mickey Rooney." Whatever they're up to, they've left me here to keep dancing. And so here I sit, writing about others and, in the end, reclaiming my own memories of my dancing body.

postscript: lisa doolittle

I began this project to choreograph my own history because I couldn't find it anywhere else. I want to talk back, move back. My own dancing life is a succession of exits and returns. I left Yoné's company in Calgary for the "real" thing — dancing in New York. Then back, to found a dance collective, and forth again to Europe, then back again.

As I move back in, I need to know better how to make the next move. It is a dance of diaspora, division, and disappearance. And every move I make is shaped by that earlier dance, thirty years old now, my muscles and bones know the score — the same old steps, here and now. Even though I have little contact with my teachers and mentors, even when I improvise, the old patterns continue to emerge. The patterns they gave me, and the ones that didn't have to be given because I was, and they were, already part of a bigger choreography.

By the way, where were they, those nurturing mentors and passionate teachers who first gave me courage and could have (if only they had been there!) whispered "Come on, you can do it" as I peered out from my outpost onto that huge main stage? Where were the modern dance studios, the university programs, the theatres and galleries, the critics, the magazines, the film documentaries, the scholarly analyses, the festivals, the presenters, the dancing colleagues? My dance waited in the wings for its walk-on role, while the grand sweep of dance history was happening out there on centre stage. I stood on the sidelines. The stars entered and exited. I studiously and respectfully absorbed trends and propped up both aging and shiny new dance ideologies — those impeccable *entrechats!* those ultracool urban combat boots! Wow, what a great show!

Can I now take that step forward? Can I own my own dancing? Can I walk past the middle class of modern dance and into a more polyglot dance party? I look ahead, but I'm not sure yet because behind me is a void. I'm floating, not a leg to stand on. I need to ground myself, get back, move back and take another look at that old territory. The North-West Territories.

acknowledgement

We are indebted to Susan Leigh Foster for providing comments on early stages of this paper that led to a radical redirection of our analysis. We also thank Susan Bennett and Ches Skinner for alerting us to important work on post-colonial theories applied in the context of Canadian theatre history. Thanks also to Eliane Silverman for her ongoing mentoring and encouragement and for the specific comments and useful suggestions she made after reading several drafts of this paper.

notes

1 Caption for cover photo, *Calgary Herald Magazine,* 6 February 1970. Cover article by Allan Connery, 2.

2 Interview with B. Poulsen, December 1998.

3 Correspondence with Norma Wood (dancer in Yoné Kvietys-Young's university company 1969–71), November 1998.

4 Elisabeth Grosz, 1990. Quoted in Helen Gilbert and Joanne Tompkins (eds.), *Post-Colonial Drama* (London: Routledge, 1996), 204.

5 Our approach draws on the notion of corporeality, which "conceptualize[s] dance as a cultural practice, and not as a formal endeavour that must be situated *within* culture" (Susan Leigh Foster, *Choreography and Narrative: Ballet's Staging of Story and Desire* [Bloomington: Indiana State University Press, 1996], 263). For other variously elaborated examples of this approach, see Susan Leigh Foster's introduction to *Corporealities* and her essay "Choreographing History" from *Choreographing History,* as well as Mark Franko's *Dance as Text: Ideologies of the Baroque Body,* Susan Manning's *Ecstasy and the Demon: Feminism and Nationalism in the Dances of Mary Wigman,* and Cynthia Novack's *Sharing the Dance: Contact Improvisation and American Culture.*

6 Susan Leigh Foster, *Choreography and Narrative: Ballet's Staging of Story and Desire* (Bloomington: Indiana State University Press, 1996), 263.

7 The "North-West Territories was the name applied to the territory acquired in 1870 from the Hudson's Bay Company and Great Britain — Rupert's Land and the North-Western Territory — which lay northwest of central Canada . . . Large portions were subsequently removed to create the (prairie) provinces . . . [Alberta in 1905] and to add to Manitoba, Ontario and Quebec" *Canadian Encyclopedia,* 2nd ed. (Edmonton: Hurtig Publishers, 1988).

8 The North-West was for some time seen as the basis of power for the whole British Empire. See Douglas Owram, *Promise of Eden: The Canadian Expansionist Movement and the Idea of the West 1856–1900* (Toronto: University of Toronto Press, 1980), 718. R. Douglas Francis argues that as settled under Utopianism, the West represented the new and ideal society — and the romantic image of the West as "the garden of the world" prevailed ("Changing Images of the Prairie West," in Francis/Palmer (eds.), *The Prairie West,* 2nd ed. [Edmonton: Pica Pica Press, 1992], 726). Francis also points out, however, that barren and desolate land was equated with the lack of trees in the minds of Englishmen and English Canadians. The Canadian prairies were and are covered with grasses and shrubs, not trees. So despite the obvious capacity of this landscape to produce useful grains, the wasteland image could persist in the settlers' imagination.

9 Alan Filewood (ed.), *Introduction to the CTR Anthology: 15 Plays from Canadian Theatre Review* (Toronto: University of Toronto Press, 1993), xii. Shelley Scott directed us to Filewood's insightful analysis of regionalism as a force in the shaping of Canadian theatre.

10 Max Wyman, *Dance in Canada* (Vancouver: Douglas and McIntyre, 1989), 127.

11 This is the voice of painter Maxwell Bates in "Some Problems of Environment," from the *Alberta Society of Artists Highlights* 2, 8, December 1948: 2; quoted by Christopher Varley, "Winnipeg West: The Postwar Development of Art in Western Canada," in A. W. Rasporich (ed.), *The Making of the Modern West: Western Canada Since 1945* (Calgary: University of Calgary Press, 1984).

12 See Howard J. Richards, "The Prairie Region," in John Workentin (ed.), *Canada, A Geographical Interpretation* (Agincourt: Methuen Publications, 1968), 396.

13 Filewood, *Introduction to the CTR Anthology,* xiv.

14 Ibid., xiii.

15 John Gray's remarks are quoted in Diane Bessai, "The Prairie Theatre and the Playwright," in A. W. Rasporich (ed.), *The Making of the Modern West: Western Canada Since 1945,* 216.

16 Ann Wilson, "Notions of Nationalism," *Canadian Theatre Review* 62, Spring 1990, 3. Quoted in Filewood, *Introduction to the CTR Anthology,* xv.

17 In 1970–1 the National Ballet received a $435,000 operating grant and its associated school received an additional $115,000. Both the Royal Winnipeg Ballet and Les Grands Ballets Canadiens each received $210,000. In contemporary dance, Toronto Dance Theatre received $15,000; Le Groupe de la Place Royale received $7,500; and Winnipeg Contemporary Dancers received $5,000. The Montréal folk group Les Feux-Follets received $60,000. Ironically, the $900 spent west of Winnipeg was given to the University of Alberta in Edmonton to support performances by the Toronto Dance Theatre.

18 Edward Said quoted in Robert Young, *White Mythologies* (London: Routledge, 1990), 11.

19 Max Wyman, *Dance in Canada,* 16.

20 Bill Ashcroft, Gareth Griffiths, and Helen Tiffin, *The Empire Writes Back: Theory and Practice*

in Post-Colonial Literatures (London: Routledge, 1989), 3.

21 Wyman, *Dance in Canada,* 82–4.

22 Timothy Plumptre, *Simply Dance: Inside Canadian Professional Dance,* a report commissioned by the Department of Communications in cooperation with The Canadian Association of Professional Dance Organizations (Ottawa: The Department of Communications, 1982). Plumptre articulates the interests of the existing professional dance elite in central Canada. "The difficulty with concepts like democratization or decentralization with reference to dance is that if misapplied they could be very damaging to other principles such as professionalism and quality, principles which have been the backbone of Canada Council policies toward the arts" (108–9). He explains further that "federal priorities should focus on events and activities that are not specific to a particular region or province" (109). Examples of good "regionalist" activities that he maintains are worthy of federal support are the cross-country audition tours of the National Balley Company. "Although dance companies may be located in larger urban centres, they draw their dancers from all parts of the country." Here we see the colonial/imperial logic of raw materials (dancers) from the hinterland being provided for the manufacturing/production of the centre (National Ballet Company), and also how easily he conflates central Canadian urban arts with the neutral "standard" — "not specific to a particular region or province."

Plumptre recognizes that policies of redistribution to "the regions" are a very real threat to the hegemonic power bestowed on centre-based dance activity by historical/imperialist patterns. "There is a very real danger that larger dance companies and schools would collapse were policies of decentralization and regionalism applied with insufficient sensitivity and understanding of the nature of professional dance" (109). Resources for dance must be concentrated in existing centres, he states, because of Canada's relative rarity of talent (dancers, teachers, and choreographers). Only 400 or 500 dancers he claims are sufficiently proficient to be called professionals, and less than a couple of dozen choreographers "have demonstrated consistent ability to add interesting, challenging new works to the dance repertoire" (112). Also, because the art form requires a long lead time for development, centralization of resources is "naturally" the best strategy. Further, any deviation from current funding patterns means finding new money, because reductions to existing institutions will reduce "standards."

The report characterizes professional dance as a rare and somewhat fragile art form that totally depends on the large urban centres in which it occurs. Plumptre implies that the new policies of the federal government are *not* at all appropriate to dance, because such a "naturally" urbanized art form would languish in the culture-poor nether regions. He says, however, that the decentralization and democratization initiatives might be all right for other art forms. Perhaps he cannot deny, at this point, the strength of regional theatre impulse. In a relieved tone of voice, he says that thankfully "such themes as 'democratization' and 'regionalization' have not been permitted to impair the overriding principle of artistic merit" (110).

23 See Filewood, *The CTR Anthology,* xii.

24 Ashcroft, Griffiths, and Tiffin, *The Empire Writes Back,* 9.

25 Anne Flynn interview with Yoné Kvietys-Young, 28 August 1991.

26 Wyman, *Dance in Canada,* 122–3, 125, 130.

27 Ibid., 83. Wyman quotes the negative assessments by two critics, Ken Winters in the *Toronto Telegram* and William Littler of the *Toronto Star.*

28 Ibid., 14.

29 Margaret Dragu, e-mail correspondence to Lisa Doolittle, 24 October 1998.

30 Norma Wood, e-mail correspondence to Lisa Doolittle, 23 November 1998.

31 Yoné Kvietys-Young quoted in Allan Connery, "Dance Program Credit to Dancers and Idea," *Calgary Herald,* 13 February 1970.

32 Wendy Woodford, "University's Dance to Dada is 'Far Out Stuff,'" *Albertan,* 25 March 1971.

33 Allan Connery, "Dance Program Credit to Dancers and Idea," *Calgary Herald,* 13 February 1970.

34 Jamie Portman, "Artful Spontaneity Hits Stage," *Calgary Herald,* 25 March 1971.

35 H. Palmer with T. Palmer, *Alberta: A New History* (Edmonton: Hurtig Publishers, 1990), 338.

36 Anne Flynn interview with Yoné Kvietys-Young, 28 August 1991.

37 Anne Georg, "Two Heads, One Vision, Ten Years," *Dance Connection,* 8, 5, 1991: 22.

38 Alan F. J. Artibise, "Boosterism and the Development of Prairie Cities, 1871–1913," in Alan F. J. Artibise, (ed.), *Town and City: Aspects of Western Canadian Urban Development* (Regina: Canadian Plains Research Centre, 1981). (Reprint. R. Douglas Francis and H. Palmer (eds.), *The Prairie West,* 2nd ed. [Edmonton: Pica Pica Press, 1992], 520.)

39 H. Palmer with T. Palmer, *Alberta: A New History,* 238–239.

40 Jamie Portman, "Ballet Lessons Are Defended," *Calgary Herald,* 13 September 1963, 31.

41 Jamie Portman, "Young Canadians Are a Talented Troupe, But Deficiencies Shouldn't Be Ignored," *Calgary Herald,* 10 January 1975.

42 Linda Curtis, "Danced to Help Her Heart," *Calgary Herald,* 5 November 1971.

43 Anne Flynn interview with Yoné Kvietys-Young, 28 August 1991. In subsequent conversations, Yoné has repeatedly emphasized that her decision to change careers to become a visual artist was strictly personal and not necessarily influenced by the sparse dance environment in Calgary. She stated that she enjoyed switching to an art form that, unlike the performing arts, does not involve intensive collaboration with others in the creative process. She also emphasized her success in this new medium.

44 For instance, both women are now single, having separated from their partners at the height of their professional dance activity, both have only one child, both are currently self-employed.

bibliography

Anderson, Carol (ed.). *This Passion: For the Love of Dance.* Toronto: Dance Collection Danse Press, 1998.

Artibise, Alan F. J. "Boosterism and the Development of Prairie Cities, 1871–1913." In Alan F. J. Artibise (ed.), *Town and City: Aspects of Western Canadian Urban Development.* Regina: Canadian Plains Research Centre, 1981. (Reprint. R. Douglas Francis and H. Palmer (eds.), *The Prairie West.* 2nd ed. Edmonton: Pica Pica Press, 1992.)

Ashcroft, Bill, Gareth Griffiths, and Helen Tiffin. *The Empire Writes Back: Theory and Practice in Post-Colonial Literatures.* London: Routledge, 1989.

Connery, Allan. "Dance Program Credit to Dancers and Idea." *Calgary Herald,* 13 February 1970.

Curtis, Linda, "Danced to Help Her Heart." *Calgary Herald,* 5 November 1971.

Filewood, Alan (ed.). *The CTR Anthology: 15 Plays from Canadian Theatre Review.* Toronto: University of Toronto Press, 1993.

Foster, Susan Leigh (ed.). *Choreographing History.* Bloomington: Indiana State University Press, 1995.

—. *Choreography and Narrative: Ballet's Staging of Story and Desire.* Bloomington: Indiana State University Press, 1996.

— (ed.). *Corporealities: Dancing, Knowledge, Culture and Power.* New York: Routledge, 1996.

Georg, Anne. "Two Heads, One Vision, Ten Years." *Dance Connection,* 8, 5, 1991.

Gilbert, Helen and Joanne Tompkins (eds.). *Post-Colonial Drama.* London: Routledge, 1996.

Gould, Stephen J. "The Invisible Woman." *Natural History,* 6,1993.

Francis, R. Douglas, and Howard Palmer (eds.). *The Prairie West.* 2nd ed. Edmonton: Pica Pica Press, 1992.

Litt, Paul. *The Muses, the Masses and the Massey Commission.* Toronto: University of Toronto Press, 1992.

Palmer, H., with T. Palmer. *Alberta: A New History.* Edmonton: Hurtig Publishers, 1990.

Owram, Doug. *Promise of Eden: The Canadian Expansionist Movement and the Idea of the West 1856–1900.* Toronto: University of Toronto Press, 1980.

Plumptre, Timothy. *Simply Dance: Inside Canadian Professional Dance.* A report commissioned by the Department of Communications in cooperation with the Canadian Association of Professional Dance Organizations. Ottawa: Hickling-Johnston Limited, 1982.

Portman, Jamie. "Artful Spontaneity Hits Stage." *Calgary Herald,* 25 March 1971.

—. "Ballet Lessons Are Defended." *Calgary Herald,* 13 September 1963.

—. "Young Canadians Are a Talented Troupe, But Deficiencies Shouldn't Be Ignored." *Calgary Herald,* 10 January 1975.

Rasporich, A. W. (ed.). *The Making of the Modern West: Western Canada Since 1945.* Calgary: University of Calgary Press, 1984.

Rubin, Don (ed.). *Canadian Theatre History: Selected Readings.* Toronto: Copp Clark Ltd., 1996.

Tembeck, Iro. "Early Modern Montréal: 1929–1970." *Dance Connection,* 8, 5, 1991, 26–32.

Wallace, Robert. *Producing Marginality: Theatre and Criticism in Canada.* Saskatoon: Fifth House Publishers, 1990.

Woodford, Wendy. "University's Dance to Dada is 'Far Out Stuff.'" *Albertan,* 25 March 1971.

Wyman, Max. *Dance in Canada, An Illustrated History.* Vancouver: Douglas and McIntyre, 1989.

contributors

Cheryl Blood- (Rides-at-the-) Doore is a Blackfeet, Blood, Dene First Nation; however, she prefers her people's original name Nistsitapii — Real people. She lives in southern Alberta with a healthy, growing family, blue skies, chinook winds, golden prairies, mountains, buttes, and rivers. She believes it is a beautiful process of discovery to create through different mediums, such as writing, music, dance, stories, painting, theatre, film, and multimedia.

Sarah Davies Cordova, assistant professor of French at Marquette University, is the author of *Paris Dances: Textual Choreographies in the Nineteenth-Century French Novel* (International Scholars Publications, 1999). She is currently working on autobiography and the dancer of the Romantic ballet as issues of identity in nineteenth- and twentieth-century Francophone literatures. She holds a Ph.D. in French literature from UCLA.

Thomas DeFrantz earned degrees from Yale, the City University of New York, and the Department of Performance Studies at New York University. He is an assistant professor of Theatre Arts at the Massachusetts Institute of Technology and coordinates the dance history program at the Alvin Ailey American Dance Center in New York City. His current writing projects include a book-length exploration of Alvin Ailey's choreography, titled *Revelations: Alvin Ailey's Embodiment of African American Culture,* and the anthology *Dancing Many Drums: Excavations in African American Dance History.* Also a performer and choreographer, DeFrantz recently choreographed the Ossie Davis play *Paul Robeson, All-American* for Theatreworks/USA and the burlesque musical *Pure PolyEsther* for Boston's Theatre Offensive, and performed the *Morton Gould Tap Dance Concerto* with the Boston Pops, conducted by Keith Lockhart. He is an active member of the Drama League of New York.

Lisa Doolittle is an associate professor in Theatre Arts at the University of Lethbridge. She initially trained as a contemporary dancer and worked as an independent dancer/choreographer and multidisciplinary artist in Canada and Italy. At Wesleyan University, where she obtained her MALS in Movement Studies, her research on fitness and female bodies focused on movement as an enculturation process. She was a co-founder of the internationally distributed *Dance Connection* magazine and was a contributing editor for five years. She currently curates an ongoing dance and physical theatre performance series, which integrates visiting professional artists into the academic curriculum. Her publications focus on Canadian dance, intercultural performance, and theatre for social change.

Anne Flynn is a dancer, teacher, writer, and advocate/organizer. An associate professor of Dance in both the Faculties of Kinesiology and Fine Arts at the University of Calgary, she has lived in Calgary since 1978. Performing and choreographing with partner Denise Clarke for most of the 1980s, she co-founded *Dance Connection* magazine in 1987. She has contributed articles on Alberta dance history and dance and philosophy to several books, written numerous articles for *Dance Connection,* and organized several conferences. She completed most of her professional training at the studios of Merce Cunningham and Viola Farber and with Cynthia Novack and Richard Bull at SUNY Brockport, where she obtained a B.A. in Dance. She holds a MALS in Movement Studies from Wesleyan University.

Kristin M. Harris has an M.A. from York University in Dance History, Theory, and Criticism and is currently a Ph.D. candidate in the Folklore Department at Memorial University of Newfoundland. During a leave of absence from 1998 to 2000, she worked as an ESL instructor in Taiwan and, most recently, as a visiting professor at Koje College in South Korea. Her current research interests include issues relating to gender and dance (especially ballet), gender and folklore, dance and material culture, and women's roles in occupational folklore. Harris' future dissertation research will focus on community identity and empowerment relating to vernacular dance in outport Newfoundland.

Michelle Heffner Hayes holds a Ph.D. in Dance History and Theory from the University of California–Riverside. She taught at the University of California–Riverside and at the University of California–Irvine, and performed with the postmodern dance companies of Susan Rose and Stephanie Gilliland, and the flamenco company of Armando Neri. Publications by Heffner Hayes include scholarly reviews of contemporary flamenco studies (*Dance Research Journal,* 1996), parallels in postmodern dance improvisation and flamenco (*Choreography and Dance,* forthcoming 2000), and issues in cultural identity and dance (*Encyclopedia of Homosexuality,* 1998). An avid aficionado of tango, flamenco, and baile popular, she has commissioned or advocated for the presentation of new work in these genres. Previously the artistic director of the Colorado Dance Festival, Heffner Hayes is currently the executive director of Cultural Affairs at Miami-Dade Community College.

Naomi Jackson received her B.A. in Philosophy and Art History from McGill University, her M.A. in Dance Studies from the University of Surrey in England, and her Ph.D. in Performance Studies from New York University. Jackson has taught at the Juilliard School and is currently an assistant professor at Arizona State University in Tempe, Arizona. She has served on the board of the Society of Dance History Scholars, and her reviews and articles appear in *Dance Connection, Dance Research Journal, Dance Chronicle,* and *Dance Research.*

Marrie Mumford is the artistic director of the Aboriginal Arts Program at The Banff Centre for the Arts. She has more than twenty-five years of experience in professional theatre in Canada and the US as an actor, director, producer, and instructor. She taught at professional acting studios and at the University of Toronto. She has an M.F.A. from Brandeis University in Boston and a B.A. in Theatre from the University of Alberta in Edmonton. During her tenure as artistic director of the Aboriginal Arts Program, Mumford has initiated and facilitated innovative professional development programs in dance, visual arts, new media, writing and publishing, and music. This work includes initiating the Chinook Winds Aboriginal Dance Program, Aboriginal Women's Voices, and the Aboriginal Curators series at the Walter Phillips Gallery.

Kate Ramsey is a Ph.D. candidate in Anthropology at Columbia University and holds an M.A. in Performance Studies from New York University. She was associate director of the multidisciplinary arts collective Pepatián from 1992 to 1996. Her work has appeared in the anthology *Meaning in Motion: New Cultural Studies of Dance,* edited by Jane C. Desmond (1997); *Women & Performance: A Journal of Feminist Theory;* and the *Village Voice,* among other publications. She is the author of *The Making of a Mosaic: An Introduction to the Music and Dance of the Americas* (National Dance Institute, 1992). Her dissertation studies the construction of "superstition" through law and performance in late-nineteenth to mid-twentieth-century Haiti.

Jacqueline Shea Murphy is an assistant professor of Dance at the University of California–Riverside, where she teaches courses in dance history and theory, and in yoga. She has a Ph.D. in English from the University of California at Berkeley, and is co-editor of the collection *Bodies of the Text: Dance as Theory, Literature as Dance* (Rutgers, 1995). She has published and taught in the field of Native American literary studies and is currently working on a book-length study of Native American and Aboriginal dance in North America and its relation to modern dance history.

M. J. Thompson is a Canadian writer working on dance, display, and everyday aesthetics. She is currently a Ph.D. candidate in Performance Studies at New York University. Her articles have appeared in *Dance Ink, Dance Connection,* and *Dance International.*

B. J. Wray is a Ph.D. candidate in the Department of English, University of Calgary. She is currently finishing her dissertation, "Imagined Citizenship: Nationalism and Sexuality in English-Canadian Lesbian Texts." Her work has appeared in *Performing the Body/Performing the Text,* edited by Amelia Jones and Andrew Stephenson (Routledge, 1999); *Decompositions,* edited by Philip Bret, Sue-Ellen Case, and Susan Leigh Foster (Indiana State University Press, 2000); and *Torquere: Journal of the Canadian Lesbian and Gay Studies Association,* among other publications.

index

index

a

b

e

f

g

h

n

o

p

q

r

s

t

u

v

w

y

photo credits

p. 4 (top and bottom), courtesy M. J. Thompson, NYC; p. 9 (top), courtesy M. J. Thompson, NYC; p. 9 (bottom) © The Museum of London, London, UK; p. 19, courtesy M. J. Thompson, NYC; p. 32, courtesy The National Film Board of Canada; p. 49, 59 (top and bottom), 60, courtesy Lola Piedra Ruiz, Brepi films, S. A., Madrid, Spain; p. 70, 71, 72, 74, video stills from *Napoli* performed by The Royal Danish Ballet, © National Video Corporation Ltd.; p. 86 (left), "Le Banc des analeurs," lithograph by Honoré Daumier, used with permission of the Musée Carnavalet, Paris, France; p. 86 (right), "Adèle Dumilâtre in the pas de Diane chasseresse," lithograph by Joseph Bouvier, used with permission of the V&A Picture Library, London, UK; p. 86 (overlay), letters from the Archives Nationales, Paris (Dossier AJ XIII 194) 21 janvier 1830 & Avril 1835; p. 109, Heather Elton; p. 112 113, Richard Agecoutay; p 115, 117, 118, Heather Elton; p. 120, 121, 123 (top and bottom), 125, 126, 127, 129, 153, 154, 158, 159, Don Lee — The Banff Centre; p. 181, print by Bruno of Hollywood used with permission of the Dance Division, The New York Public Library for the Performing Arts, Astor, Lenox and Tilden Foundations, NYC; p. 186, print by Walter E. Owen used with permission of the Dance Division, The New York Public Library for the Performing Arts, Astor, Lenox and Tilden Foundations, NYC; p. 189, print by Martha Swope © Time Inc.; p. 190, photograph © Jack Vartoogian, NYC; p. 198, photo used with permission of Northwestern University Archives, Evanston, IL; p. 199, used with permission from the Katherine Dunham Papers, Special Collections/Morris Library Southern Illinois University Carbondale; p. 224, print by Maria Nasif is used with permission of Naomi Jackson; p. 233, The Calgary Exhibition and Stampede, Calgary, AB; p. 234, Bill Simpkins; p. 235 (top), The University of Calgary Drama Department, Calgary, AB; p. 235 (bottom), The Calgary Exhibition and Stampede, Calgary, AB; p. 236, Ken Sakamoto.